HAUNTED
IDOL

HAUNTED IDOL

THE STORY OF THE REAL CARY GRANT

Geoffrey Wansell

Quill
William Morrow
New York

Library of Congress Cataloging-in-Publication Data

Wansell, Geoffrey, 1945–
    [Cary Grant, haunted idol]
    Haunted idol : the story of the real Cary Grant / by Geoffrey Wansell.
      p.   cm.
    Originally published: Cary Grant, haunted idol. London : Collins, 1983.
    Includes bibliographical references and index.
    ISBN 0-688-11910-7
    1. Grant, Cary, 1904–1986. 2. Actors—United States—Biography. I. Title.
[PN2287.G675W3   1992]
791.43′028′092—dc20
[B]   92-8785
                                                                                CIP

Printed in the United States of America

First Quill Edition

1 2 3 4 5 6 7 8 9 10

BOOK DESIGN BY JO BONNELL

For Daniel

PREFACE

There are a thousand Hollywoods. There is the one that everybody sees: the dream factory with its silent white-walled studios, its carefully watered estates in Bel Air and Beverly Hills and the crowds outside the Chinese Theatre beckoned by a great wooden sign in the hills; but there are other Hollywoods. There is the Hollywood of tiring apartment blocks: where Ramon Novarro was battered to death and Mae West died at the age of eighty-seven; the Hollywood where knots of old men stand on the sidewalks living on their memories. There is the new Hollywood of manicured young men in designer jeans climbing casually into convertibles and checking in their driving mirrors to be sure their hair is in place, the Hollywood of deals struck in aerobics classes, of meetings in romper rooms and Jacuzzis. But in the end there is only one Hollywood that really counts: the Hollywood of legend.

That is the eternal Hollywood, where the stars have never stopped shining and their names have never been forgotten. Some may have disappeared into rest homes and private clinics to die, but many, many survive, living quietly behind their high walls, lingering in the flesh as well as in the memory.

Astaire and Rogers, Dietrich and Davis, Stewart, Colbert and Hepburn all epitomize this unforgettable Hollywood, where glamour and style mattered more than reality, and all of them are still alive. But no one survivor of this breed captures the nonchalant, effortless charm of the old Hollywood as well as Cary Grant.

On the screen he was unmistakable. In more than seventy films he always seemed to play himself: the ageless, elegant, witty sophisticate with whom many of the cinema's most beautiful women fell hopelessly in love. Perhaps more than any other star he represented what Hollywood meant in its golden days: an indelible personality with a style and class all of its own.

Yet Cary Grant paid a perilous price for his celebrity: he became entombed in the legend he had so effectively created. Although he will remain forever one of the movie greats, he has spent most of his career trying to forget his childhood, to erase the poverty of his upbringing by a relentless pursuit of wealth, and to overcome the paralyzing fear of women instilled in him by his doting but mentally unstable mother.

When I started to write this biography I hardly guessed the difference between the public and private Grant. All I knew was that none of the interviews or books that I had read about him prepared me for the nervous, haunted man I actually met when I went to interview him early in 1981. I decided then to try to put the record straight and find out what lay behind the flawless mask he had so painstakingly adopted, to discover why he was both hypnotized and terrified by his own creation, and to present, as well as any biographer can do, the real Cary Grant.

The search took me to Hollywood and to New York, back again to England to Grant's hometown of Bristol and then to London. In the process I interviewed more than two hundred people and spent months of research in libraries in Britain and the United States. To all those I talked to I owe a vast debt of gratitude for their courtesy and patience and for the help they gave me in piecing together a picture of one of the cinema's most intensely private personalities.

It would be invidious to pick out particular individuals from so many, but I feel I must especially thank James Stewart and Katharine Hepburn, Doris Day and José Ferrer, Samantha Eggar, Moray Watson and Laraine Day, to name only a few of the distinguished performers who shared Cary Grant's career. Of the producers, directors or writers who worked with him, Robert Arthur and Pandro S. Berman, Stanley Kramer, Delbert Mann and Sol Saks were especially kind; while in the Hollywood studios I received a great deal of help from Vernon Harbin and John Hall at RKO, Andy Leigh at Universal and Kellam de Forest at Paramount.

I am also deeply grateful to the members of the staff of the library of the Academy of Motion Picture Arts and Sciences in Los Angeles, who not only helped me sift through a vast amount of material but also gave me access to two of their special archives: the George Stevens and Hedda Hopper collections.

I owe a similar debt to the staffs of the American Film Institute Library in Hollywood and the film libraries of the University College of Los Angeles and of the University of Southern California, and to Dr. Bob Knutsen of USC who allowed me to delve into the Warner Brothers archive there.

In England I also have to thank the staff of the London Library, the British Film Institute Library, the Public Records Office in London and a series of newspaper libraries in Fleet Street.

But there is another group of people who contributed enormously to this book yet whom I cannot thank publicly. These are the men and women, co-stars, friends and acquaintances of Cary Grant who agreed to talk to me on the understanding that I would not reveal that we had spoken. In consequence, I can only offer them all my profound but private thanks.

Finally, I must thank my editor and friend Rivers Scott, my agent, Leslie Gardner, in London and her associates, Joy Harris in New York and Ken Sherman in Los Angeles, and my editors, Robin Baird-Smith at Collins and Harvey Ginsberg at William Morrow. This book could not have been completed without the support and encouragement of Coutts Bank, in whose debt I shall be forever, and whose faith in the project almost rivaled mine; nor could it have been finished without the advice of my own psychoanalyst, Giles Clark, who helped me to understand myself in relation to the man about whom I was trying to write.

Most of all, it could never have been written without the help of my wife, Jan, who worked as a research assistant and typist for eighteen months and who put up with my obsession with Cary Grant without the slightest complaint.

No one should be held responsible for my conclusions, however; those are mine alone.

G.W.
London, June 1983

CONTENTS

PROLOGUE

Fame has also this great drawback, that if
we pursue it we must direct our lives in
such a way as to please the fancy of men,
avoiding what they dislike and seeking what
is pleasing to them.

Spinoza

The room in the London flat was small, drab and almost un-
bearably hot. Thick net curtains kept out the bright winter
sunshine, and even the two glowing table lamps only added to
the gloomy air of reticence and suspicion. There were no glittering chandeliers, no huge vases of flowers, not even a bottle of
champagne—just the slight scent of fear. It was the room of a
man intent on hiding himself from the world, although I did
not know then how true that first impression would turn out to
be. It was, above all, a most unlikely setting for one of the
world's most cherished and enduring movie stars.

"Hel-lo, I'm Ca-ry Grant," he said in his unmistakable voice,
and he smiled his unforgettable smile.

The time was January 1981, and he had just turned seventy-
seven. His hair was white rather than the luminous black that
had shone out of the screen in the thirties, but in most other
ways he was still as his fans remembered him: six feet two
inches tall, immaculately dressed and with a perfect suntan.
But his handshake was cautious, like that of a small child who
has never found his courage with strangers.

"De-light-ed to meet you," he said, yet his eyes did not quite match his words. They revealed something elusive, private about him. Millions of moviegoers may have felt they knew him as a friend, as (the description is Pauline Kael's) "the fairy-tale hero who always played himself." But did this character bear any resemblance to the man sitting opposite me? Little seemed to connect the two.

I knew that Cary Grant disliked discussing the past (he had never given either a television or a radio interview). "He will only talk about his interest in Fabergé; that is the only reason he is seeing you," I had been sternly warned before meeting him. "And he will not be tape-recorded under any circumstances." How could anyone who had been a star for half a century and who had appeared with almost every great leading lady the cinema had ever produced not look back on the pleasure he had brought to millions with the greatest delight and pride?

By coincidence Mae West, one of his first co-stars, had just died in Hollywood. They had appeared together in her first major film, *She Done Him Wrong*, in 1933, and it had launched her international career. Almost without thinking I said, "You must be very upset about Miss West's death."

There was silence.

"I don't think about it."

A pause. Then, "Is there anything I can get you, cof-fee, tea? Can't drink much coffee myself these days."

The words were as faultlessly and as effortlessly enunciated as in his best screen dialogue, the courtesy perfect.

"Having starred with her . . ."

Cary Grant did not shudder visibly, but it struck me that it was as if someone had stepped on his grave.

"I never think about it. Never."

The spell was broken by the appearance of the young English public relations officer, Barbara Harris, who had become his constant companion. They were not married then, but her affection for this man, who was fifteen years older than her father and forty-seven years older than she was, was very apparent. Brown-haired, calm and with a clear, soft complexion, she was preparing to leave for the passport office, and Cary Grant became relaxed, comfortable in her presence.

14

"You've never written your autobiography," I said. "You must have been asked many times."

"Don't think anyone would be in-ter-ested, and I don't want to waste my time writing about the past, or talking about it now, I'm too busy living."

I knew quite well he had said the same thing before, countless times, in newspaper interviews. "I've only got a few thousand hours left, I'm not going to waste them," and "Nobody is ever truthful about his own life." It was as though he was choosing to conceal things from himself, as though the memory of his appearance on thousands of movie screens over more than thirty years had come to appall him. Perhaps that was why he had been fascinated by psychotherapy, and why he had experimented with the drug LSD. Certainly, when I told him that I had been in Jungian therapy for a year and asked about his own experiences, Cary Grant, for the first time, responded positively.

"I've tried all sorts of things in the States, and I've been to a couple of places in England. One of them was very good, a country house where you can spend a week taking LSD and discovering about yourself. It made me realize things I never knew. It's made an enormous difference to me." As he said this, he looked down, a frail man rather than a movie star. I regarded this look as another telltale sign that his screen personality was a fortress he had constructed to protect himself from the world outside.

In the hour and a half that followed we talked about the parts of his life before he realized the price of fame; about the English music hall still flourishing in his youth, about the acrobatic troupe he had joined as a boy from Bristol, about vaudeville in the United States and finally about why he had given up acting at the moment when he was the biggest box-office star in the world in order to become a businessman.

"It's no surprise. Actors have always been businessmen. Do you know a more complicated business than films? Or any other where a man can earn three million dollars for ten days' work?"

He dated his change of heart about the movies to the birth of his only child, his daughter, Jennifer, in 1966.

"She's the greatest production of my life. I decided I wanted to spend all my time with her, and I couldn't do that if I was making films."

Gradually, he retired behind the facade of his practiced charm. When I left, we shook hands again, a little more calmly but no less cautiously than before; and I walked down the stairs and out into the bright watery sunlight of the cold London street. The soft heavy scent of the room was still in my nostrils, and in my mind was the thought that Cary Grant had not enjoyed being a star.

As I walked back through Mayfair I remembered another meeting, also in London. In January two years before, I had waited for half an hour in another small, stuffy flat while Dyan Cannon, who had been Cary Grant's fourth wife, prepared herself for our interview.

"I feel so different now," she had shouted through the half-open door to her bedroom. "My hair has just got to be right."

Dyan Cannon had not been keen to talk about her life as the former Mrs. Cary Grant.

"I'm me, an actress in my own right," she had said firmly as she swept into the flat's chintz drawing room to hug her and Cary's daughter, Jennifer, the bright-eyed twelve-year-old who had been sitting quietly beside me on the sofa.

Fewer than two weeks after seeing Cary Grant, I interviewed Stewart Granger, another English actor who had gone to find fame in Hollywood. He had just published the first volume of his autobiography, and parts of it were about Grant, who had been a friend of his in the 1950's and had introduced him and his former wife, Jean Simmons, to the reclusive millionaire Howard Hughes. Without prompting, Granger suddenly had said, "Cary is exactly the opposite of what he appears to be, you know. He isn't carefree or debonair at all."

At that moment I decided to write a biography of this enigmatic star and to try to unravel the enigma at the heart of his life and career.

The undertaking did not prove easy. I wrote to Cary Grant in Beverly Hills and received a polite reply from his lawyer and close friend, Stanley Fox, advising me that Grant did not want any book written about him. That was hardly a surprise, but I wrote back again saying that I believed any biographer had a duty to treat his subject fairly and courteously, and that I wanted to allow Grant to give his own interpretation of his life, as a balance to the views of others. There was no further reply until May 1982, when Grant himself telephoned me in London.

"I know who I am," he said, sounding as apprehensive as ever, "and I know what people say about me. I even know what my enemies think of me. So I have no intention of collaborating or authorizing you to write this book."

Then, suddenly, as if his screen personality still hypnotized him and he wanted to discover what I thought of it, he added, "But I will talk to you."

I went to California and spent three months tracing his old colleagues, searching through dusty studio archives, talking to people in the movie business. My activities were punctuated by a string of telephone calls from Grant.

"You're only writing this book because you think I'm going to die," he announced one day. "Don't try to tell me you aren't."

In fact, by that time I was convinced that Cary Grant would live as long as his remarkable mother, who had survived almost to her ninety-sixth birthday.

"I think you'll go on for years," I replied. He clearly did not believe me.

"It's because you're trying to write the definitive book, that's the only reason you're doing this."

"The only people who'll talk to you will be those whose autographs I've refused to sign, or the ones I've sacked," he declared on another occasion.

That was not true. His own friends had already begun to volunteer information. But the phone calls continued.

"I've told Doris Day she could say what she wanted about me."

"Jimmy Stewart told me he was going to speak to you."

Then, after a few days' interval: "No one's ever talked to my friends before."

"We should meet, but I don't want to appear to be authorizing you."

After I returned to London to start writing in October 1982, the telephone rang again.

"Sorry I didn't see you when you were here. Perhaps when I'm in London in May or June, perhaps then!"

I explained that I quite understood and that I hoped he'd had a happy birthday.

"I'm eighty next year, you know. I've every intention of getting to that birthday." He sounded almost astonished by the thought, but pleased.

"I spend every birthday and New Year's at home, it's a time for reflection, I find. But now I'm going on a cruise. I feel a little tired, I've been working too hard."

Talking to his old friend Howard Hughes, I thought to myself, must have been much like this, the same disembodied, elusive voice on the telephone, the strange fascination at what the world thought and the same apparent disregard for its conclusions.

Just as the manuscript was finished Grant called again. We had still not met since the January day two years before. He was still being elusive.

"I've been in London for a few days, but busy all the time."

I told him I quite understood, and asked how he planned to spend his birthday.

"No dinners, no television, no interviews, I'm just going to sit at home. I've turned down all the requests. Birthdays are a time for meditation and reflection, don't you think?"

We exchanged good wishes, but I could not quite understand why he had bothered to call. In spite of the calls and his apparent invitations, we never did meet again. Once again it seemed to me to be the reaction of a man obsessed with his right to privacy, and yet afraid of being forgotten.

Cary Grant may not speak about the past, but he has preserved it meticulously in his home. In a fireproof vault hidden behind a secret panel and protected by a series of alarms, he has carefully accumulated memories of his lifetime: the school blazer he wore as a child, the box of cap badges he collected as a boy scout, the contracts and the fan letters, the film stills and the press clippings of a career that began while Marie Lloyd was still alive and finished several years after Marilyn Monroe's death. There he keeps his five marriage certificates and photographs of his wives, his passports and his birth certificate, his father's waistcoat pocket watch and his mother's rings. He has hoarded these objects like a miser's gold.

And so I began to discover the haunted human being behind this ageless, debonair and effortlessly charming star of the movies' golden age. One of the last of Hollywood's acknowledged aristocrats, he has counted among his friends Noel Coward and Cole Porter, Louis Mountbatten and Aristotle Onassis, Robert Kennedy and Ronald Reagan. He is still a welcome guest at Buckingham Palace and the White House, as well as at Frank Sinatra's estate in Palm Springs. Marlene Dietrich, Katharine Hepburn, Jean Harlow, Irene Dunne, Carole Lombard, Ginger Rogers, Ingrid Bergman, Grace Kelly, Sophia Loren and Audrey Hepburn, among others, have been his co-stars through the years.

Strange to think that hidden from the world and, in so far as he can manage it, from himself is a small, sensitive boy who began life in Bristol as Archibald Alec Leach, the only child of an obsessed and doting mother.

PART 1

Archibald Alec Leach

I became an actor for the usual reason—
a great need to be liked and admired.
                                        Cary Grant

CHAPTER 1

She never told her love,
But let concealment, like a worm i' the bud,
Feed on her damask cheek: she pin'd in thought;
And with a green and yellow melancholy,
She sat like patience on a monument.
Smiling at grief.

William Shakespeare, *Twelfth Night*

Elsie Maria Kingdon was a Victorian by birth and by disposition. She favored prim, high-necked blouses, muttonchop sleeves, starched petticoats and hard work. She did not care for alcohol, tobacco or, all that much, for men. A short wiry woman, blessed with beautiful olive skin, sharp brown eyes and a slightly cleft chin, she appeared shy, almost innocent to those that did not know her. Those who did realized her dutiful manner concealed a waspish temper and a frightening determination.

Elsie stayed at home to look after her parents while her four older brothers left to make their way in the world. Then, at twenty-one, she felt it was time to create her own family. The man she chose to be her partner in this task was Elias Leach, a tailor's presser by trade, the son of a local potter. Her own father, a shipwright, was a cut above his future son-in-law, and there were those who whispered that his daughter was a bit of a snob. But when she and Elias went to the altar in their local parish church on Saturday, May 30, 1898, she felt she would be able to make something of him.

Elsie and Elias Leach moved into a respectable small terraced house they had rented a mile or so north of the center of the town. The lighting was all by gas. What heating there was came from small coal fires in every room and from the black range in the kitchen. But the house had a perfectly respectable parlor in which they could entertain their relatives at tea. The new Mrs. Leach took care to see that her brocade and the antimacassars were clean, her dark table polished and her piano topped with framed photographs to give the correct impression of stability and pride that every family insisted upon in those last years of Queen Victoria's reign. Elsie also insisted that every Sunday she and her husband should attend their local church.

To their friends the Leaches looked a perfectly matched couple: he, a tall, blithe and handsome young man of twenty-five with a fine, if rather fancy moustache and a benevolent sense of humor, and she, frailer, with black hair, a splendid selection of hats and a proud, slightly wistful mien.

The reality was less romantic. As their only son was later to remember, "My father had an inwardly sad acceptance of the dull life he had chosen," while his mother's appearance failed to reveal what he called "her will to control—and her deep need to receive unreservedly the affection she sought to control."

When she realized she was pregnant only a few weeks after her marriage, Elsie triumphantly began to prepare for motherhood with a studied intensity. In the bottom drawer of the tall wooden chest in her bedroom she assembled baby clothes, and a cot was installed in the house at 30 Brighton Street.

For his part, Elias Leach pressed as many trousers, coats and waistcoats at Todd's Clothing Factory as his employer would allow him to. He was determined to provide for his new family. Yet no matter how much overtime he worked, his income was never quite enough for his single-minded young wife.

At home in the afternoons Elsie Leach contented herself with the thought that, no matter what happened to her husband, the child she was about to bear would be a credit to her. She would see to that. But she also knew that no matter how fiercely determined a mother might be, no child born in 1899 was guaranteed life. The death rate among infants was still appallingly high; and, at the back of Elsie's mind, there was a tiny nagging fear that did not entirely abate when the child, a boy, christened John William Elias, was born at home on February

9, 1899. Elsie felt exceptionally close to her first son, who was born the day after her own twenty-second birthday, and for the first few months of his life, she spent every waking moment with him. He suffered from coughs and occasional bouts of fever, but she would always nurse him back to health, sitting beside his cot at night as he fought to catch his breath, feeding him carefully and never leaving his side. When her husband came home from work, he would find her sitting with the child in her arms, willing him to live.

But in the months that followed, the convulsions and fever did not abate, and when the family doctor called to see Elsie on February 6, 1900, he told her firmly that there was nothing more she could do. Staying up night after night had only exhausted her. The best thing for both mother and child was that she should rest.

Elsie Leach never revealed what went through her mind that evening as she climbed into bed beside her husband. The memory was to become too painful. By the time she woke, her son, John, had died of tubercular meningitis. It was the day before her twenty-third birthday. In just two days he would have been one year old.

Elsie Leach was probably never the same after that night, but she conducted herself with calm dignity as she arranged for her son's funeral in the local churchyard. Although she wore the black shawl of mourning with the bearing that her brothers expected of her, she did not allow herself to give way to tears. She had already decided that she would have another child.

Grief and morbid fear that her son's death had been her fault were emotions that Elsie could not reveal even to her husband in the privacy of the parlor in the new terraced house to which they had moved on Hughenden Road. She pushed the memory of her son's death deeply within her, hoarding it just as she hoarded his tiny clothes. To Elias, his wife seemed less and less the frail, feminine woman he had married and more the stiff embodiment of someone made strong by death and duty. He left her to her solitude. Walking down the hill toward Portland Square each morning, past the pony-drawn milk carts with their churns on the back and the ladies in wide-brimmed hats and long skirts, he looked forward to the cheerful freedom of his work.

Finally, in the late spring of 1903, only a few months after King Edward VII's often-postponed coronation, Elsie Leach told her soft-voiced husband that she believed she was pregnant again.

"It's not before time," she added firmly, "and I can only say that I'm glad."

"So am I. So am I." Elias's sad face for once was wreathed in smiles.

Elsie's meticulous preparations began again. The back bedroom was cleaned and the baby clothes assembled. As the autumn turned to winter the cot was brought out to be reassembled from its pieces. White linen sheets were tied around it, and a proper canopy erected over it to keep out drafts. This time Elsie was going to see to it that her child survived.

One cold wet January day in 1904, only two weeks before her twenty-seventh birthday, Elsie Leach suffered the first pains of labor. She made sure that her cousins had called the doctor and the midwife and had run down to the factory to tell Elias. Then she retired to the upstairs front bedroom and settled herself calmly in the brass bedstead.

As the night progressed the room grew hotter and hotter as more and more coal was heaped onto the small open fire in the black leaded grate. Shortly after one o'clock the following morning, January 18, with the rain blowing against the double-sashed windows, the midwife delivered the child. To his mother's intense satisfaction, it was a boy whose eyes, when he first opened them, were exactly the same color as her own, a dark engaging brown.

Elias Leach was suitably proud. He insisted on everyone's sharing a small glass of whiskey "to wet the baby's head" and to "keep out the cold." In the neat front bedroom upstairs Elsie Leach retired gratefully to sleep, the small boy in her arms. The effects of the chloroform the doctor had given her to dull the pain had not quite worn off.

Six weeks passed before she would allow her husband to

record their son's birth. She was superstitiously afraid that a fatal weakness might strike him down as it had her firstborn, and she had no wish to jeopardize the reward of her patience and nightly prayers by prematurely announcing the arrival of her second son.

Not until February 29, 1904, did Elias Leach journey down to the Bristol Register Office in Quaker's Friars to register the birth before the superintendent registrar, Mr. D. E. Bernard. He told him the boy's name was to be Archibald Alec Leach.

Elsie Leach was determined that Archie would be her testament. Everything else might fail her, but she would see to it that he never did. She would keep him with her at all times, supervise his activities, choose his clothes and make sure that the friends he made lived up to her expectations. This child would be the only reason for her life. She had already decided that there were to be no more births.

For Archibald Alec Leach this upbringing was claustrophobic. As the black-haired baby grew into a small, sad-eyed little boy, Elsie Leach's fascination with him deepened into an obsession. Her son was kept in a baby's dress with his hair falling around his shoulders in ringlets long after he had grown out of the carriage in which she wheeled him around Bristol. The white girlish dresses confused more than one unsuspecting passerby, and at times his mother would add to the confusion by calling him Alexandra.

It was not that she wanted her son to be a girl, it was more that she wanted a doll, a dependent being who would be unable to exist without her love and affection. In return she required him to worship her alone. The intensity of their relationship was to scar the boy's attitude toward women throughout the rest of his life, even though he was to spend more than fifty years being pursued by some of the most beautiful women in the world.

Elias Leach, who preferred his friends to call him Jim, worked longer and longer hours at the clothing factory in Portland Square and took to coming home a little later in the evenings after a drink or two in the local pub on the way. Even his small son noticed that his father's face was sad after a Sunday spent at home, and the atmosphere in their meticulously neat house descended gradually into gloom.

"My father progressed too slowly to satisfy my mother's dreams," he said years later. "The lack of sufficient money became an excuse for regular sessions of reproach, against which my father learned the futility of trying to defend himself."

The parental bickering left an indelible impression on the boy. He blamed himself for their quarrels and vowed never to let himself fall into similar financial difficulties. Yet, at the same time, he longed to have his mother all to himself. It was her praise and her reaction that he needed, no matter how much sympathy he instinctively felt for his father.

When Archie was four, the family moved to a better house. Elias himself was not particularly keen to do so, but Elsie was anxious that everyone should realize that her son was going to be something special in the family. She had already started to teach him to sing and dance. Before long he was taking piano lessons.

In the afternoons she would take him for walks on the Downs, then toward the River Avon and the superb Georgian terraces of Clifton, where she herself had been born. The walks were an experience the boy was never to forget, for they filled him with the dreams of the affluence and success that his mother wanted for him. She longed to return to the elegant crescents of Clifton, and more than sixty years later her son was to see to it that she did so. But for the moment both mother and child concentrated on making young Archie every bit as much a "little gentleman" as the sons of the solicitors and merchants who lived there.

Not that the frail boy, whose right shoulder was slightly lower than his left, did not sometimes defy his mother. He could, she told her friends, "be the very devil with his temper," and his cousins would remember him as proud and willful, stubborn and inventive. He was given to petulance and to the small deceits of an only child.

"My earliest memory," he later confessed, "is of being publicly bathed in a portable enamel bathtub in the kitchen before the fire at my grandmother's house, where my mother was, I

ARCHIBALD ALEC LEACH

suppose, spending the day. It was quite an old house which
either had no bathroom or, more likely, was unheated and too
cold for me to be there. I was just a squirming mass of protesting flesh, protesting against being dunked and washed all over
in front of my grandmother."

Bristol had always been a God-fearing town, and its traditions of strict churchgoing and hard work had not been abandoned. Children in such a town were taught to be polite to
strangers, to respect authority and "to speak only when spoken
to." Elsie Leach also impressed upon her son that his father was
not "made of money," that money "didn't grow on trees" and
that he must "brush the mud off your shoes before you come
into the house" and look after his clothes because "they're not
made of iron." When he stood in the hall before going out,
waiting for Elsie to straighten the folds of his coat and smooth
his long hair, the boy felt proud and vexed at the same moment, wanting to be independent and yet desperate to please
her. He thought himself then, as he would many times in the
future, very special, that he was his mother's little prince. It
was their shared secret.

Besides, his father could frighten him. Elias Leach would
sometimes take him out into their leafy garden to a swing he
had made in the branches of an apple tree and push him higher
and higher on it until he became terrified. His father wanted
him to be "a real boy" who got into trouble and whose knees
got dirty. But the garden swing, instead of effecting the transformation, only made his son frightened of heights.

There were brief moments when all came right. In the fine
June of 1909, the Leach family would sit together in their garden under the apple tree and have Sunday lunch from a trestle
table. The boy would bob up and down in his seat, his father
would remark how well the lilies of the valley he had planted
had done and how nice the fuchsias looked, while his mother
would relax visibly in the afternoon sun. Archie Leach remembered later, "They were the happiest days for the three of us."

But, in general, the relations between Elsie and Elias grew
more and more distant, and Archie felt afraid and different
from the other children he met every afternoon on the Com-

mon. They used to tell him, "If you pick daisies, you're a pansy," and, "If you pick dandelions, you'll dampen the bed" (he actually did wet his bed from time to time).

One night that autumn, Archie Leach woke up in his small, cold bedroom to hear the sound of singing from downstairs.

"As I walked along the Bois de Boulogne with an independent air . . . / You should hear the girls declare. . . ."

It was his father's voice.

"He must be a millionaire" was chorused by several other voices he did not recognize. He squirmed down under the sheets. Then he heard his mother's firm high tone.

"Do be quiet, you'll wake the boy."

"I will indeed, lass," he heard his father say, and then the sound of footsteps approaching up the stairs. His beaming father opened the dark wood door to Archie's bedroom and said softly, "Are you awake, lad? Have we wakened you?" Archie sat up in bed and nodded.

"Never mind, you come and show us what you can do." And with that his father picked him up, wrapped him in one of the blankets and carried him downstairs into the hot, stuffy front room. The smell of smoke in the air made him cough.

After he was put down on the table and had looked around nervously, he recognized some of his uncles and aunts among a number of strange faces. Then, suddenly conscious of an angry scowl from his mother, he averted his eyes.

"Now, lad, show 'em how well you know your poem," his father told him.

The boy, his bare feet strangely pink against the white linen tablecloth beneath him, still refused to return his father's gaze.

"Go on, lad, you know, 'Up in a Balloon.' "

Archie Leach remained silent, only too conscious that he should not have been out of bed at all, least of all "performing," as his mother used to call it.

Suddenly she lunged toward him and tried to pull him off the table into her arms. His father intervened.

"No, no, Elsie, the lad's all right," he said soothingly. "He'll enjoy it."

But Elias Leach did not take the chance that his wife might

try to snatch the boy away again. He took his son into his arms and raised him so that his head almost touched the gas mantle hanging from the ceiling.

"Come on, Archie, you know it."

Faintly, and with a slight lisp, the boy began to recite the first poem he had ever learned, "Up in a Balloon so High." As he looked around at the faces of the adults in the smoky room, his confidence grew. For the first time he realized the excitement of being praised, the taste of the thrill of applause.

As he settled back between the sheets of his bed, clutching the apple he had been given as a present, he was exultant. And in the last moments before he dropped off to sleep he murmured the first words of the poem to himself again, "Up in a balloon so high. . . ."

He hoped his mother had not thought he had spoken it too badly.

At last the boy escaped the smocks and dresses of his first four years and found himself dressed instead in dark shorts with thick woolen socks almost up to his bare knees. He was to go to school. The new Education Act stated that a child should start school at five, but Elsie Leach wanted better. *Her* son must begin at once. So, an apprehensive Archie Leach was marched off to the Bishop Road school at the age of four and a half. A stern, tall building, with the tiled walls and high ceilings of the time, it stood in the shadow of the town's prison. Archie was to recall years later how frightened he was when he first saw his classroom with its uncovered floorboards and rows of double desks. He was instructed to use his chalk and slate and reminded that lack of attention would bring a wooden ruler down hard across his knuckles. The sensitive, spoiled boy was terrified.

There were compensations, however. Between lessons he discovered for the first time that he could join in with other boys of his own age and play football.

"Very gradually I grew accustomed to associating with other children," he said years later, "or, rather, mostly with other boys. Little boys. In fact, I was, to my surprised delight, invited to play goalkeeper in the football team—a rather scrubby group who hadn't sufficient bravery to play with the girls during recreation time and kicked a soccer ball around instead." This was not so very surprising, for the city of Bristol had two new football teams in the recently formed English Football League, and their games were attracting bigger and bigger crowds each Saturday afternoon.

"We had no goalposts, just chalk lines marked on a jagged stone wall at each end of the playground to denote where they should be," the former Archie Leach went on. "Whenever the ball struck the wall between those lines, that was considered a goal. I whacked into that wall countless times, skinning bare knuckles and knees and snagging my clothes, desperately trying to stop the other side from scoring, until it dawned on me why no one was eager to be goalkeeper, and why, probably, they had invited me." The shy, neat boy with his shoes shined and his hair parted on the left could not escape the feeling of being alone even in the hubbub of the school playground.

"If that ball slammed past me, I alone—no other member of the team but I alone—was held, to my mystification, responsible for the catastrophe." But as he stood there waiting for the ball to fly toward him, he also felt, as he was always to feel, very special, singled out.

If he managed to keep the ball from banging into the wall behind him, he was cheered and hugged by his own team. As he was to say almost sixty years later, "Right then and there I learned the deep satisfaction derived from receiving the adulation of my fellow little man. Perhaps it began the process that resulted in my search for it ever since."

"No money, no material reward is comparable to the praise, the shouts of 'well done' and the accompanying pat on the back of one's fellow man."

At home, however, there was no applause and little laughter. Elsie Leach did not want her son to be praised by anyone except her. He was still to be controlled. He was to wear Eton collars made of stiff celluloid, raise his cap politely, polish his shoes and not get dirty under any circumstances. Most important of all, he was to do precisely what Elsie wanted.

Elias Leach worked on at Todd's Clothing Factory. He described his wife as a "good woman" to his friends at work, and added, "She looks after the boy properly," even if he privately thought that she tended to be a bit too strict. On Saturdays the boy would run down the road to meet him when he came home from work and, as they walked up the hill together, Archie would search eagerly through his pockets for the present his father usually brought him at the end of the week. Sometimes the two of them played games on the parlor table in the evenings, pushing the colored counters up the snakes or down the ladders or hurrying them into the safe squares of the ludo board.

The boy's pocket money was sixpence a week, but he rarely got it. His mother would fine him two pence for each mark he made on the stiff white linen tablecloth she put on the dining table for Sunday lunch, and he could be clumsy. The terror of spilling the slightest drop of food or water on the cloth was to remain so fixed in his mind that for years afterward he would refuse even to own a dining table.

There were diversions. By the time Archie had reached the age of nine more than two hundred companies in England had registered with the Board of Trade as film exhibitors and had started more than thirty-five hundred cinemas. The grand music halls were still filled every day with audiences glad to wallow in their warm affectionate atmosphere, but seats in them were more expensive and the entertainment more adult. For Archie Leach, as for most of his school friends, the new, cheaper cinema provided their weekly fun.

Inevitably, in their case, his parents took him separately. Elias Leach favored the comparatively humble Metropole, a vast barnlike building with hard seats and bare floorboards where the audience hissed as they watched silent serials like *The Clutching Hand* with its beautiful new heroine, Pearl White. This cinema smelled of raincoats and Wellington boots, and the boy remembered for years afterward being given a bag of peppermints or a bar of chocolate by his father before they went inside for the afternoon.

"We lived and loved each adventure," he was to say, "and each following week I neglected a lot of school homework conjecturing how that hero and heroine could possibly get out of

33

the extraordinary fix in which they'd been left." Indeed, so hooked was he that he would go to Pringles Picture Palace to see another serial on Saturday afternoons, as well as Mack Sennett's new short comedies. "The unrestrained wriggling and lung exercises of those Saturday matinees, free from parental supervision, was the high point of my week," he later recalled.

Elsie Leach, however, felt her son was a cut above such common pleasures. She preferred to take him to Bristol's more expensive Claire Street Cinema, where the customers took tea and cake in wicker armchairs in the balcony while they watched the films. There he was instructed in the correct use of a pastry fork and expected to sit up straight and pay attention. It was a bleak contrast to the joy of Saturday afternoons at the Metropole when his father and he started stamping and shouting to warn the unsuspecting heroine that the villain was creeping up behind her.

By the time of King Edward's death in May 1910, Archie had began to realize that his parents were not at all happy. "I remember the grief of my father and mother the morning King Edward the Seventh died, and saw them sharing a common bond of sympathy," he was to say. "A rare moment."

That night, as if to presage the upheavals that would soon overtake the world, Halley's comet shot through the sky for the first time in a hundred years. Within a few months, the streets of the cities of England were plunged into rioting. Soon the railwaymen, the sailors, the firemen, the dockers and the miners were all on strike, protesting that the real value of their wages had been falling steadily for the past decade. In some places the violence was so intense that the army was called in to restore order: two men were shot dead in Liverpool and another two killed in Llanelli in Wales. In Bristol, nervous local police kept vigil over the pickets at the dock gates.

For Elias Leach the mood was infectious. He too wanted to make sure that life in the future was going to be different. In 1912, at the age of forty, he decided to leave his wife.

It was the most momentous decision he had ever taken. For he would also be leaving his son, his house, his job and his home. Though he had cycled around the vales of Gloucestershire and Wiltshire over the past twenty years, he had never lived anywhere but in the town in which he had been born. And now, while Home Secretary Winston Churchill was proclaiming that workers deserved "time to look about them, time to see their homes by daylight, to see their children, time to think and read and cultivate their gardens—time in short to live," Elias Leach was telling his wife that he was moving eighty miles away to Southampton.

He did not tell her that he had also found a woman with whom he thought he might be able to be happy. He simply explained that he had been offered a job in a new factory making khaki army uniforms and would be a fool not to take the chance to better himself. He told his friends at work the same story, and they saw no reason to doubt him. In any case, it was partly true.

The clothing firm was sorry to see Elias Leach leave. He had worked there for more than twenty years, and the seamstresses and cutters collected enough money to buy him, as a parting gift, a pocket watch engraved with his name for his waistcoat. Elsie Leach was less disturbed at her husband's decision. She had already taken to greeting his late return from the factory each evening in silence. After watching him eat his supper without a word, she would leave him alone while she retired upstairs to bed in the still, somber house.

"Odd, but I don't remember my father's departure from Bristol," his son was to say later. "Perhaps I felt guilty at being secretly pleased. Or was I pleased? Now I had my mother to myself."

But within six months Elias Leach was forced to return to Bristol and to the home he thought he had left for good. The cost of his two houses and his two lives had proved to be more than the increased salary he had earned in Southampton could sustain. The caution that the newly cheerful, moustached man had thrown to the wind turned to dust as he crept back under the thumb of his wife. His son was never to forget the humiliation his father had to suffer as the price for his return. Long after Elias's death, Archie was to keep the engraved pocket watch locked in a drawer in his Hollywood home.

35

As the cold winter of 1913 began and Archibald Alec Leach celebrated his ninth birthday, Elias Leach sank into a gloom from which he was not to recover for more than a year. He would sometimes lift his small son onto his knee in front of the parlor fire, but nothing seemed to cheer him as he smoked his pipe in the thickening darkness. On the other side of the fire his wife sat with her hands firmly clasped on her lap, particularly when she was in a temper. And she was often in a temper.

Taller now, and with the confidence of a boy eager to find his own feet, the nine-year-old Archie would go to the tuck-shop opposite his school when classes ended at four o'clock and buy jam tarts with his pocket money. "Or Five Boys Chocolate that was made by Fry's in Union Square in Bristol and then go home for tea, " he recalled. After sandwiches or a poached egg he would go back into the street to play cricket or football with the other boys in the neighborhood. He had become an untidy child, the neatness his mother had tried to instill scuffed off by the rebelliousness of childhood, his quietness replaced by an enthusiasm for hitting and kicking balls as far as possible. The subdued, self-conscious child who had gone to school at four and a half had become boisterous and restless. "I was not turning out to be a model boy," he said later. "It depressed me to be good, according to what I judged was an adult conception of good."

"The worst thing I ever did as a child," the actor confessed not long after his mother died, "and it was dreadful, was to set fire to a little girl's dress with a match. It was a Bengal light. She ran off screaming to her mother, who put her out! But I didn't set fire to her on purpose."

In spite of his rebelliousness, Archie and his mother remained suffocatingly close. After months of pleading, he was finally allowed to have his first pair of long trousers: white flannels, very much the fashionable thing for any young man in 1913 to wear in the summertime. He was to take the tickets at the merry-go-round at the annual church bazaar on Redland Green, and it was agreed that this might be a proper occasion for a new pair of trousers. But his delight at escaping from shorts was not to last. Ever conscious of the need to save money,

Mrs. Leach had decided to make his flannels herself rather than buy them.

"How can I be expected to get these to fit you properly if you will insist on fidgeting about," she complained as she tucked the white cloth around his legs.

The boy stood in the kitchen, as still as he could, while she finished with her pins.

"What on earth you want white flannels for I will never understand," she muttered, smoothing the flannel through her fingers.

He did not explain—she would never understand, he told himself—he had fallen in love for the first time. The object of his affections was the local butcher's daughter, whom he had, in fact, not seen for several weeks, the last time being when he had walked past her house to deliver a message to his grandmother. It was out of his way, but he could not resist the temptation, because he knew she usually played in her front garden when she came home from school. And there she was, sure enough, looking at him, not saying a word. Equally speechless and totally transfixed, he walked slowly past her and collided with a new iron lamppost. He heard the plump, pretty girl laugh, but when he raised his head again, she was gone.

His passion had not dimmed, however, and he hoped there was a chance she might visit the merry-go-round and see his new white trousers.

"There, satisfied, are you?" his mother said finally, inspecting her work with the sharp-eyed look he knew well. "They seem all right to me."

The boy did not know what to say. The trousers felt strange, and yet he liked the idea that he was no longer a child. Would he see the girl again as the Wurlitzer organ played and the carousel's wooden horses rose and fell behind his ticket booth?

But alas for dreams. "Those homemade trousers didn't seem to fit or appear as well, nor was the flannel of the same quality at the shop-bought ready-made version of white flannels I saw on other boys," he was to remember. "I was crestfallen."

Secretly, he could not rid himself of the suspicion that his mother had made his trousers ill fitting on purpose. He would never admit it. Instead, the boy who was later to become one of the best-dressed men in the world simply vowed to own some well-cut white flannels of his own one day.

But Elsie Leach, unnoticed by her son, was undoubtedly growing stranger. She was getting even more obsessively fastidious and had started locking every door in the house. She took to hoarding food and to asking no one in particular, "Where are my dancing shoes? What's happening to my dancing shoes?" At other times she would sit motionless in front of the fire, staring at the coals, with the gas mantle turned down so low that only a halo of light hung around her. Archie did notice that she washed her hands again and again, scrubbing them brutally with a bristle brush. What he could not know was that the fragile balance of her mind, for so long precariously maintained by his dependence on her, was beginning to fail. But Elias did know: in the spring of 1914, when his son was occupied playing with his marbles and considering becoming one of Lord Baden-Powell's new boy scouts, Elias decided he should consult his own doctor and the local magistrates. Afterward, without telling his son, Elias Leach commited his wife, Elsie Maria, to the local mental institution at Fishponds.

For the remaining twenty-one years of his life, Elias was never again to share the same house with Elsie, nor was he ever to discuss with his son why he had taken this painful step.

One bright, cold Friday morning he arranged for the hospital's staff to take her from their home, and he quietly stayed away from the factory that day to travel with her. After settling her in, he returned to work since now, especially, he could not afford to lose a day's pay.

At school, his son had no idea what was happening, no inkling that his mother would not be there to get him his supper when he returned home shortly after two o'clock.

As the gaslit streets were growing dark, Archie Leach ambled slowly up the hill to the claustrophobic terraced house. He rang the bell and waited for his mother to open the door without realizing that the woman who had dominated his life in the ten years since he was born would not be part of it again for the next twenty. He was never to know whether she had left the house that morning quietly or screaming at the top of her voice. No matter how much he tried, he would never shake off the despair that her absence bred in him, the feeling of guilt that her departure might have been his fault. The memory of that day would be with him for the rest of his life.

Two of Archie's cousins were staying at the house, and when there was no reply at the front door, he set off to find them. They told him his mother had gone off to the local seaside town of Weston-super-Mare for a short holiday, but would be back soon. His father's answer was equally bewildering.

"Gone away for a rest, lad," he said when he returned home from work.

"Where to?"

"Not far, lad, she needed it."

"When will she be back?"

"Not long." And Elias Leach busied himself with the task of looking after his son. Over the weeks ahead he would say to him from time to time, "Your mother's well; sends you her love." But he would never tell the ten-year-old boy with the olive skin, cleft chin and brown eyes anything else.

Gradually, Archie realized that his mother would never return; and as he climbed between the cold, slightly damp sheets in his upstairs bedroom night after night, he asked himself why she had left him. What had he done wrong?

"No sense in worrying yourself, lad," his father would murmur occasionally, but the boy could not shake off the fear and the guilt. Nor could he escape the feeling that it was dangerous to trust anyone, particularly a woman, again.

As he put it bleakly half a century later, "I was not to see my mother for more than twenty years. By which time my name was changed and I was a full-grown man living in America. I was known to most people in the world by sight and by name, yet not to my mother."

The ghosts that were to haunt Archibald Alec Leach for the rest of his days had begun to take shape.

39

CHAPTER 2

I can remember, I can remember,
The months of November and December
Were filled for me with peculiar joys
So different from those of other boys
For other boys would be counting the days
Until end of term and holiday times
But I was acting in Christmas plays
While they were taken to pantomimes.
I didn't envy their Eton suits,
Their children's dances and Christmas trees.
My life had wonderful substitutes
For conventional treats such as these.
I didn't envy their country larks,
Their organized games in panelled halls:
While they made snow-men in stately parks
I was counting the curtain calls.

Noel Coward, *The Boy Actor*
Copyright © 1967 by Noel Coward

The sadness that enveloped the boy drove him deeper and deeper into himself. The pain of his mother's loss sharpened the lonely restlessness he had always felt. He took to wandering through the streets of Bristol and sitting for hours at the town's quayside, watching the ships ease out into the Channel toward the Atlantic on the evening tide, their sails slapping in the breeze. Then he would walk home in the dusk.

Finally, as the early spring of 1914 turned to summer, he ran away from home. He took his wooden scooter and pushed off down the Gloucester road toward the River Avon. But his nerve failed. He came home again after dark, having abandoned his idea of stowing away on a schooner; but he was not to forget the experience. Next time, he would plan his flight more carefully.

His rebelliousness continued. One afternoon he was marched down to the local police station by an angry neighbor who had caught him throwing sticky India rubber balls at unsuspecting passersby. But he also joined Bristol's first troop of boy scouts shortly after it had started in the Young Men's Christian Association Hall in St. James's Square. The troop would assemble for parade on Wednesday evenings, and meet again on Saturday afternoons for the maneuvers known as "exercises." Once a month a church parade would be held on Sunday morning, and the troop of about forty boys aged between ten and seventeen would attend one of the local churches. After the service, they would line up in their uniforms of green woolen sweaters and short brown shorts and, proudly carrying broomsticks over their shoulders, march through the streets.

His fellow scouts later remembered Archie as "rather small for his age and somewhat untidy and disheveled in appearance," although his patrol leader in Hounds Troop, Bob Bennett, said, "He was just an ordinary bloke who seemed cheerful enough, although he was a bit of a loner." Once the parades were over, most of the boys would go to the movies. "But," says Bennett, "he'd disappear off." However, the boyish camaraderie that the movement inspired, with its strongly patriotic tone, made a great impression on Archie; when war was suddenly declared on August 4, he and the others were anxious to be pressed into service. The sixteen-year-olds were soon to be encouraged to leave for France, but the younger ones were given duties at home. Archie Leach and his troop became junior air-raid wardens.

Before the somber casualty lists of men killed in the trenches of Flanders began to dim the jingoism of an England where three quarters of a million men had volunteered to fight for their country in the first seven weeks of the war, Archie Leach and his father were forced to leave their home. His two cousins had moved out, and Elias Leach found that he could no longer afford to keep himself and his son there. He and the boy went to live with Elias's mother on Picton Street, a narrow lane of two rows of tiny, terraced houses barely wide enough to allow a horse and cart to pass. Archie and his father shared the down-

stairs front room and the upstairs back bedroom, while his
grandmother lived in the bigger front bedroom upstairs.

"I didn't see a great deal of her," Archie was to say later,
"and I took care of my needs as best I could, sharing with her
and father each Saturday and Sunday breakfast and midday
dinner, and scrounging around in the kitchen, or stone larder,
for other meals on my own." He would never lose this habit of
scavenging for food.

Perhaps the move convinced him he had to leave Bristol as
quickly as he could. In any event, even without his mother's
high-pitched exhortations ringing in his ears every day, he suddenly started to study for the school scholarship examinations.
In the first months of 1915, he won one of the Liberal government's "free" places to the Fairfield Secondary School, not far
from his home.

Fairfield was a respectable Victorian school less than a mile
from the center of Bristol in the middle of a new estate of de-
cent terraced houses, cramped on one side by a line of the
Great Western Railway. Since 1906 Fairfield had been obliged
by the government to offer free places to children whose parents could not otherwise have afforded to send them there. It
was hardly the dignified "academy" that Archie Leach described in the later years of his life. Nevertheless, there were
special ties, caps and blazers to be worn in the school colors of
plum with blue and yellow stripes, gym clothes to be bought
and bicycle shed fees to be paid. "I economized wherever I
could, but just the required books each term were really more
than my father could afford," Archie Leach was to recall.
When he finally went to the school in September 1915, he bar-
gained for secondhand copies of any books he needed and sold
them again as soon as he had used them, to keep his father's
expenses to a minimum. In the process, he recalled, "My aspi-
rations for a college education slowly faded. It was obviously
too expensive to consider."

With the knowledge that he had little hope of going to one of
England's universities came the realization that, like most
other boys of his age, he was probably destined for the trenches
of France. School, for him and all the boys who saw their cous-

ins and uncles going away to war, became a supreme irrelevance; his heart was not in his books.

He hated mathematics in particular—algebra, geometry and trigonometry—and he was loathed by his Latin mistress for his idleness. But he did not mind geography, "because I wanted to travel," and did fairly well at history, art and chemistry, although even they hardly captured his imagination.

For most of the time he was simply a mischievous, willful boy with a rebellious and insolent streak that brought him into regular contact with his headmaster's cane. When he was caught at some misdeed, he had the ability to open his dark brown eyes and raise a single eyebrow quizzically, as if in proof of his innocence. As he stood waiting for his punishment in his scruffy sweater, twisting his ink-stained hands behind his back and with his socks pushed down to his ankles, he seemed desperate to be noticed. A frail boy with sad eyes and an almost girlish face, he looked like a belligerent fawn.

Back at the gloomy house on Picton Street he was growing more and more aware of his father's melancholy. "He was a dear, sweet man," Archie would remember, "and I learned a lot from him. He first put into my mind the idea of buying one good superior suit rather than a number of inferior ones. Then, even when it is threadbare, people will know at once it was good." But even the comradeship of his son could not overcome Elias Leach's despair.

Archie was to tell a magazine nearly half a century later, "I thought the moral was—if you depend on love and if you give love, you're stupid, because love will turn around and kick you in the heart."

The shadow of Elsie hung over them both. And, as it did so, the scruffy boy, whose scout patrol once forcibly washed his neck after his dirtiness had lost them a troop competition, developed, like her, an obsession with being clean.

"I washed myself constantly, a habit I carried far into adulthood in a belief that if I scrubbed hard enough outside I might cleanse myself inside, perhaps of an imagined guilt that I was in some way responsible for my parents' separation."

The journey into adolescence brought with it a vanity that

was to remain throughout his life. When another boy knocked him over accidentally in the school's playground that winter, he fell face forward onto the icy ground. "My front tooth snapped in half. Straight across."

Anxious not to let his father discover what had happened and wanting to preserve the features that he was aware were beginning to attract some attention among the girls at the school, he decided to have the remaining piece of his broken front tooth pulled out at the local dental hospital. The price of an extraction there was low enough for him to pay for it out of the pocket money he had started saving.

For weeks after the extraction he kept his mouth closed as much as possible while the gap between his front teeth slowly closed; as a result, he perfected the rather tight-lipped smile that became famous. But he was never to replace the tooth.

At the end of his second year at Fairfield School in 1917, he volunteered for war work during his summer holidays. "I was so often alone and unsettled at home," he remembered later, "that I welcomed any occupation that promised activity."

He was given work as a messenger at the Southampton docks, where his father still had friends from his own stay in the town three years before. There, the thirteen-year-old boy helped thousands of young men into the ships waiting to take them to France. He could not fail to notice the look of apprehension on their faces as they climbed the long wooden gangplanks and he handed them a life jacket.

When he returned to Bristol, he could not slip back into the life he had led before. The image of the men lying on the floor of the sheds, or sitting with their packs and rifles behind them, playing cards or singing, lingered in his mind. He started haunting the docks and wharves of the River Avon, as he had done when his mother had first disappeared. The sadness he had felt then still clung to him like a shroud. "Once, I even applied for a job as a cabin boy, but was turned down, not only because I was too young, but because I couldn't bring permission from my parents," he was to say later.

Yet it was not the ships carrying sugar, cocoa, tobacco or coffee that would finally help him escape, but a part-time assistant teacher in the school's chemistry laboratory, who invited him to go backstage on Saturday afternoon at the Bristol Hippodrome. The jovial, middle-aged man had just installed the theater's new electrical switchboard and lighting systems to replace the original gas lamps.

As the boy, so often sullenly wrapped up in himself, followed the man through the stage door and along the narrow tiled corridors that led past the dressing rooms toward the stage, he realized there was another life.

"I suddenly found myself in a dazzling land of smiling, jostling people wearing and not wearing all sorts of costumes and doing all sorts of clever things," recalled the future Cary Grant. The sickly smell of grease paint and the faint aroma of sweat hung in the air. The warmth, color and friendliness of it all captivated him. "That's when I knew. What other life could there be but that of an actor?"

It was what he had longed for without even knowing it existed. Actors traveled and toured. They were classless, cheerful and carefree. But most of all they could present to the world the face they chose, and no one wanted to know how they felt. The audience adored them for what they appeared to be, not what they were. To the insecure Archie Leach, who had been presenting a brave face to the world for as long as he could remember, this idea was a revelation.

He took to hanging around the Hippodrome at every opportunity, until the electrician introduced him to the manager of another of the town's theaters, the Empire. While the Hippodrome specialized in spectaculars in the style of its more famous counterparts in London, the Empire offered a more traditional music hall, spiced with the new fashion for revue. The shows, with titles like *Jingles* and *Spangles,* were filled with comedians, magicians, singers and chorus girls.

At the Empire Archie was allowed to help the men work the new arc lights mounted at each side of the stage. Unpaid but utterly content to have found somewhere to go, he felt at home at last. He was spellbound, so stagestruck that one evening he absentmindedly allowed an arc light he was holding to reveal the mirrors secretly assisting the famous illusionist The Great

Devant. He was fired on the spot. Undeterred, he went back to the Hippodrome.

He ran messages again and was finally rewarded with a job as a callboy in the early evenings, summoning the performers when the time came for them to appear. He was delighted, although, as he confessed later, "I was most annoyed I couldn't do the Wednesday matinee because of school." He was paid ten shillings a week, and when he finished work he would walk home. "I didn't want to spend my earnings on a tram."

In fact, he started working Wednesday matinees and missing school as a result. There was no one at home to reprimand him. His father left before he did in the morning and came back after he did in the evenings. His grandmother did not know where he went. No one seemed to care what he did, except at the theater. It became the home he no longer had.

One evening at the Hippodrome he met Bob Pender, a stocky, cheerful man of forty-six, who had been running a troupe of boys specializing in slapstick comedy, known as Pender's Knockabout Comedians, since he was nineteen. The boys acted comic sketches in mime. They ran and fell, balanced and tumbled, jumped and walked on stilts. More than twenty years later, Pender recalled, "A young fellow came up to me and said he wanted to go on the stage." It was Archie Leach.

What the boy did not tell Pender was that he was still only thirteen, and therefore not quite old enough to leave school legally. When the jovial man told him that there might be a chance of his joining the act if he could get his parents' permission, because so many of the troupe were going off to war, Archie remembered the lesson of his application to be a cabin boy. "Before I knew it, I was writing a letter purportedly from my own father to Mr. Pender, and I conveniently neglected to explain that I was not yet fourteen," he said later.

Within ten days a reply came back from Pender inviting him to Norwich, where the troupe was performing, for an interview. Even better, Pender had sent the railway fare. But Elias Leach never saw that letter, even though it had been addressed to him. His son Archie had intercepted it at the front door.

That night Archie Leach could not sleep. Unable to decide

whether or not to go, he packed and then unpacked, until finally, just before six o'clock in the morning, he made up his mind. He stole quietly out of the house, knowing that his father would probably not miss him for days. As he closed the door behind him and walked through the empty streets toward the railway station, he realized that one part of his life was ending.

As the terrible war ground on, the music halls of England were filled with people only too anxious to take their minds off its horrors. Warm, cheerful and bathed in an affection for happier times, the songs of Harry Lauder and Marie Lloyd, of Florrie Forde and Vesta Tilley, the jumble of jugglers and acrobats, conjurors and unicyclists, made the halls a haven of cheerful refuge. Sophisticated audiences in London might prefer the new musical shows like *Chu Chin Chow,* but for most people the music halls provided a sense of belonging shared by audiences and performers alike, and certainly shared by the boy who had run away from his home in Bristol.

Bob Pender had spent his life in this boisterous, uninhibited world. When he was a child his father had toured with a portable wooden theater, and by the time he was fourteen Bob was playing a monkey on the music hall stage. He used to say proudly, "And I did that act for fourteen years." At eighteen, he started his own troupe of boys to play in pantomime sketches. He may never have enjoyed the success of Fred Karno, but he was every bit as successful as most of the other knockabout troupes touring the halls, troupes like Charlie Manon's Knockabout Comedians or Joe Boganny's Lunatic Bakers.

Pender understood how attractive the music hall could be to boys who were unhappy at home. He and his wife, Margaret, who had been a dancer at the Folies-Bergère, were distinctly skeptical about the nervous boy who presented himself at the Theater Royal in Norwich shortly after ten o'clock one cold winter morning in 1917. Privately, Pender was prepared to bet that the letter he'd received had been written by Archie rather than by his father, but he also knew that his act urgently needed replacements. "After looking me over carefully they agreed that if it was still all right with my father they would apprentice me to their troupe," Archie was to recall. "They gave me a short, handwritten contract stipulating that I was to receive my keep and ten shillings' pocket money a week."

The next morning the new recruit began to learn how to be an acrobat, an art he was never to forget. Together with a dozen other boys, most of them older, he was taught the essence of tumbling and the basis of the acrobatic dances he would need in the act. He was taught how to fall convincingly, how to balance and how to take an imaginary blow. Pender's sketches did not need words; they simply needed boys who could turn a backflip without a moment's hesitation. When the morning's rehearsals were over, the new boy was expected to stand at the back of the theater, or, if he was lucky, in the wings, and watch the act. He had to know what he might have to do if he suddenly had to go on, and there was always the chance he would.

"So I practiced making up and thickly covered my face with grease paint that took hours to apply in imitation of what I took to be the prevailing theatrical mode," he was to say later. He did not enjoy this experience. Indeed, he would eventually prefer to avoid wearing any makeup at all, and would feel embarrassed in the company of actors and actresses who insisted on doing so. But, at this stage, he was intent on diving headfirst into the traditions of the theater.

At the end of the week the troupe moved forty miles south to the slightly larger town of Ipswich in Suffolk for the next week of twice-nightly performances. The routine of practice and watching the act each night continued, but Archie had not yet appeared on stage.

One evening, between shows, the theater's stage-door keeper told him that there was a man waiting to see him. "Says he's your father," the old doorkeeper told him, and it was.

Before father and son could say anything to each other, the stocky figure of Bob Pender emerged from his dressing room and shook hands with Elias Leach. Although the boy did not know it, the meeting was not unexpected, for Pender had taken the precaution of writing another letter to Elias Leach to make sure he felt happy about his son's new apprenticeship. He had invited him to come and see them.

In fact, there were great similarities between the two men. They were almost exactly the same age, and each was given to wearing bowler hats, waistcoats and rather flamboyant wing collars and ties. They were also both subscribers to the teachings and practices of the fraternal order of Free and Accepted Masons, the largest secret society in the world. Bob Pender did not know that when he wrote about his latest recruit. But once he caught sight of the insignia hanging from Leach's watch chain he was relieved. Between Masons, he knew, there was not likely to be a disagreement.

Without telling the by now pale-faced boy what they intended to do, the two men left the theater together for a drink. Standing in the wings, Archie looked across the empty stage and wondered whether he would ever see it again. He need not have worried. After some discussion, the two men agreed that he had better finish his education, although, in fact, he would be fourteen in a matter of weeks and nothing could keep him at school after that. "If he leaves, I'd be happy to take him back," Pender concluded.

Elias Leach returned with his son to Bristol on the train the following morning. Back at school, Archie reveled in being a celebrity. He demonstrated the cartwheels, handsprings and backflips he had learned with the troupe, and carefully concealed the fact that he had never actually appeared in front of an audience. Gradually, however, his mind returned to wandering in its familiar lonely darkness. He could not forget the release and fantasy of the Pender troupe. "I did my unlevel best to flunk at everything," he was to say. "The only class I attended with any interest and alacrity was the twice-weekly instruction in the gymnasium."

For the rest of the time he played truant and caused disruption. The singing teacher actually threw a bunch of keys at him during one lesson, so appalling was his behavior. Once again, but now with much greater regularity, he began to appear in front of the school's formidable headmaster, Augustus Smith— "And he could lay it on," recalled Archie—but the canings and reprimands had no effect. He had inherited his mother's stubbornness.

Finally, in March 1918, matters came to a head. One afternoon, Archie and a close pal of his sneaked into the girls' lavatories while the rest of the school was studying and were discovered there by one of the women teachers. Now, Archie Leach found himself in front of his dreaded headmaster for the last time.

"The following morning when the school filed in for morning prayer," he wrote later, "my name was called and I was marched up the steps onto the dais and taken to stand next to Gussie Smith, where with a quivering lip that I did my best to control, I hazily heard such words as 'inattentive . . . irresponsible and incorrigible . . . discredit to the school' and so forth, and through a trancelike mixture of emotions realized I was being publicly expelled in front of the assembled school."

The rather tall boy—he had grown four inches in the past year—walked across the playground, took his bicycle from the shed and went home. He was just fourteen. Three days later he was back on the train and rejoining the Pender troupe.

His father had not put up any resistance to the idea. For one thing, he had been expecting it. For another, to have the financial burden of his son off his hands meant that he had a little more money for himself. For, although he would never divorce his mentally ill wife, he had begun to realize that he could not stop living a normal life just because she was no longer there to share his home. He had already found the woman who would be his wife in all but name.

For his part, the son was glad to be finally escaping from the wintry shadow of his mother. He had never seen her since the day four years before when he had come back from school to discover that she had gone. There had not been even a letter from her, even though his father had told him from time to time she was asking after him. He still felt desolate at her loss, and he had no idea at all where she was. So he grabbed the opportunity to find a new family who would welcome his presence and indulge the feeling his mother had fostered in him of being a special boy without her habit of cutting him down to size and denying him the praise and admiration he longed for.

Three months later, in August 1918, Pender and his troupe

came back to the Bristol Hippodrome. This time their latest recruit was performing onstage with them. The act still relied on pantomime, as it had always done, but that did not detract from the pleasure Elias Leach enjoyed at seeing his son perform.

Before the second house at the Hippodrome that night, Elias Leach had another drink with Bob Pender and asked if Archie could stay at Picton Street while the troupe was in Bristol. Pender agreed. After the final curtain, Leach and his son walked home in the warm night air together to the gloomy house they no longer shared.

"We hardly spoke," the boy was to write, "but I felt so proud of his pleasure and so much pleasure in his pride, and I remember we held hands for part of that walk."

At the end of the week Archie Leach went back to the Penders, and back on the road touring the music halls. The warmth and affection that he craved were still there, and, most important of all, Pender's troupe provided him with an identity. They taught him the pantomime art of timing, of knowing how to get a reaction from an audience. But they also taught him that he did not need to be alone.

When they were in London, playing the Gulliver circuit of music halls, most of the boys lived with the Penders in their house in south London, a district traditionally beloved of music hall performers. Sleeping in dormitories like pupils at an English boarding school, they were subject to a not-dissimilar regime. Lights were put out at ten P.M., and the boys had to be washed, dressed and ready for breakfast at seven-thirty the next morning. Hardly the bawdy, bohemian actors of popular imagination.

When the armistice was signed on November 11, 1918, Bob Pender's boys were in Preston in the north of England, still performing their elaborate clowning acts but now as part of a show in which the newly popular moving pictures were an added attraction. The boy remembered later that the theater was almost empty that night, not as a result of celebrations in the streets but because of the postwar flu epidemic that was beginning to claim its first victims. Before the epidemic abated, a quarter of the population would have caught the disease and 150,000 would be killed by it.

By Christmas, the Pender boys had split into two groups of eight. The more experienced troupe spent the holiday period playing the great industrial city of Liverpool, while the less experienced, which included Archie, were performing on the pier at Colwyn Bay, a small seaside town in north Wales.

In the next eighteen months, Archie Leach ruthlessly taught himself to be a performer, and to conceal his own personality as he did so.

"At each theater I carefully watched the celebrated headline artists from the wings, and grew to respect the diligence it took to acquire such expert timing and unaffected confidence, the amount of effort that resulted in such effortlessness," he was to say later.

"I strove to make everything I did at least appear relaxed. Perhaps by relaxing outwardly I thought I could eventually relax inwardly, sometimes I even began to enjoy myself on-stage."

The determination to succeed paid handsome dividends when Pender told his young stars that he had booked the troupe for New York. They were to join a Charles Dillingham show at the Globe Theater on Broadway, but he could take only eight boys. One whom he chose was the determined Archie Leach, a close friend of Pender's younger brother, Tommy, who was also to be included.

The sixteen-year-old Archie realized that there was nothing to keep him in England. He still did not know where his mother was, and his father was creating another life for himself. Standing on the deck of the magnificent SS *Olympic* as she nosed carefully out of Southampton Water in July 1920, he had no tears in his eyes. As he watched the chalk cliffs of the Needles fall away slowly behind him, he knew he might not see them again. He also knew that he did not much care.

When she was launched in 1911, the White Star Line's SS *Olympic* had been called "the world's wonder ship." The first-class stairway was paneled in mahogany, with a wooden symbol representing Honor and Glory inlaid at the main landing.

The first-class dining room had Louis Seize chairs and close carpeting. At forty-six thousand tons she was bigger and faster than the Cunard Line's famous *Mauretania*, and exactly the same size as her famous sister ship, the doomed *Titanic*, which had sunk on her maiden voyage in April 1912. Since that disaster, the *Olympic* had been specially fitted with double sides and "additional watertight bulk heads extending from the Bottom to the Top of the Vessel."

Perhaps it was this opulence that drew actors to the ship. The *Olympic* had taken Charlie Chaplin and the Fred Karno company to New York for the start of their second tour of the United States. Clara Bow, Pola Negri and Maurice Chevalier had traveled first class on it, although in a few years many of them were to transfer their affections to the French liner *Ile de France*, and then later to the beautiful SS *Normandie*.

Archie Leach, however, was not traveling first class, but, like Charlie Chaplin before him, second. Nevertheless, he would occasionally glimpse some of the liner's more celebrated passengers on their morning walks around the deck. Among them were the world's most famous honeymooners, Douglas Fairbanks and Mary Pickford, who, having just launched with Chaplin and D. W. Griffith the United Artists company in Hollywood, had been married in a blaze of publicity a few weeks before.

Needless to say, they captivated the boy from Bristol. "They were gracious and patient in face of constant harassment by people with cameras and autograph books whenever they went on deck," he would remember. "Once I even found myself being photographed with Mr. Fairbanks during a game of shuffleboard and, as I stood beside him, I tried to tell him of my adulation." The athletic actor smiled and accepted the compliment, thanking the boy for his kindness.

The star's generosity stuck in Archie Leach's mind, and so did his deep suntan, which he then and there determined to imitate. That morning he began a regimen he was to keep up for the rest of his life, a regular period of sitting in the sun to make sure he looked as healthy, and as relaxed, as Fairbanks. It was not to be the only parallel between the two men's careers.

Twenty-two years later the boy was to have almost as celebrated a honeymoon with the "richest girl in the world," Barbara Hutton.

As he played deck tennis, watched the daily tug of war and
listened to the band while the ship sailed sedately across the
summer calm of the Atlantic, Archie could hardly believe his
luck. When the ship entered New York harbor, he stayed up all
night to see, with wonder tinged with terror, the new towers of
Manhattan shimmering in the early daylight. He had no idea
what lay in store for him, but here at last was the city where
reputations were made at a stroke, where every barman, newspaper seller and shoeshine man on Broadway and Forty-second
Street had only one topic of conversation—show business.

Originally, Bob Pender and his troupe had been booked to
play the Globe Theater, but soon after they made their way
down the canvas-covered gangplank they learned there had
been a change of plan. The eight boys, together with their eternally cheerful boss, now resplendent in a dogtooth check suit
with his wife, Margaret, flaunting her best fur beside him, set
off instead toward the majestic Hippodrome on Sixth Avenue.
Called "the largest theater in the world," it could seat nearly
forty-five hundred people and played two shows a day six days
a week with a matinee on Sundays. The immense stage concealed forty-eight dressing rooms, each named after a state in
the Union. Best suited to exhibition acts like the Penders, who
relied on pantomime and not dialogue, "the Hipp" was now to
house Charles Dillingham's new spectacle *Good Times,* with a
cast of almost a thousand and a backstage company of eight
hundred.

Archie celebrated his newfound independence in America by
falling in love. As he was to do many times in the future, he
chose a girl utterly unlike his small, dark-eyed and wiry
mother. Gladys Kincaid was blond, blue-eyed and generously
endowed; and when the time came for the show to close, he was
in a state of despair. While the other boys waited impatiently
outside, he languished inside, longing for a last look at the girl
who had become the focus of his adolescent passion.

"When she appeared, I remember standing there tongue-tied

and fuddle-headed while people milled around us and those nitwits kept putting their heads around the door yelling, 'Hurry up' and 'Come on.' ''

They were to stand there for what seemed like an hour before both blurted out, "I do hope we see each other again" at precisely the same moment. They had never even held hands, although he had given her a multicolored woolen sweater for Christmas. She rushed out of the stage door, leaving him looking bashfully after her. They never met again. But the seventeen-year-old Archie mooned about her for weeks.

It was the spring of 1921, a time of Prohibition and speakeasies, of King Oliver and a young Louis Armstrong, when young women with short skirts and bobbed hair wished they could shimmy like their sister Kate. Jack Dempsey was the world heavyweight champion, Big Bill Tilden the greatest tennis player of the day and Warren Harding had just been inaugurated President. It was the beginning of an era that F. Scott Fitzgerald would name the Jazz Age.

A quarter of the American population was going to the silent movies every week, and the vaudeville houses were suffering as a result. Not that B. F. Keith's theaters, for which Pender had booked his troupe next, were doing badly. They were the major circuit in American vaudeville and had their own fierce rules and regulations to keep them on top. Groucho Marx used to recall, "They fined you for everything," and many others were frightened by the sign that hung backstage at every theater: DON'T SAY "SLOB" OR "SON OF A GUN" OR "HOLY GEE" ON THE STAGE UNLESS YOU WANT TO BE CANCELED PEREMPTORILY.

For the next year Pender, his wife and their eight English boys toured Keith's East Coast circuit. They played in theaters from Cleveland to Boston, Chicago to Milwaukee and Washington to Philadelphia, happily sharing the same bills as the Foy family or Eddie Cantor, unaware that vaudeville would ever come to an end.

The pinnacle of the Keith circuit was the Palace in New York. In the ten years since it had opened on Broadway at Forty-seventh Street it had become a vaudeville legend. Jack Benny, who played there as part of a double act known as

Benny and Woods, described it as "the theater every actor was nervous about," because it was acknowledged as the top of the vaudeville tree. Performers would arrange to meet on the pavement outside its entrance, on what became known as the Palace Beach, and the restaurants and cafés on the block were called "the corn exchange for comedians." When the Pender troupe played the Palace in June 1922, they knew they had conquered vaudeville. What they did not know was that they were about to split up.

Bob Pender and his wife had decided to take a holiday before starting another tour. No one went to vaudeville in the summer anyway, and traditionally the weeks until Labor Day in early September were the time to work out a new act. But both Archie Leach and Tommy Pender, who was still in the troupe, felt the time had come to break out from the Pender dormitory. They told Pender they were homesick and wanted to go back to England. Generous as ever, he gave them their fare home. But the two boys had no intention of returning to England. They had decided to work on their own.

With no prepared act, they set themselves up as an unofficial Pender troupe, relying on the stilts, tumbling and slapstick routines they already knew. Even this did not seem to upset their old boss, who was by then in California. The stocky man with the ready smile and the loud check suits had been on the road as an entertainer since he was born. So what did he care? Later that year, while his younger brother and Archie Leach were still doing a version of the act he had created in New York, he sailed back to England. Within two years he was to give up the music hall altogether and retire to run a small toy shop in the English resort of Southend-on-Sea, down the Thames from London, where he was to die in 1939.

Vaudeville was dying too, but if Archie Leach noticed it, he had no intention of trying anything else, at least not for the moment. He was determined simply to survive.

CHAPTER 3

There were no more wise men;
there were no more heroes.
F. Scott Fitzgerald, *This Side of Paradise*

Coney Island in the summer of 1922 was everything the greatest amusement park in the world should be. The rides were the
fastest, the Ferris wheel the tallest and the new roller coaster
the most frightening in the world. There was no traffic on the
main streets, and the policemen who patrolled them were
rarely troubled. It was the place where every family in New
York knew it could be sure of a good time. Since the subway
had reached it two years before, the boardwalk looking across
the sand toward the Atlantic Ocean had been packed, especially on Saturdays and Sundays.

In fact, it was Coney Island that provided Archie Leach's
first job after he left the Pender troupe. One evening that summer he had been invited to a dinner party on Park Avenue.
The fact that he was eighteen, tall and darkly handsome meant
an increasing number of invitations. His face may have been a
little fleshy and his nose a little wide, but Archie Leach was attractive enough to grace any dinner table. That evening he was
seated beside George Tilyou, whose family owned and operated
the Steeplechase Park on Coney Island.

"I remembered seeing a man walking on stilts along Broadway advertising something or another, and I heard myself suggesting to Mr. Tilyou that perhaps I could do the same for
him," he recalled. Within a week he found himself walking up
and down outside Steeplechase Park on six-foot-high stilts
wearing a bright green coat with red braid, a bright green cap
and exceptionally long black trousers.

"I got three dollars a day on weekdays, but after the first Saturday and Sunday I struck for five dollars a day. Mr. Tilyou

wouldn't give it to me at first, but I took him outside and showed him that the weekend crowds were so terrific that I was knocked down regularly, and that was worth five dollars." Before long he had doubled that to five dollars for weekdays and ten dollars for each weekend day, for a total of forty-five dollars a week.

He supplemented his income by making a deal with the proprietor at a hot-dog stand. "I got five hot dogs a day just for walking by his stand. So then I fixed up a deal with a restaurant and an ice-cream place and I got all the food I wanted free."

The only drawback was that his stilts provided a target for the children who toured the park looking for less conventional amusement. "I used to walk in fear, constantly afraid some hoodlums would dash between my legs, knock me down and break my knees, so that I wouldn't be able to find a job that fall." He was upended half a dozen times a day, but he stuck it out. Any job was better than none.

Fortunately, a new opening presented itself in vaudeville. The director of the New York Hippodrome, R. H. Burnside, was preparing a spectacle on the lines of Dillingham's *Good Times*, which he called *Better Times*. The new version of the Pender troupe, Tommy Pender and Archie Leach, began to practice together again, and in September they returned to the theater where they had started two years before, calling themselves The Walking Stanleys. This time Archie Leach was a little more confident with the chorus girls in the cast. He started to go out with one of them, who lived with her family in Brooklyn.

"One night," he recalled forty years later, "we attended a late party in someone's apartment. Prohibition was in force so naturally we drank. I drank hard apple cider, thinking it least likely to affect me, and in no time at all was laid to rest in a spare bedroom, where I was hazily joined, thanks to the maneuvering of some well-meaning friends, by the lady in question. We awakened to find ourselves falteringly, fumblingly and quite unsatisfactorily attempting to ascertain whether those blessed birds and bees knew what they were doing." It was the first time he had ever tried to make love to a girl, but as he was to recall, "I cannot add it was an occasion for song."

For the next few weeks he tried to do what he thought a suitor should do and escort the girl home to her parents' house in Brooklyn every evening after the show, but gradually the problems of finding a way of getting back into Manhattan again persuaded him to give up. Instead, he took to having supper with some other former members of the Pender troupe to talk about what sort of act they could put together after *Better Times* closed. For Archie Leach, women were not as serious a business as making a living.

Burnside's spectacle at the Hippodrome closed in the first months of 1923. It was the last time any New York producer would ever try to mount anything so extravagant, and it forced the former members of the Pender troupe to put their plans into action. After trying out their new mime show, with its familiar mixture of tumbling, stilt walking and slapstick farce, they got a booking with the Pantages circuit. The experience came as a considerable shock after the comparative luxury of the Keith circuit on the East Coast.

Alexander Pantages had started out as a waiter in a concert hall on the West Coast during the Klondike gold rush in 1896 and, after teaming up with a burlesque producer called Jack Flynn, who supplied the chorus girls, had started opening vaudeville theaters. The first two were next door to each other in Seattle. This circuit was principally on the West Coast, from Washington down to California and up to western Canada. Working his theaters could mean up to five shows a day on Saturdays and Sundays, with four on weekdays. But Alexander Pantages did give Archie one great gift. On this tour Archie first saw the town that would become his home, Hollywood.

When Horace Henderson Wilcox bought 120 acres of cactus and palm trees, orange groves and poinsettias northwest of Los Angeles in 1887, he had wanted to found a religious community based on sober principles. He was, after all, a Kansas Prohibitionist. His wife, Daeida, gave the place the name Hollywood, but it did not develop quite the way Wilcox had hoped.

59

In 1906 the American Mutoscope and Biograph Company set up in the sunshine of central Los Angeles, eight miles away down a rough country road; and, in 1907, the director of some early one-reel films, Francis Boggs, turned up from Chicago with a handful of actors from Colonel William N. Selig's motion picture company. Selig had decided to send them to California because the state boasted it had 350 sunny days a year. With Hobart Bosworth, a former Broadway actor who had lost his voice, in the starring role, Boggs made *The Power of the Sultan* on a vacant lot next to a Chinese laundry. Four years later the first studio to settle in Hollywood itself was opened on Sunset Boulevard by the Nestor Company, run by two English brothers, William and David Horsley. Within a few months, fifteen other companies from the East Coast had joined them in Hollywood, to take advantage not only of the fine weather but also of the cheap rents.

By 1919, Hollywood had incorporated itself into Los Angeles as a result of a paralyzing drought (the city had provided it with water), and four out of every five films made anywhere in the world were being made in Southern California. The electricity and coal shortages during World War I had sent more and more film companies hurrying across the continent, and by the time Douglas Fairbanks and Mary Pickford arrived back from their honeymoon trip on the SS *Olympic* in 1920, they were at the center of a worldwide industry.

Cecil B. De Mille, Jesse Lasky and Sam Goldwyn had made *The Squaw Man,* D. W. Griffith had directed both *The Birth of a Nation* and *Intolerance,* Mack Sennett had launched the Keystone Kops and Charles Chaplin had created "the little fellow" well before Archie Leach's train pulled into the Los Angeles station early in 1924. The city was already a modern Babylon, a place of scandal and excess, where rumor fueled the wildest fantasies. There were no art galleries or museums, few bookshops and no traditional theaters to give a young Englishman a sense of home. But like so many of the other hopefuls who had flocked there, Archie Leach wanted a new life, not memories.

"I saw palm trees for the first time," he recalled. "I was impressed by Hollywood's wide boulevards and their extraordinary cleanliness in the pre-smog sunshine. I didn't know I would make my home there one day. And yet, I *did* know. . . .

"There is some prophetic awareness in each of us. I cannot remember daring consciously to hope I would be successful at anything, yet, at the same time, I knew I would be."

Nearly eight years would pass between this first visit and his return. For the moment he was still playing four shows a day as a silent comedian for Pantages, still climbing onto his stilts when the act demanded it and still not speaking a word on-stage. As the troupe slowly worked its way up the California coast into Canada and then started back east, Archie began to want to do more than that. As the columnist Hedda Hopper was later to point out, "He figured out that performers who talked got more money so, just like that, he decided to talk."

For years afterward he was to suffer a nightmare about his search for a speaking part that summer. In the dream, he would remember "standing on the lighted stage of a vast theater facing a silent, waiting audience. I am the star, and I am surrounded by a large cast of actors, each of whom knows exactly what to do and say! And I can't remember my lines! I can't remember them because I've been too lazy to study them. I can find no way to bluff it through, and I stand there inept and insecure. I make a fool of myself. I am ashamed."

When he began to tour the Broadway booking agents' offices looking for speaking parts in plays, the question he was asked was usually the same.

"You ever spoken lines?" the girls behind the small wooden railings would ask in slightly bored voices. Tall, athletic looking and flashily handsome, Archie was striking enough to make them look up, but he could not deny his inexperience. Nor could he control the insecurity he always felt. He tended to answer meekly, "None at all, I'm afraid."

There were occasional jobs, however. In one company he was supposed to portray "The Spirit of the Theater" by dressing in a leotard and emerging from a trapdoor in the center of the stage at the opening of the show to explain what the audience was about to see. One night, as he was descending again, the trapdoors shut prematurely, and he spent the first act with his

61

head sticking up above the floor of the stage with the chorus line kicking around him. The stage manager had no intention of bringing down the curtain just to rescue a walk-on player.

There were also some slapstick routines which called for him to use the tumbling he had refined with the Pender troupes, and he still got one or two bookings as a mime because of his slightly bowlegged walk, which had earned him the nickname "Rubber Legs" in some vaudeville houses.

Between bookings, he returned to Coney Island, once as a lifeguard, more usually as a "barker," encouraging the customers to try the thrills of the Red Mill, sample the delights of the Tunnel of Love or, on one occasion, pay to gawk at a bearded lady. He even spent time on Sixth Avenue selling hand-painted ties, which a young Australian, John Kelly, had been making in his apartment in Greenwich Village.

Kelly, who was to go on to Hollywood and become famous as the designer Orry-Kelly, said later, "He was a very likable kid who had rather a thick English accent, although he was losing it fast. He lived in my apartment in Greenwich Village for a time. He was trying to act but he was god-awful, and other friends of mine thought so too."

Gradually, he began playing the straight man to any comedian who would take him on tour, or working around New York for the minimum rate of $62.50 between the two of them. As he put it later, "Eventually, I played practically every small town in America, and, as the straight man, I learned to time laughs. When to talk into an audience's laughter. When to wait for the laughs. When not to wait for the laugh. In all sorts of theaters, of all sizes, playing to all types of people, timing laughs that changed in volume and length at every performance." It may not have been quite the "speaking" he had thought of when he left the Pantages tour, but it taught him his technique. He also started watching the great straight men work, like George Burns, who was playing with his wife, Gracie Allen, and Zeppo Marx, part of "the greatest comedy act in show business," as the Marx Brothers called themselves.

Eventually, an old friend, Don Barclay, turned up and suggested that Archie become his partner in a mind-reading act. At a beach cottage on Long Island the two men tried out their routine, using the children next door as an audience. As it happened, these children were used to the ways of vaudeville, for their father, Walter Winchell, was still working in it.

"Gentlemen," Barclay would say from the midst of the audience, "this is a serious test of thought transmission. Professor Knowall Leach will endeavor to call anyone in the audience by name."

The comic would then ask selected victims their names before shouting to his partner on the stage.

"This gentleman's from Buffalo."

"Bill," the straight-faced stooge would shout back.

"Now here's a stickler, Professor. For the love of . . ."

"Pete."

"No, no, the other kind."

"Mike."

"This girl is an upper and a lower, Professor."

"Bertha."

"And here's one not deaf but dumb."

"Dora."

"Dumber than that."

"Belle."

Then Barclay would vary the routine slightly. He would shout to his partner, "Where is this man's father?"

There would be a pause.

"At this minute your father is in Denver, Colorado."

The member of the audience would then shout, "No, he's not, he's in Memphis."

Another slight pause. Then the puzzled professor would reply from the stage, "Your mother's husband may be in Memphis, but your father's in Denver."

Years later Barclay would say, "Archie always felt that was bad taste. But bad taste or not it always got a big laugh."

In the summer of 1927, the two men took their act on the road. They started in Toledo, but got no farther than Newark, New Jersey, where the theater manager told Barclay to get another straight man or the act was canceled. Sadly they broke up, and a disheartened Archie Leach took the train to New York. It was an experience he preferred to forget.

The speakeasies were still there and the young men still

63

paraded in their snap-brimmed hats and spats, but the Broadway Archie Leach came back to in the summer of 1927 had changed. Audiences were no longer desperate to relieve the thought of war with the laughter of the vaudeville theater. Now they preferred more sophisticated entertainment. The loud jackets and baggy trousers of vaudeville were giving way to the white tie and tails of musical comedy. Archie Leach could hardly know it, but the change was to make him a star.

Being English was no longer a handicap. Gertrude Lawrence, Beatrice Lillie and Jack Buchanan had already taken New York by storm in André Charlot's *London Revue of 1924,* while Noel Coward's *The Vortex* had been breaking box-office records for five months. Almost any young Englishman who looked dashing in tails had a chance of success.

Romance, too, was in the air. The most popular songs from *No, No, Nanette,* "Tea for Two" and "I Want to Be Happy," seemed somehow to capture the spirit of the times. This was not England recovering from the general strike, it was the America of Fred and Adele Astaire glittering in George Gershwin's *Lady Be Good.* It was the country of Valentino and Theda Bara, not John Galsworthy and George Bernard Shaw. The ladies in the theaters wanted their leading men to be tall, dark and handsome, and preferably as mysterious as the Red Shadow in Sigmund Romberg's *The Desert Song.*

The twenty-three-year-old Archie Leach was undeniably tall, and with his brooding eyes and olive skin he was unquestionably handsome. His hair was every bit as dark as Valentino's, and while his face may have been fleshier than Coward's or Astaire's, it had an almost Mediterranean voluptuousness that theirs lacked. Archie realized that if he could master their clipped, elegant and fundamentally English style, it would add to his appeal. As a step toward this goal, he started dressing more conservatively. His suits became better cut, his shirts white and his ties restrained. He took to standing with one hand in his pocket, adopting a studied nonchalant stare in an awkward parody of Coward. He looked graceless at first, but he knew that to succeed he had to become someone else, and he was not to be put off.

As his transformation evolved, he was invited to more and more parties as an escort for unattached ladies. Manhattan hostesses knew he would light their cigarettes with a practiced movement of the wrist and take their arms at precisely the right moment, although perhaps a little too cautiously. Like one of the young men in Margaret Kennedy's new novel *The Constant Nymph,* he was brittle, charming and always "frightfully" gay. This pose became a mask he was steadily more reluctant to take off.

When he wasn't invited out to dinner, he would go to Rudley's Restaurant on Forty-first Street and Broadway, where a circle of actors and writers gathered. At a corner table there was always gossip about jobs. Preston Sturges was a member of the Rudley's table, so were Moss Hart, George Murphy, Edward Chodorov and Humphrey Bogart, then still assisting the independent producer William A. Brady. Later, Moss Hart was to describe the Archie Leach of those years as "disconsolate," and Edward Chodorov was to say, "He was never a very open fellow, but he was earnest and we liked him."

Still relying on the discipline he had had since childhood, he kept quiet most of the time, learning as much as he could from the conversation around him, eager for any intellectual education and even spiritual leadership. Not that he neglected vaudeville. It still provided him with a steady, if not handsome, living. He played dates here and there at small theaters and private clubs, and he would sometimes do Sunday-night benefits. One Sunday evening his partner was too drunk to stand up, and the desperate stage manager persuaded Archie to go on by himself. He sang two songs, told a couple of jokes, did a short acrobatic dance and retired gratefully to the wings. But the experience convinced him that he could probably survive alone, and that he might have a future in musical comedy if he could learn to sing.

One of his friends, Max Hoffman, was already in musical comedy. Hoffman was a not particularly successful juvenile, but he was a friend of Reggie Hammerstein, the stage director whose elder brother was Oscar Hammerstein II, composer of the lyrics for Jerome Kern's *Show Boat,* Rudolf Friml's *Rose*

65

Marie and Romberg's *The Desert Song.* One night Reggie Hammerstein spent some time persuading the young Archie Leach that he had a future in musical comedy. It was unusual for Archie to take the advice of anyone his own age, but he was a little in awe of the young man whose grandfather had owned the famous Victoria Theater and whose Uncle Arthur was about to open another theater that would bear the family name. The arguments, moreover, sounded all the more attractive when linked with the high salaries musical performers commanded. As Archie put it years later, "I went into musicals because, frankly, they paid more money than the drama in New York."

Archie began to take singing and voice lessons, and in the evenings he and Reggie would discuss the best way for him to get his first part in a musical. In September 1927, the obvious opportunity presented itself. The young stage director took his friend to meet his Uncle Arthur, who had just announced he was to stage *Golden Dawn,* a new operetta, with lyrics by Oscar. The story might have been a little hackneyed, but there was a good juvenile part that could suit the newly trained Archie Leach. "It was the nicest thing anyone ever did for me."

Arthur Hammerstein did not object to the idea of Archie for the part and signed him to a contract. Since the character he would be playing was supposed to be an Australian prisoner of war, it would not matter too much if Broadway audiences were slightly baffled by Archie's English accent. Hammerstein's main worry was whether his leading lady, Louise Hunter, was a big enough name to draw the crowds at the box office, and whether the somewhat erratic leading man, Paul Gregory, would turn up at the theater on time regularly enough to star opposite her.

Late in October Hammerstein sent *Golden Dawn* out on the road for a month of previews. Two weeks in Boston were to be followed by two weeks in Philadelphia, then would come the Broadway opening on the last day of November.

Boston was not a success. Oscar Hammerstein and Otto Harbach fiddled with the lyrics and amended the story daily, and everyone became increasingly confused. In Philadelphia things went better, and the cast relaxed a little. By the end of the second two-week run they were even beginning to feel they had a chance of being a hit. But Archie was taking no risks on the prospect of a long run. He was carefully saving as much as he could from the salary of $250 a week that Hammerstein was paying him. He didn't intend to end up in the Bristol workhouse.

Golden Dawn opened on November 30, 1927, to distinctly cool reviews. The critics praised a "lavishly mounted" spectacle but thought that it failed to "realize its promised potential" and that the cast had to struggle with the "material they had to work with." Archie Leach was noticed as a "pleasant new juvenile" and a "competent young newcomer," and there were one or two other bright spots. In any case the public ignored the reviews. The name Hammerstein was enough. *Golden Dawn* ran for more than five months before closing after 184 performances. It had not been a bad start to Archie's new career. At the corner table in Rudley's the regulars took to calling him "Kangaroo" and "Boomerang," and maintained that Archie actually sounded Australian because he was struggling so intently to improve his English accent. Archie took the hint. When looking for work, he began calling himself Australian. No one need know he was a lonely boy from Bristol, less carefree and debonair in the private darkness of his apartment than he liked to appear to his friends.

He was distinctly cheered when Arthur Hammerstein offered him a part in *Polly,* a musical version of *Polly with a Past,* the American comedy written by George Middleton and Guy Bolton, in which Ina Claire had been a great success seven years before. Archie was to play the role that Noel Coward had taken in London.

But as soon as rehearsals started he began to worry, and to worry in public. He fussed interminably: his clothes weren't right, there wasn't enough for him to do, the "business" he was supposed to use to make the audience laugh wasn't funny enough, his lines didn't work. It was the meticulous niggling of a privately insecure man who desperately wanted to succeed, and this fussing was to become one of his hallmarks.

On this occasion, it was not unjustified. *Polly* may have boasted the considerable talents of Fred Allen, one of vaudeville's best deadpan comics, as well as the coyly pretty Inez Courtney, but it did not really work as a musical. Archie himself did not shine. As the critic in Wilmington, Delaware, put it when the show was on its six-week tour before New York, "Archie Leach has a strong masculine manner, but unfortunately fails to bring out the beauty of the score."

Later he was to admit ruefully, "My musical comedy inexperience was too evident to go unnoticed, and I was taken out of *Polly* and replaced before it opened on Broadway." Once there, it was greeted by a deadening silence and closed after fifteen performances. His sacking had shocked him, but the show's failure softened the blow, and so did the six-week guaranteed income at $250 a week.

Indeed, the possibility of making even more money had just presented itself. Marilyn Miller, who had started as one of the chorus girls in Florenz Ziegfeld's hugely successful *Follies,* wanted a replacement for her leading man in the musical comedy *Rosalie,* and she thought that the "promising juvenile" from *Golden Dawn* might be just right.

A leading lady with a clear idea for the new leading man she wanted was not unfamiliar to Ziegfeld. Twenty years of "glorifying the American girl," as his publicity called it, meant that he had heard most things from the ladies in his productions. But for once he was not all that averse to the proposal, especially since Archie would cost him a good deal less than the comedian Jack Donahue, whose part he would be taking, and he would certainly not ask anything like the $2,500 a week being paid to Marilyn Miller. So the autocratic Ziegfeld asked his archenemy, Arthur Hammerstein, to release Archie from his contract.

Hammerstein was not amused. To Ziegfeld, he said there was not the slightest chance of his letting him have Archie Leach. But to Archie he said, "I'm selling your contract to someone else." The man he sold it to was J. J. Shubert, who with his brother, Lee, to whom he was reputed never to speak, was Broadway's biggest but hardly most distinguished theatrical producer.

Ironically, nothing could have been better for Archie's career. Within a few weeks the Shuberts had cast him in a new musical with Jeanette MacDonald and had agreed to pay him $350 a week. For a man who had been in only two previous productions and had been summarily fired from one of them, this was no small stroke of fortune. But even then Archie Leach took no chances. The salary with the Shuberts was settled upon before he even set foot inside the theater to rehearse. He was still determined never to be penniless.

"I had great disdain for working for the Shuberts. I wanted to be with Ziegfeld, you see, so that I had no fear of Mr. J.J. because they were beneath me." When it had opened in Atlantic City, the musical had been called *Snap My Garter,* but the confident new juvenile told J. J. Shubert, "That sounds like a burlesque show," and the impresario eventually changed the title to *Boom, Boom.*

But now the Broadway musical itself was being threatened. Talking pictures had begun to take away the audiences that the theaters had come to rely on. The newly merged Metro-Goldwyn-Mayer was already making the first all-singing, all-dancing, all-talking musical, *Broadway Melody.* The movie opened in February 1929, only three weeks after *Boom, Boom,* and overshadowed everything around it.

Jeanette MacDonald remembered later, "The heavy in our show was a dark-eyed, cleft-chinned young Englishman, who, in spite of his unmistakable accent, was cast as a Spaniard. We did a fandango together, during which he tossed me over his arms. He was absolutely terrible in the role, but everyone liked him. He had charm." So much for Archie's performance. Of the show itself, *The New Yorker*'s critic declared, "It can teach one more about despair than the most expert philosopher." It closed after seventy-two performances at the Casino Theater.

Nevertheless, the play brought the Latin-looking Archie Leach and the sometimes petulant Jeanette MacDonald one benefit. During the run Paramount Famous Lasky Corporation decided they should both be given screen tests at the Astoria studios in New York. Paramount had built its reputation on bringing stage stars to Hollywood ever since its chairman, Adolph Zukor, had persuaded Minnie Maddern Fiske to leave New York in 1916 and star in *Tess of the D'Urbervilles.*

In the hysteria after the opening of *Broadway Melody,* the audition was an opportunity neither of the two young players wanted to miss. Riding across the East River toward Queens and the studios, they agreed the suspense about the outcome was "torture" but that it was worthwhile. In Archie's case, the verdict did not prove to be favorable. The studio told him he would never make a movie star. His neck was too thick and his legs were too bowed. But they liked Jeanette MacDonald and swept her off to Hollywood where her first film, *The Love Parade,* was directed by Ernst Lubitsch in his first experiment with sound, with Maurice Chevalier as her co-star.

To console himself, Archie Leach bought a Packard Phaeton, a large and expensive automobile designed for touring, with an open top and a 143-inch wheelbase that made it difficult to steer around corners. He had hardly even sat behind the wheel of a car before, and he certainly could not drive this one, but whatever Paramount thought, he did not intend to be ignored.

The Shuberts kept him under contract and put him into *A Wonderful Night,* a reworking of Johann Strauss's *Die Fledermaus* starring Gladys Baxter and Mary McCoy. The play opened at the Majestic on October 31, 1929, two days after the Wall Street crash. Archie played Max Grunewald, a dressy, vain, superficial and romantic young man, basically the same character he had played before. One New York critic called him "woefully unfunny," although he went on to say that the rest of the men in the cast were no better. Another stated that he "sometimes manages to miss the proper note entirely," while a third added, "Archie Leach, who feels that acting in something by Johann Strauss calls for distinction, is somewhat at a loss as to how to achieve it." Not that the notices mattered all that much. Miraculously, the show survived for 125 performances, playing to largely empty houses before the Shuberts put it out of its misery.

So far Archie's career mainly had consisted of being fired, not getting the part and struggling in mediocre musicals. He was, however, surprisingly undismayed. He was living with three other young men in an apartment in Greenwich Village, sporting a fashionable racoon coat, which he was never to part with, and learning to drive the Packard. He was enjoying a good life for a young man of twenty-five.

Yet one thing was wrong. He was not at all comfortable in the company of women of his own age. With his female partners in the theater, he was calm, superficially charming, reserved and, some thought, pompous. Outside the theater, however, he was gauche, moody and given to adolescent bouts of showing off.

Years later he was to say sadly, "That was my trouble. Always trying to impress someone. Now, wouldn't you think that with a new, shiny, expensive open car and an open-neck shirt, with a pipe in my mouth to create a carefully composed study of nonchalance, sportiveness, savoir faire and sophistication, I would cut quite a swath among the ladies? Nothing of the sort. . . .

"In all those years in the theater, on the road and in New York, surrounded by all sorts of attractive girls, I never seemed able to fully communicate with them."

A romance in Boston fizzled out. Other women whom he tried to court seriously ended up telling him he was conceited and self-satisfied. He felt more comfortable with men. He liked to joke with them after the show was over, drink with them in the Broadway bars. No matter how attractive he may have been to the women on the other side of the footlights, he was more than a little afraid of the sex as a whole.

Soon the Shuberts were employing him again, this time in the touring company version of the musical *The Street Singer* opposite Queenie Smith. For the next nine months he traveled around the country. His baritone voice, however unsatisfactory, was at least keeping him out of the clutches of the Depression; yet, as he strolled awkwardly through the performances, he seemed to be tortured by the sense of being trapped by the debonair personality he had adopted for the stage.

Defensive and moody, he could be awkward with his fellow performers, distant for days at a time and then given to sudden bursts of charm, never sure whether anyone really liked him. In the afternoons he would take bus rides around whatever city he found himself in, just as he had done in London and New York,

71

or he would drive into the country in his Packard to be alone. He also saved his money carefully.

In the first months of 1931 the Shuberts were paying him $450 a week, more than ten times the wage of the average working man in America—if the man were lucky enough to be working at all. More than ten million Americans were out of a job. For them, a Packard Phaeton and a racoon coat were impossible dreams, but Archie Leach's salary enabled him to begin to erase the memory of the cold, gloomy rooms of his grandmother's house, although the damp smell of her pantry sometimes came back to him.

On tour he subdued the recollection with elaborate meals in the company of the most beautiful young women in the show's chorus. Diffident as he was, and occasionally helplessly tongue-tied, he felt this was the sort of thing a twenty-six-year-old leading man should be doing.

On November 5, 1930, Ernst Lubitsch and Maurice Chevalier were both nominated for Academy Awards for their work on *The Love Parade,* the film Jeanette MacDonald had left New York to make after her screen test the year before. The musical had also been nominated for the best picture of the year, only to lose to Lewis Milestone's brilliant antiwar film, *All Quiet on the Western Front.* In the spring of 1931, only a few months after this saddening reminder that other people's careers had fared better than his own, the tour of *The Street Singer* came to an end.

Because he still had Archie's contract to pay, J. J. Shubert proposed that Archie spend the summer in St. Louis, where the brothers ran the open-air municipal opera in Forest Park. Rather than let go of a comfortable salary, Archie Leach accepted. But times were hard and the season had barely begun when the Shuberts asked every member of the company to take a cut in pay. The dancer Frank Horn, a member of the St. Louis company who was to become Archie's secretary for more than twenty years, recalled, "Everybody did—except Archie Leach. He asked for a raise, so when his contract expired, he was through."

Through or not, he completed the season of eighty-seven performances, playing everything from *Music in May* to *Rio Rita,* from *A Wonderful Night* to *Irene* and *Countess Maritza*. He was always the handsome juvenile and managed to look dashing, even when not displaying much talent. Indeed, with his dark hair and olive skin, he cut such a romantic figure that *Variety*'s midwestern correspondent was inspired to write a glowing piece about him.

The piece caught the eye of another Broadway producer, William Friedlander, who was on the verge of casting a new musical play, *Nikki*. He not only sent someone to St. Louis to see Archie but then asked the Shuberts if he might borrow him.

Written by John Monk Saunders for his wife, Fay Wray, who played the female lead, *Nikki* opened at the Longacre Theater in New York on September 29, 1931. Loosely based on a magazine story about flyers in Paris after World War I, earlier that year it had been made into a popular film entitled *The Last Flight* by First National Pictures, with Richard Barthelmess in the role of Cary Lockwood, which would be taken by Archie Leach. But as a musical, this thin mixture of romance and forgettable melodies did not endear itself to audiences for whom the theater was now an expensive luxury. Although Friedlander moved it to the George M. Cohan Theater in a desperate bid to keep it going, *Nikki* closed on October 31, 1931, after just thirty-nine performances.

Archie Leach next accepted an offer to make a one-reel film called *Singapore Sue* at Paramount's Astoria studios, playing opposite the Chinese character actress Anna Chang. It was the first time he had been inside the studio since his ill-fated screen test two years earlier. As one of four American sailors visiting Chang's café in Singapore, Archie smiled and murmured his few words of dialogue. On the screen, dressed in a white uniform, he looked almost Oriental himself, with his heavy sallow features and ripe lips bared in a wide, false smile. The short's director, Casey Robinson, who was later to go to Hollywood as a screenwriter, was sufficiently impressed as he recalled later, to send "a note to the important executives at Paramount, none of whom I knew at the time, urging them to screen the short, not for my work but for that of a young actor whom I felt to be a surefire future star." But the short was not screened until the middle of the following year, and by that time its leading man had reached Hollywood by another route.

Meanwhile, Fay Wray, his co-star in *Nikki*, was packing for California to play the part of the beauty who hypnotizes the beast in the film that RKO Radio was planning from Edgar Wallace's story, *King Kong*. "Why don't you come out on a visit?" she said to Archie almost in passing.

Together with his friend the composer Phil Charig, Archie had originally planned to take a golfing holiday in Florida. The regular salary he had been receiving over the past year meant that he had more than enough money to live on, and he wasn't anxious to jump back into another Shubert contract. Billy Grady of the William Morris Agency, always known by his nickname "Square Deal," had advised Archie not to sign another contract, telling him, "You must become a leading man. Why don't you go to California?"

So Archie and Phil Charig went to California instead of Florida, setting out in mid-November 1931 to drive three thousand miles across the continent. The Packard was crammed with so many suits they could hardly squeeze into it themselves, but they were in no particular hurry. After ten days, driving some of the time with the tiny glass windshield folded down to help them get a tan in the wind, they arrived in Hollywood, settled themselves into a suite at the Château Elysée, where Katharine Hepburn had stayed when she had first arrived, and set out to discover what California had to offer to two handsome young men.

Billy Grady had arranged for Archie to see the Hollywood agent Walter Herzbrun, who in turn introduced him to Marion Gering, a former Broadway stage director who was then directing films. Two evenings later Gering invited Archie to dine with him and his wife at the home of the production chief of Paramount, the fearsome B. P. Schulberg, who had not only helped launch the Famous Players company with Adolph Zukor in 1912 but had also started the film careers of both Clara Bow, the "It" girl, and Gary Cooper, by then the studio's biggest star. Given to massive fits of temper, Schulberg was reputed to receive a salary of $500,000 a year from Zukor. The dinner was intimate and, inevitably, sumptuous.

74

"I'm going to make a screen test of my wife tomorrow," Gering murmured to Archie after the main course had been cleared away. "She thinks she'd like to be in movies, and B.P. agreed I could do it."

"Why don't you make it with her," suggested Schulberg, peremptorily addressing Archie from the head of the table. "She'll need someone to act against. You only have to feed her the lines. Nothing too difficult."

Archie smiled and replied that he would be delighted. As he left Schulberg's house to drive back to the hotel, he resolved to make sure that the test caught his right profile and that the lighting did not make his neck look too thick.

For Archie, the test, which took place at Paramount Publix's studios on Marathon Street, right in front of the Hollywood Cemetery, involved nothing more than the reading of a few lines and a series of entrances and exits. Throughout, he remembered to relax and to keep his eye on the camera so that it would catch him in the best light. By comparison, the pretty but flustered Mrs. Gering was a good deal less in control. Less than a week later Schulberg called Archie.

"How would you feel about a contract? We could start you at four hundred fifty dollars a week with options for five years. Standard, everybody signs it."

Archie had taught himself never to agree to anything too quickly. "I'd like to think about it."

"Do that. Only one other thing. You'll need to change your name."

At that moment the only son of Elsie Maria Leach realized that it was possible to put aside his unhappy past as if it had never happened, to become someone new. He could begin life again six thousand miles away from the chill memories of home. He and his father still wrote to each other, but Elias had set up house with another companion who, he said, was expecting a child. Archie's mother was a subject they never discussed. Now Archibald Alec Leach knew exactly what he was going to do. He was going to cease to exist.

PART 2

The Matinee Idol

I see Hollywood as a precarious sort of
Streetcar. Call it Aspire. There's only room
for so many, and every once in a while, if
you look back, you'll see that someone has
fallen off. When Tyrone Power got on it
meant someone was left sprawled out on the
street. Ronald Colman sits up with the
motorman. Gary Cooper is smart, he never
gets up to give anybody his seat.

Cary Grant

CHAPTER 4

The movies. It's everything, money, fame, adventure—
the thrill of a lifetime.
        Robert Armstrong to Fay Wray in *King Kong*

No matter how gay the stars seemed, and no matter how hard
the studios tried to reassure the world, Hollywood at the end of
1931 was distinctly nervous. Gone were the carefree days of the
late 1920's, when even the taxi drivers had acted like million-
aires, and Garbo, Chaplin and Swanson had gathered at the
Coconut Grove to hear Paul Whiteman and The Rhythm Boys
with Bing Crosby. Movies were no longer "Depression proof."
They were beginning to lose money. The mighty Warner
Brothers, in spite of its success with *The Jazz Singer* and the first
talking pictures, was contemplating an estimated loss of eight
million dollars. Even tiny RKO, which had just won the Academy Award for best picture of the year with its elegant western
Cimarron, starring Richard Dix and Irene Dunne, had slipped
more than $5.5 million into the red. And it looked as though
things were going to get worse.

At Paramount, Adolph Zukor, its chairman and creator, was
less worried than most. His company was about to report a
profit of six million dollars and his stars had done well at
the fourth Academy Awards ceremony in November. Jackie
Cooper and Fredric March had been nominated, while the
director Norman Taurog had been honored for his work on the
studio's film *Skippy*.

Even more satisfying to Zukor was the fact that Josef von
Sternberg and Marlene Dietrich had won him a string of nominations for *Morocco,* the first film on which they had worked together in America. The movie had not only been as visually
dazzling as Sternberg's *The Blue Angel,* but it had given Zukor a
foreign star to rival Garbo, Louis B. Mayer's prize at Metro-

79

Goldwyn-Mayer. One film magazine had carried out a poll of its readers in which they were asked, "Who will be the greater star of tomorrow, Dietrich or Garbo?" A majority had chosen Dietrich.

But Mayer and Zukor were the only studio heads in Hollywood whose companies were comfortably in profit, and they both knew that those profits depended on the appeal of their stars. Mayer could boast Clark Gable, Marie Dressler, Norma Shearer and Joan Crawford, but Zukor had Gary Cooper, Dietrich's co-star in *Morocco,* as well as Fredric March, Claudette Colbert and Carole Lombard. Always anxious to improve his stable, he had also recently approached Tallulah Bankhead and Herbert Marshall, and Zukor saw no reason why Archie Leach might not prove useful if he agreed to change his name.

Universal had just proved the importance of the right name with the success of its film *Frankenstein,* whose star, Boris Karloff, was an Englishman whose real name was William Henry Pratt. MGM had insisted that Lucille Le Sueur become Joan Crawford and had conducted a fan magazine contest for the new name. Fox had encouraged Jane Peters to become Carole Lombard and Zukor's Frank Cooper had had the sense to change his first name to Gary, after the city in Indiana.

Schulberg himself had suggested to Luis Alonso that he might call himself John Adams, though the actor had finally settled for Gilbert Roland. So when he told the cautious but enthusiastic Archie Leach that if he accepted the studio's contract he would have to find a new name, the only question was, which one?

The first suggestion came from his friend Fay Wray and her husband, John Monk Saunders. "They said it might be nice if I used the name by which I'd been known in their play, Cary Lockwood," he recalled later. The studios liked the first part but objected to the second. "There's already a Harold Lockwood in pictures," said Schulberg firmly, when Archie presented his idea. "We need something short, sharp and easy to remember, like Gable or Cooper." And without a pause he produced a typewritten list of alternatives.

One of the names on it was Grant. "That's the name we'll

put on your contract," he told Archie. "It should be ready shortly."

Schulberg and his colleagues had another reason for liking the name, which they did not tell their new player: it could be confused with Gary Cooper. They already had it in mind to use their fledgling, Grant, as a dark-haired version of Cooper, their most popular leading man, and to star him in the roles that Cooper turned down. They also hoped that Cooper might be made just a little nervous by Grant's arrival at the studio, for the hardworking, hardheaded, six-foot two-inch ex-cattle rancher had them seriously worried. He had gone off in a huff to Africa on safari and was refusing to come back unless Zukor and Schulberg agreed to his right to decide which pictures he made and with whom. As Cooper put it later, "I had made twelve pictures in a year for Paramount; I hardly had time to eat. I really hadn't had a vacation since I started there five years before, so I just went to Africa and vowed to stay there forever if need be. They knew I meant it."

He had been out of town barely four weeks when Paramount signed Cary Grant. As the fan magazine *Photoplay* noted not long afterward, "Cary looks enough like Gary to be his brother. Both are tall, they weigh about the same, and they fit the same sort of roles." Bringing in a newcomer as a potential threat to an established star was nothing new in Hollywood. In 1931 MGM had brought in Robert Young as hedge against Robert Montgomery; ten years later Metro brought in James Craig as a threat to Clark Gable. Such moves were insurance. If things worked out with the original star, the substitute could be paid off without too much fuss and bother. However, no studio could risk having a confrontation with a major star unless it was prepared to replace him.

It was some time before Archie understood this state of affairs. As he signed "Cary Grant" on his new contract in January 1932, he was more interested in being paid $450 a week to become another person. Fourteen years before he had been a moody, frightened boy in Bristol. Now he was a carefree young man in white tie and tails who smiled confidently at beautiful girls. He understood at once that what mattered in the picture business was the image an actor presented on the screen. No one was anything except what he appeared to be and, even more important to Archie, in Hollywood the past did not exist.

The moviegoing public did not want to know that its hero was drunk more often than not, or that the heroine it fervently worshiped had become addicted to morphine. Each studio's lavishly staffed publicity department was paid to see that the image never slipped. That was what mattered.

For Archie Leach, the glamorous mask was a deliverance. As the motion picture fan magazines were soon to report, Cary Grant was suave, distinguished, graceful in every move he made before the camera. The word *polished* fit him as closely as one of his gloves. He was also "handsome" and "virile," blushed "fiery red" when embarrassed and possessed the "same dreamy, flashy eyes as Valentino." Not a bad jump from Picton Street.

Nevertheless, he took pains to protect his new personality. As a reporter noted during his first few months at Paramount, "Anything he says about himself is so offhand and perfunctory that from his own testimony you get only the sketchiest impression of him." And Elisabeth Goldbeck wrote in *Motion Picture* magazine, "Seldom have I seen a man so little inclined to pour out his soul, and you have to scratch around and dig in order to discover even the bare facts of his life from him."

He betrayed only one sign of his buried past. After the contract was signed, he bought a small Sealyham terrier and called it Archie Leach. The act was his only recognition that he had not always been Cary Grant.

As the effects of the Depression cut deeper and deeper into movie attendance, Hollywood relied more and more heavily on its stars. Early in 1932 MGM's production genius Irving Thalberg put five of the studio's biggest names into a film version of Vicki Baum's successful novel and play, *Grand Hotel*. Greta Garbo and John Barrymore headed a cast that also included Joan Crawford, Wallace Beery and Lionel Barrymore. The gamble paid off. *Grand Hotel* won the year's Academy Award as best picture and took in more than $2.5 million at the box office from audiences fascinated both by Crawford's hotel secretary and by Garbo's mercurial ballerina.

But the studios also realized that they must offer something else, a hope of better times and a reassurance to the public that things would turn out all right in the end. This optimistic philosophy lay at the heart of Frances Marion's beautiful script for MGM's *The Champ,* and it was one with which Schulberg at Paramount heartily agreed.

As if to underline this policy, Schulberg decided to launch Grant in as optimistic a film as he could find. His choice was George Marion, Jr.,'s adaptation of Avery Hopwood's Broadway play *Naughty Cinderella,* to be directed by Frank Tuttle and retitled *This Is the Night.*

Cary was cast as Lily Damita's naive husband, an Olympic javelin thrower whose frequent travels leave her time for a romance with her co-star, Roland Young. Essentially a feeble French bedroom farce, the piece called for Grant to look foreign and faintly puzzled as the action moved from Paris to Venice. But beside the blond Miss Damita, Cary was sufficiently striking to provoke *Variety*'s critic to note, "He looks like a potential *femme rave.*"

Grant did not share the critic's good opinions. Early in April 1932, the morning after he had seen the first preview of the film, he called a friend in the Paramount publicity department.

"Good morning, I've called to say good-bye," he told her. "I'm leaving town."

"What?"

"Yes, I'm checking out fast. I saw the preview last night. I've never seen anything so stinkeroo in my life, and I was worse."

The publicity woman finally convinced him not to put his suits in the Packard and drive east to the comparative safety of the Shuberts and Broadway. It was not to be the last time that his insecurity would make him difficult to deal with when a film was about to be released. To many people who would work with him, he seemed to be an actor "virtually paralyzed with fear."

The *Daily Variety* critic made matters worse by calling him Gary Grant in his review, thereby increasing the confusion with Gary Cooper. Mordaunt Hall described him as "efficient" in *The New York Times.* He certainly did not feel it.

Nevertheless, he went straight into making *Sinners in the Sun,* in which, looking conventionally glamorous in a white tie and tails, he supported Carole Lombard. Even Lombard, in the role of a hardworking fashion model, could not save the film. One critic, summing up the views of the rest, said, it was "a weak picture with an unimpressive future before it."

By the time *Sinners in the Sun* was released, Cary Grant had almost completed a third mediocre picture for Paramount, *Merrily We Go to Hell.* Starring Fredric March, this was another feeble story of unrequited love in luxurious surroundings, and Grant was not even to play a part in the principal story. Instead, he portrayed the leading man of the stage play that the drunken journalist, March, had written. Directed by Dorothy Arzner and co-starring Sylvia Sidney, who was then having an affair with B. P. Schulberg, the movie received less than enthusiastic reviews.

His first three films had done little more for Cary Grant than teach him technique of film acting, but he had already started to invest his money wisely. He had bought an interest in two haberdashery shops, one in New York and the other in the rapidly developing Wilshire Boulevard area of Los Angeles, fruits of the interest in tailoring and cloth he had acquired from his father. More importantly, he had met two men who were to play a central part in his life for many years. One was Randolph Scott, who had become a featured player for Paramount shortly before Cary's arrival there. The other was a tall, shy man, reserved with women and wary of talking about himself. His name was Howard Robard Hughes, Jr.

"We met at Paramount," Randolph Scott was to tell Hedda Hopper some years later. "We were having lunch with some of the publicity girls; Cary had just come out from New York as Archie Leach, and he came over to our table and said he was looking for a place to live, so we got bachelor quarters together and lived there for five years."

Born in January 1903, in Orange County, Virginia, the son of a textile engineer, tall, blond-haired and athletic George Randolph Scott was only a year older than Cary Grant but he shared none of his insecurities. He was extroverted and relaxed, liked playing golf and riding and thoroughly disliked worrying. He had five sisters at home, and a nasty back injury, sustained in his junior year of college, had ruined his chances of becoming an all-American in football. After he graduated from the University of North Carolina, he talked his father into letting him tour Europe before starting work in Charlotte, North Carolina, where his family then lived. After the tour he found he still could not settle down, and in 1928 he and a friend took a holiday in California.

He knew no one in Los Angeles and had no particular interest in the movies, but he did have a letter of introduction from his father to Mrs. Ella Hughes, then the wife of a strange young motion picture producer who had arrived in Hollywood in 1925. The tanned, easygoing Scott stayed as a guest with the Hugheses for a couple of weeks.

"Just about the time our stay was up," Scott later told Hopper, "I asked if he could get us on a movie set so we could see how pictures were made. He said to me, 'Why not work in a picture? That'll be better.' "

Hughes called the casting director at United Artists and got Scott and his friend jobs as extras on *Sharp Shooters,* one of the last silent films made. They were to play Australian soldiers. Dressed in uniform, the tall, handsome Scott caught the eye of the director, James Ryan, who told him to take a screen test. But it was Cecil B. De Mille, just about to start making his first talking picture, *Dynamite,* who convinced Scott that he might have a future as an actor. "He advised me to stay here, said I had many things in my favor for becoming a movie actor and suggested that, since talking pictures were coming in, I go to the Pasadena Playhouse and study for a while."

Cary Grant and Randolph Scott were to live together, with only a few interruptions, for nearly ten years. Early on in their friendship, Scott introduced Grant to Hughes.

Hughes was confident, completely self-contained and utterly unconcerned about what Hollywood thought of him. One of his first ventures was *Hell's Angels,* a film that began as a silent in 1928, switched to being a talkie, cost vastly more to make than any previous Hollywood effort, lost, in spite of denials, a cool $1.5 million dollars, but ended up, after its opening on

June 30, 1930, firmly establishing the reputation of Jean Harlow and the legend of Hughes, who then went on to make *The Front Page* and *Scarface*.

Superficially, Howard Hughes, the maverick filmmaker, and Cary Grant, the cautious contract player, were the antithesis of each other. Beneath the surface, however, they were remarkably alike. Both were Capricorns, as was Scott. Both were reticent, careful with their money, shy with women and given to outbursts of peevishness. For Hughes, Cary Grant would become a friend who would help him meet some of the most beautiful women in the world, a follower of his philosophy that women were there to make love to rather than to love. For Cary Grant, the twenty-seven-year-old Texas millionaire would become an adviser and confidant whose opinion he would always listen to, a silent guide for his career.

But Howard Hughes had another attraction for the young Cary Grant. He was unashamedly rich, even though he chose not to behave as some believed a rich young man should, and through him Grant came to realize that he enjoyed the company of wealth. It was an appetite he was never to lose.

Not even Howard Hughes's money, however, could prevent Gary Cooper from affecting Cary Grant's career. In the early summer of 1932 Cooper had made a regal return to Hollywood, carrying a monkey he had brought back from Africa. The photograph of Gary and the monkey made every front page in town.

A relieved Adolph Zukor gave Cooper all he wanted, including the right to choose his films and to have the power of veto over cast and director. He and Schulberg decided he should star opposite Tallulah Bankhead in a picture to be directed by Marion Gering. They had also decided to use the vehicle for the American film debut of the British actor Charles Laughton. To add to the mixture, they gave their new young man, Cary Grant, a significant enough role to allow them to see how he compared with Cooper on the screen. At the same time, his presence would serve to remind Cooper that no one was indispensable.

As *Photoplay* magazine was to point out a few months later,

"Both Gary and Cary knew what was happening. They know that they're pitted against each other, and when the final gong sounds, one of them will be on the floor."

The Devil and the Deep marked Cooper's triumphant return. After its opening in New York in August 1932, *Variety* commented, he was "looking better than he has in a long time, and making a stunning figure in the uniform of a British naval officer." From start to finish a melodrama that had Laughton as the insanely jealous submarine commander who finally drowns himself in his cabin after he has rammed the submarine into a passing liner, it gave Grant little or no chance to prove whether he could act or not. Once again he was required only to look foreign and flashily handsome.

Even so, the film convinced Schulberg to give Grant a chance to star beside Marlene Dietrich. She had just finished making *Shanghai Express* with Clive Brook, and her director, Josef von Sternberg, had a pronounced liking for "Britishness" in his leading men. The actor who was to play Dietrich's husband was the wistful Herbert Marshall, just arrived in Hollywood from success on the London stage.

Blonde Venus, as the film was called, did not start happily. Dietrich was extremely nervous. Shooting began just after the kidnapping of Charles Lindbergh's infant son, and Marlene had received a series of letters threatening to abduct her own daughter, Maria. In addition, Josef von Sternberg was locked in argument with Schulberg. Paramount wanted one ending. Sternberg wanted another and refused to budge. Paramount replaced him as director and fined him $100,000. In a rage he stormed out of Hollywood for a trip to Berlin. Dietrich announced that she would not work with any other director and refused to discuss the picture.

After weeks of transatlantic argument Sternberg accepted a compromise; and when *Blonde Venus* was released, it won Cary Grant the best reviews of his career. Mordaunt Hall in *The New York Times* said, "Cary Grant is worthy of a much better role than that of Townsend." On the first day of filming Sternberg had grabbed a hairbrush and parted Grant's hair on the right-hand side, the side opposite from his usual, changing his appearance dramatically. He now looked thinner and a little frailer on the screen, gallant rather than flashy. He was never again to part his hair on the left.

Around the same time, Cary and Randolph Scott found a house they could share on West Live Oak Drive that was larger than the apartment they had been living in and certainly larger than Cary could have afforded on his own, with a swimming pool and a staff of a maid and black cook. Carole Lombard, who knew them both, called it "Bachelors' Hall." But she maintained that when they told their friends that they shared expenses it meant "Cary opened the bills, Randy wrote the checks, and if Cary could talk someone out of a stamp, he mailed them."

The magazine *Silver Screen* noted after a few months, "Cary is the gay, impetuous one. Randy is serious, cautious. Cary is temperamental in the sense of being very intense. Randy is calm and quiet." Neither man chose to live alone as many of Hollywood's other young bachelors did.

Shortly after Scott had finished *Sky Bride,* the picture he was making for Howard Hughes, the studio agreed that he and Grant should co-star opposite the red-haired ingenue Nancy Carroll in the film *Hot Saturday.* Grant revived the role of rich playboy he had played in *Blonde Venus* while Scott was asked to be the boyhood sweetheart who walks out on his marriage because he had heard rumors that Nancy had fallen for Grant.

Grant now put to good use the lessons he had learned from Sternberg. He stopped acting so ostentatiously and allowed the camera itself to discover the inflection or movement he made. It worked. As *Variety* noted, he "stands ahead of Miss Carroll and Scott in performance. He exercises extreme restraint toward his part," while Mordaunt Hall in *The New York Times* liked his "nonchalant young libertine."

Grant had made six films in Hollywood in less than a year, and Zukor intended to keep him just as busy in the future. As soon as *Hot Saturday* was finished, he sent Cary straight back onto the set of another Marion Gering picture, once again starring Schulberg's mistress, Sylvia Sidney. It was a film version of Puccini's opera *Madame Butterfly,* and Grant was to play Lieutenant Pinkerton. He had to sing and look impulsive, and he did not manage either too well. *Variety* thought him "rather cold" and said tersely, "He sings one song and it isn't so hot." Gary Cooper had turned down the role, as he had turned down *Sky Bride.* But by the time *Madame Butterfly* opened in New York, just before the New Year of 1933, Cary Grant's fortunes were about to improve. He had met Mae West, the woman who was to convince Hollywood that he had a talent for comedy.

When Mae had arrived from New York in June 1932, Hollywood's preeminent gossip columnist, Louella Parsons, had called her "buxom, blond, fat, fair and I don't know how near forty." In fact, she was thirty-nine and one of Broadway's biggest and certainly most voluptuous stars. Almost single-handedly she had made sex respectable on the stage by "taking it out in the open and laughing at it."

Broadway in 1932, however, was hardly more stable financially than Hollywood. After getting an offer from Zukor to play a small role in a film he was planning for George Raft, who had become a star in Howard Hughes's *Scarface,* Mae decided to accept ten weeks' work at a guaranteed $5,000 per week. "Broadway was in real trouble," she wrote in her autobiography. "Maybe, I decided, I'd take a fling at Hollywood."

But for her first eight weeks in California the tiny blonde did nothing. Paramount had not been able to settle on a script; and when they finally decided on one, Mae West refused to perform in it. After a protracted argument, during which she offered them her salary back, she rewrote the part for herself.

Her first words on screen, uttered to an awestruck hatcheck girl who had exclaimed, "Goodness, what beautiful diamonds!" were, "Goodness had nothing to do with it, dearie." Her performance made her a star overnight and provoked Raft to remark, "In this picture Mae West stole everything but the cameras."

Cary Grant first met Mae on a Friday night at the American Legion Stadium in Hollywood, where he and Randolph Scott went regularly to the boxing matches. Several movie stars made a habit of going: Chaplin was usually there and so was one of Gary Cooper's girl friends, Lupe Velez, who liked to climb into the ring and encourage the boxers. All the same, Mae West's story, which she held to for years, was that she first caught sight of Cary on the lot at Paramount while she was talking to Al Kaufman and William Le Baron, who were to produce her new film.

"I saw a sensational-looking young man walking along the studio street," she later wrote in her autobiography. "He was the best thing I'd seen out there."

"Who's that?" she had asked.

Kaufman recognized him. "Cary Grant."

"He'll do for my leading man."

Kaufman protested, but Mae West went on. "If this one can talk, I'll take him."

She said later, "I could see he had poise, a great walk, everything women would like."

Cary Grant came to resent this version. As he told *Screen Book Magazine,* "It seems that during her search for a suitable leading man she had seen me getting out of my studio car and decided I was the type to play opposite her. I suppose it was because she is blond and I am dark and we make a suitable contrast." He also pointed out that Lowell Sherman, the director she had selected for the film, had liked his performance in *Blonde Venus.*

With costumes especially designed for her by Edith Head, Mae West started work on the film, titled *She Done Him Wrong,* on November 21, 1932, immediately after Grant finished *Madame Butterfly.* The actors rehearsed together for a week before going in front of the cameras, and shooting was then completed in eighteen days without any overtime.

Grant was The Hawk, a government agent who poses as a captain in the Salvation Army; and for the first time Hollywood put his vaudeville training as a straight man to use.

"Haven't you ever met a man who can make you happy?" he asked at one point.

"Sure, lots of times," she replied.

Other parts of the dialogue also passed into Hollywood legend. During the film West referred to him as "warm, dark and handsome" and explained, "You know I—I always did like a man in uniform, and that one fits grand. Why don't you come up sometime, see me? I'm home every evening." Then, pausing only for a moment, "Come up, I'll tell your fortune. Aw, you can be had."

His quizzical half-surprised reaction and faintly raised eyebrow proved that he was capable of much more than the wooden parts he so far had been given by Paramount. It showed he was one male star whom the greatest leading ladies could pursue without looking foolish.

Released in February 1933, *She Done Him Wrong* was an immediate success, earning more than two million dollars at the box office and temporarily rescuing Paramount from dire financial straits. The studio had been comtemplating selling its seventeen hundred theaters throughout America and merging with MGM, but *She Done Him Wrong* enabled it to change its plans. Within three months Mae West was being paid $300,000 a picture, while even Garbo could command only $75,000. Within a year Mae was the highest paid performer in Hollywood, living in luxury in her Ravenswood apartment with her pet monkey, Boogie. Grant, however, was put back into the strait jacket that Paramount had made for him.

Brooding at his house near Griffith Park, he became convinced that the studio was keeping him from any part that would allow him to establish his own personality on the screen; the thought made him increasingly moody and distrustful. He was angry that Gary Cooper could pick whatever parts he liked. On their side, the studio people could claim that they were being generous. Had they not just raised his salary to $750 a week? From that time on, Cary Grant determined never again to rely on the patronage of a single studio.

His suspicions were confirmed when, after he had completed *The Woman Accused* with Nancy Carroll, he was immediately put into a new John Monk Saunders flying story, *The Eagle and the Hawk,* opposite Fredric March. The film was originally to have starred Gary Cooper and George Raft, but neither actor would do it. In desperation Paramount had added Carole Lombard to the cast, but even that bait failed. *Variety* called the film "strictly a formula story."

Grant's next film, *Gambling Ship,* again showed no sign that

Paramount would ever allow him to do anything more than look handsome. This time he was to be the glamorous gangster who falls for Benita Hume in what *Variety* described as "a fair flicker."

I'm No Angel, in which he was a rich playboy who falls for a circus performer, reunited him with Mae West. It had none of the memorable exchanges that had enlivened *She Done Him Wrong,* but bad reviews did not hurt its success at the box office. It earned $2.25 million, even more than its predecessor. In less than a year, Cary Grant had appeared in the two films that had saved Paramount from bankruptcy, and he now felt he deserved recognition.

As the fan mail flooded into Paramount and the fan magazines featured him, Cary Grant remained as canny as ever about self-revelation. He was charming to the press, but he carefully avoided saying anything personal. The head of magazine publicity for Paramount, Julie Lang Hunt, was so irritated by his evasiveness that she complained bitterly about him after she had left the studio. "Cary Grant will never know peace as long as his name spells news," she wrote. "His fixation, or complex, or mania (it is difficult to find the exact words for Cary's hypersensitivity) was planted during his childhood, and it was unwittingly nurtured during a strangely solitary youth." She added that even Randolph Scott had told her, "I can't tell you why, but I've seen him actually lose sleep and weight after reading certain items that touched upon his personal life and thoughts."

The insecure boy who had gratefully adopted the debonair mask of a handsome leading man was still afraid that it might slip. As he once admitted to Hunt, he could not transfer his poise on the stage to his private life. "When I go courting," he told her, "it's a very sad performance."

Nevertheless, Grant knew his responsibilities to Paramount. Every studio liked its leading men to be seen with the young actresses on their payroll. Such dating was good for business, since it encouraged the audience to think that the romances they were seeing on the screen might be happening in real life. Cary Grant accepted the tradition happily enough. He and

Randolph Scott would regularly escort new starlets around Hollywood, entertain them at home on Saturday evenings or arrange to meet them at the Santa Monica Beach Club on Sundays.

In addition, Cary carefully cultivated the elegance that was to become his trademark. He made sure his suits were carefully chosen and tailored. He avoided hats because he thought he did not look good in them. He sunbathed whenever he could in order to preserve his tan. He kept his clothes neatly labeled, always putting them back on their hangers as soon as he had finished wearing them, and he chose what to wear with obsessive precision. He also wanted to avoid being photographed smoking, even though he often consumed three packs a day. He had no wish to spoil his screen image.

One of the young women he met regularly in public was Virginia Cherrill, Charlie Chaplin's leading lady—the blind flower girl—in his silent film *City Lights*. Frail, with hazy china-blue eyes and striking blond hair, Virginia was another regular visitor to the American Legion fights on Friday evenings. There she had first met Chaplin and first seen Cary. She had arrived in Hollywood from Chicago in 1928 at the age of twenty after a disastrous first marriage to a lawyer named Irving Adler. As Chaplin was to recall, she once met him at the beach and asked, "When am I going to work for you?"

"Her shapely form in a blue bathing suit did not inspire the thought of her playing such a spiritual part as the blind girl," Chaplin wrote later. "But after making one or two tests with other actresses, in sheer desperation I called her up. To my surprise she had the faculty of looking blind."

The seventy-second scene in which Chaplin as a tramp avoids a traffic jam by getting into a limousine and out the other side, only to be mistaken for its owner by the blind flower girl, was to be one of the most famous debuts in Hollywood and the highlight of her short career.

By 1930 Virginia Cherrill had become a familiar figure at all the smartest parties. Louella Parsons described her as "Hollywood's greatest beauty," and everyone was convinced that she was about to marry the New York millionaire William

Rhinelander Stewart, one of the most eligible bachelors in America. Amidst a barrage of publicity, she followed him to Tahiti, where he was a guest on Vincent Astor's yacht, the *Nourmahal*, and Louella Parsons reported breathlessly that "the ceremony will be performed by Vincent Astor who, as captain of the boat, has the authority of performing the marriage at sea."

In spite of speculation, however, Virginia never married "Willie" Stewart, either on the *Nourmahal* or anywhere else. Within a week she returned to the Fox studios to resume work under a contract she had signed a year earlier.

She was soon to find compensation. As Cary Grant began to tell his friends, "I fell in love with her the moment I saw her."

To a man normally nervous in the presence of women, and apparently settled in his bachelor life, Virginia proved a revelation. She was outgoing, cheerful, endlessly energetic, the embodiment of all the actor thought he should become. He contrived to meet this petite blonde, five feet five inches tall and weighing less than 120 pounds, at other people's parties; he invited her to the parties he gave at Live Oak Drive. Worldly, glamorous and yet still attractively frail, she seemed to him the ideal companion.

By the time *I'm No Angel* opened in New York in September 1933, and broke the Paramount Theater's box-office record in its first seven days, Cary Grant was beginning to wonder whether Virginia Cherrill might not make a good wife. She could be infuriating certainly, with her apparent desire to make him jealous and her habit of leaving California at a moment's notice for Honolulu, Palm Beach or Mexico City to "forget the whole thing." But she was also captivating. The more she ran, the more he pursued. On one occasion he even chartered a tug to meet her cruise liner, the *Monterey*, as it steamed back to Los Angeles from Hawaii. The young man who had hardly had a girl friend before was infatuated.

But Cary Grant was still responsible to Paramount. The studio had not had one of its best years, and Zukor had decided that he needed a major production ready for the Christmas rush at the box office. Wanting a family film that everyone would regard as a classic, he settled on *Alice in Wonderland.* A small talking version of the story had done quite well at Christmas two years before, and Zukor decided to put every available star into this new production.

To begin with, he launched a nationwide search for the girl to play Alice, with 6,800 girls applying in a series of heavily publicized auditions. The final choice was Charlotte Henry, a seventeen-year-old from New York with no acting experience. Gary Cooper was to play the White Knight, Charles Ruggles the March Hare, and Jack Oakie, Tweedledum. The great silent comedian Ford Sterling was to be the White King, W. C. Fields was Humpty Dumpty and Edward Everett Horton, the Mad Hatter.

Originally, the studio had wanted Bing Crosby to play the Mock Turtle and sing Lewis Carroll's song about "beautiful, beautiful soup," but he would not agree. Cary was drafted in his place, but the part was not to threaten his reputation as a handsome leading man. He was to play it in a large wooden mask while dressed as a turtle.

When the film opened in New York just before Christmas, *The New York Times* admitted that it was a "marvel of camera magic and staging" and thought "the lachrymose Mock Turtle highly amusing." The production was only a minor success, however, and not the major triumph Paramount had hoped for.

As the filming of *Alice* came to an end, Cary Grant decided to take a vacation. He went to Phoenix, Arizona, at the suggestion of Howard Hughes, who had bought land there, but Grant and Cherrill, who had taken separate rooms at one of the hotels, were discovered by a group of reporters.

"We are not going to marry," Grant told them angrily. Within two weeks he had flown to New York to see the small, blond actress off on a trip to England, where he was to follow her fewer than ten days later. But Virginia was not the only woman Cary Grant had left America to see. He had also decided to find his mother.

CHAPTER 5

In the real dark night of the soul it is
always three o'clock in the morning.
F. Scott Fitzgerald, *The Crack-Up*

In the Depression England of Woolworths, cigarette coupons, the wireless and factory girls who looked like actresses, Elias Leach felt uncertain and a little out of place. He was sixty-one, a saddened, weary man with white hair, who kept his memories at bay with whiskey and the comfort of a pipe. He had survived as a tailor's presser in Bristol, but his had never been an easy life. His wife was still in the institution to which he had committed her almost twenty years before, and he had lived quietly for more than ten years with a woman whom he could never marry but who had nevertheless borne him a second son.

Although his eyes sparkled in the public bar when he talked about the success of an actor called Cary Grant, he found it difficult to link that faraway figure with the small, dark-eyed boy who used to sit opposite him at the parlor table on a winter evening playing checkers. He had barely seen him since then, but now that boy was coming back a Hollywood star.

In the past few years some members of the family had suggested that perhaps the time had come for Elsie Leach to leave the mental institution, but if anyone was going to decide that, Elias believed it should be her son, Archie. He had told him so when he had written to him in California. They would decide between them what to do about the fierce, wiry woman who had ordered both their lives.

In November 1933, Cary Grant swept into Bristol like a visiting maharaja, driving up to Elias's door complete with chauffeur, suntan, immaculate dark suit and an accent his father did not recognize. Cary was friendly and obviously delighted to see Elias again, but the elderly man became shy and uncertain in the presence of someone so relaxed.

"You'll be going to see your mother?" he asked finally.

That was the question he had been waiting for. Elsie would be fifty-seven on February 8, 1934, and he had decided they would celebrate her birthday together.

Cary Grant has never spoken publicly about his feelings as he walked into the small, bare room in the mental institution to meet the woman who was his mother but whom he had not seen for twenty years. He was never to know exactly how ill she had been, or even if she had ever been legally certified as insane. His resentment at her disappearance all those years before had been replaced by his need for her just to recognize and be proud of him. They were as hypnotized by each other as they had always been, the ferociously determined mother and the anxious-to-please son. Ironically, the internationally known film actor was confronting the one person who was hardly aware of his success. To Elsie Maria Leach, Cary was still her little boy, and she came back into his life as swiftly as she had left it, as though there had hardly been a moment's pause since they had seen each other last.

The other crisis of those weeks was also personal. Should he marry Virginia Cherrill? For more than a month Grant dithered. He bought a marriage license, but postponed the ceremony. He told his cousins that he would like to marry in Bristol, but changed his mind and thought he would marry in London. He talked about going back to California, where he was to start filming again late in February, but decided against it. He fretted about what would be the right thing to do, but he could not quite bring himself to do anything. Instead he contented himself with introducing the blond actress, whom he called Ginny, to his uncles and aunts at a party for them at the Grand Hotel, Bristol. Finally, he decided he would get married in London, once he had visited his mother. But what would his mother say? The stiffness she had always had was still there, and so was the terror he had always felt that she would not approve of what he did. He told her of his plans, however, and the effort, once made, gave him an intense feeling of relief. Part of his life had returned.

Now there wasn't much time. Passages were booked on the French liner *Paris* from Plymouth, and he and Virginia even wondered whether it might not be more romantic to be married by the ship's captain once they were out in the Atlantic. But since they had already struggled with the regulations at London's then famous registry office, Caxton Hall in Westminster, they agreed it was probably simplest to have the ceremony there.

When Grant arrived at Caxton Hall just before eleven o'clock on the morning of February 9, 1934, a crowd of reporters, photographers and sightseers was waiting outside, but there was no sign of his future wife. Desperate, he ran into the building and telephoned her.

"We're getting married, aren't we?"

Slightly stunned she said, "When?"

"Right now."

It took her barely a quarter of an hour to reach the registry office, and even less time for the superintendent registrar to conduct the brief formal ceremony that married Archibald Alec Leach to Virginia Cherrill, the former Mrs. Irving Adler.

The day's confusion was not over. As he and his new wife pushed their way toward the two taxis that he had ordered to wait for them and he shouted "We're so happy" to the struggling reporters, the new Mr. and Mrs. Cary Grant were separated. He had pushed his bride into the first taxi, and the cab had promptly set off, leaving him standing in the middle of the jostling, heaving crowd. Pulling himself gratefully into the second taxi, he heard the cab driver say, "Better follow the other one, hadn't I?"

After they were reunited at the hotel, where they collected their luggage before rushing off to Paddington Station to catch the boat train, he vowed not to submit himself to such public scrutiny again. In Plymouth he told the waiting reporters, "We are both due back in California for work on pictures, and so our honeymoon will be short."

Cary Grant was not altogether pleased at the prospect of returning to Hollywood. He felt misunderstood and misused by Paramount, yet unable to escape, and he felt dwarfed by Gary Cooper. Nevertheless, within twenty-four hours of stepping off the Santa Fe Chief at Pasadena, he was back on the Paramount lot to start shooting his third film with Marion Gering as director, and his third opposite Sylvia Sidney, *Thirty Day Princess,* another light comedy. Once again he was dressed up in white tie and tails, this time as a newspaper publisher.

When he asked if there might ever be a chance of his being cast in parts that asked him to do something more than change into evening clothes, the studio retaliated by loaning him out to Joe Schenck, who had been appointed chairman of United Artists a year before. A loan-out by one studio to another was usually designed as a punishment to bring recalcitrant performers into line, and this instance was no exception.

Born to Be Bad, with a script by the actor Ralph Graves and directed by Lowell Sherman, suffered from the restrictions of the film industry's new Production Code which Mae West's ribald dialogue had helped to create. Nine minutes were cut out of the film at the eleventh hour, and only Grant's co-star Loretta Young survived unscathed in what *The New York Times* called a "hopelessly unintelligent hodgepodge." Still determined to keep him playing mindless leading men, Paramount immediately put Grant into another light romantic comedy, *Kiss and Make Up,* which was also destined to sink without a trace. There was just one small variation from the formula. Instead of white tie and tails, he was now dressed in a cravat and black jacket as the manager of a Paris beauty salon.

Again without a pause, Paramount cast Grant in *Ladies Should Listen,* based on a play that had not even survived an out-of-New York trial. In three months he had made four films, all of them disastrous.

In despair, he asked to be loaned out by Paramount to appear in the film MGM was planning of a new book, *Mutiny on the Bounty.*

Louis B. Mayer's brilliant protégé, Irving Thalberg, had approached Grant about the possibility of playing a good supporting role in the picture. Clark Gable had already agreed to play the hero, Fletcher Christian, in spite of his fear that his slightly bandy legs would look ridiculous in naval knickerbockers. The thirty-four-year-old Thalberg, who had just recovered from a serious illness, was determined to mark his return to production with a major success, and Cary Grant knew he could do what was required of him.

Adolph Zukor, however, refused to release him. "Grant stays at Paramount," he replied. Reluctantly, Thalberg announced that Franchot Tone would be given the part he had in mind for Grant, and Zukor arranged for his leading man to appear with Elissa Landi in a film with an operatic background, *Enter Madame*. All Grant had to do was to look right, Zukor argued, and he could play opposite all the beautiful young women in Hollywood. What did he have to complain about?

In the heat of the Hollywood summer of 1934, Cary Grant's moods deepened into depression. The insomnia he had always suffered from grew worse, and he started to spend evenings morosely searching through his press clippings. There had been depressions before, but even Randolph Scott had never seen one as bad. "No one seems to care about me," he would mutter bitterly to a mystified Virginia Cherrill. The unfortunate woman found herself no longer married to one of the most publicly charming young actors in Hollywood but sharing a house with a man possessed by private fears and obsessed with imagined slights; a husband who refused to let her out of his sight but would not go anywhere with her; a depressive who could not bear to hear how well Clark Gable seemed or Gary Cooper had performed.

Virginia Cherrill had become a prisoner of her husband's moods. When they did go out it was often only to see Howard Hughes or Randolph Scott. If they were invited to one of the huge parties at Marion Davies's beach house, Cary would insist that Virginia talk to no one except him. If she refused, he would accuse her of preferring other people's company to his. He would shout at her, but before the shouting began he would start to whistle. She came to dread that whistle. "I don't know how much longer I can go on," she told her mother.

Mrs. Blanche Cherrill Wilcox had no doubt what her daughter should do—she should leave her husband. At the very next outburst, she was simply to walk out of the house. Within two weeks she had done just that. In the middle of September, Virginia Cherrill told her mother that the apparently debonair Cary Grant not only was given to blind rages but had threatened to kill her if she did anything he did not approve of.

Three days later an apologetic but cheerful Cary Grant arrived to visit his wife at her mother's house. It had all been a terrible mistake, he told her; he would never behave so abominably again; he could not live without her; she was the most important person in his life. Wouldn't she come back to him? The slight twenty-six-year-old blonde looked at her dashing, handsome husband, kissed him on the cheek and walked out to the Packard with him.

The reconciliation was not to last. Just two weeks later, on Friday, September 28, 1934, fewer than eight months after their marriage, Grant sat sullenly through a dinner party he had already told his wife he did not want to attend, drinking steadily. When they got home, he accused her of ignoring him. "I won't stand for it," he told her, moving across the room toward her. Just after midnight Virginia Cherrill ran out of the house and back to her mother.

The next morning she told Louella Parsons, "Whether it is permanent or not is up to Cary. I will not discuss the reason for our trouble, but things have been going from bad to worse. I left Cary two weeks ago and consulted a lawyer, but we later patched things up, and I hoped we might make a go of our marriage because I am in love with my husband."

To the habitually secretive Cary Grant the telephone calls from the news agencies and the newspaper gossip columnists were an ordeal. Finally, he told Louella Parsons, "It's silly to say that Virginia and I have separated. We have just had a quarrel, such as any married pair in Hollywood might have. . . . I hope when I get home tonight that Virginia will be waiting for me."

She wasn't. Indeed she was never to go back to him. Gradually, the realization that he had once again been abandoned by a woman he had been prepared to trust swept over Cary Grant, followed by the feelings of guilt he had never lost since his mother had first disappeared. On the night of Thursday, October 4, less than a week after their final argument, he started drinking alone and then began telephoning his friends. As the evening wore on he became less and less coherent.

Shortly after two o'clock in the morning he telephoned Virginia Cherrill and asked her to come back to him.

"You've never understood, everything will be different. Let's try again."

His young wife tried to explain that they had already tried again.

"This will ruin me," he told her before hanging up.

Greatly worried, she called back. When the houseboy answered, she asked him to go into the bedroom and see if her husband was all right. The manservant discovered Cary Grant lying unconscious across the bed, wearing only his underpants and with a bottle of pills marked POISON on the table next to the bed. In a Hollywood all too familiar with suicide, he immediately assumed his master had killed himself. At 2:28 A.M. on October 5, he telephoned for an ambulance.

Within an hour, the police surgeon, Dr. C. E. Cornell, was using a stomach pump on the unconscious actor in the Hollywood Hospital. Because of the pills he had seen beside the bed, he was convinced he was fighting for Grant's life. Yet there was no trace of poison in the actor's stomach; and when he had awakened in the hospital, a desperate Grant convinced Paramount's publicity department to put out a story that the whole episode had been a prank. "I had been at a party with friends, and when I got home they tried to play a joke on me," he explained. "They called the police. It was all a colossal gag." In a town where gossip was still the second most important industry, he had no wish to see his reputation for carefree charm threatened by reports of a miserable suicide attempt. He was badly frightened.

Later, but some considerable time later, he came nearer to admitting the true story. "I had been drinking most of the day before and all that day. I just passed out. The servant found me, became alarmed and called the cops.

"You know what whiskey does when you drink it all by yourself," he added. "It makes you very sad. I began calling people. I know I called Virginia. I don't know what I said to her, but things got hazier and hazier. The next thing I knew they were carting me off to the hospital."

While the Hollywood gossip columns speculated about a reconciliation, Cary Grant moved back to Live Oak Drive and the friendship of Randolph Scott.

He returned to work, first in the well-worn white tie and tails as Elissa Landi's long-suffering but devoted husband in *Enter Madame,* then at last to a change of style as an aviator intent on breaking world speed records in James Hood's *Wings in the Dark,* where his co-star was Myrna Loy, straight from *The Thin Man.* In the age of Lindbergh and air races, the film's flying sequences were designed to attract the audience. But Grant's performance as the flyer blinded in an explosion attracted the most notice. *The Hollywood Reporter* called him "splendid" and *Variety* added that he "tops all his past work."

In spite of this breakthrough he could not shake off the suspicion that Paramount saw him only as a pale imitation of Cooper. When, hard on the heels of their success with Cooper's *The Lives of a Bengal Lancer,* the studio announced it intended to use Grant in another film about India, he was more than ever convinced he would never escape from his rival's shadow. Bitterly, he concluded that he was unlikely to succeed at Paramount, and Zukor, for his part, was wondering what to do with him. To him, Grant seemed an ungrateful actor who could not recognize how lucky he was.

Another problem was the impression created by the acrimonious and extremely public divorce proceedings between Grant and Cherrill. On December 11, 1934, Virginia Cherrill told Los Angeles Superior Court Judge William Valentine, "I was obliged to pawn my engagement ring and wristwatch and borrow on my automobile," and "I have been unable to work because of ill health and needed the money with which to live."

Asking the court to order her husband to pay her $1,000 a month, she explained that he had given her only $125 in the ten weeks since their separation. "I must look presentable if I work," she said.

When his own lawyer cross-examined him on the witness stand and asked why he believed his wife could get along on just $150 a month rather than the $1,000 she was asking for, Grant replied tersely, "She managed to before we were married, so she could do it again." Hardly the remark the public would have expected of Grant, the screen hero, especially since he had already told the court that Paramount had agreed to extend his contract by another year at a salary of $1,250 a week.

Judge Valentine was not impressed by the actor's testimony or his apparent charm. He awarded Virginia Cherrill maintenance of $167.50 a week, or $725 a month, pending the full hearing of their divorce, and he ordered the actor to put up a $20,000 bond to guarantee that he would pay both her and her lawyers and that he would not dispose of any property until a divorce settlement was reached.

Even that was not the end of it. A few days later Virginia Cherrill's lawyer returned to court to amend their original complaint against Cary Grant still further. The new complaint, extensively reported in the Los Angeles newspapers, included the assertions that he "drank excessively, choked and beat her and threatened to kill her." A nervous Paramount knew the time had now come to act, and on Christmas Eve lawyers for both sides agreed on a settlement. The charge that the charming actor might have beaten his wife and threatened to kill her was never to come to court, but the damage had been done.

As soon as the filming of *Wings in the Dark* was completed at the end of January, Cary Grant left Hollywood for a trip to England. Once more he intended to visit his mother on her birthday. Though he could not know it, his decision was well timed, for this would be the last time he would see his father alive.

In his absence, his divorce became final on March 26, 1935. Dressed in a blue suit and wearing dark glasses, Virginia Cherrill arrived at Judge Charles Haas's courtroom in Los Angeles shortly before ten o'clock in the morning and not long afterward recited what one newspaper called "a long list of the assorted shortcomings of her actor-husband."

When she slipped off her glasses and tucked them into her bag, she looked even more the sad waif than she had as Chaplin's blind flower girl. She began by telling the court that she had been ill. Then her lawyer, Milton Cohen, asked her to describe her life with Grant.

"He was very sullen and disagreeable," she said softly, causing the judge to bend forward toward her. "He refused to pay my bills. He told me to go out and work myself and then discouraged me every time I had a real opportunity. He was like this almost from the first."

The newspaper reporters that were packed into the back of the courtroom could hardly believe their ears as Virginia, taking out a lace handkerchief, continued in her soft voice, "He told me he didn't care to live with me anymore, a number of times."

"Please speak a little more loudly, Mrs. Grant," the judge interrupted. The frail blonde nodded and smiled at him.

"He was sullen, morose and quarrelsome in front of guests. He falsely accused me of not appreciating him or his efforts."

The courtroom was silent when Judge Haas asked if her husband drank.

"Yes, he was inclined to drink quite a bit all during our marriage."

Virginia was allowed to step down from the witness stand. Her mother took her place. Mrs. Blanche Cherrill Wilcox testified that she had indeed seen her son-in-law insult his wife, just as Virginia had described. In less than an hour, the slim, blond actress had been awarded a divorce.

There were no claims for maintenance to settle, so Virginia Cherrill walked gratefully into the spring sunshine to talk to a small crowd of reporters and photographers. She was twenty-seven years old and had been married to Grant just over thirteen months. In less than two years' time she was to become Countess of Jersey by marrying a wealthy British earl. For the moment, however, she just looked frail.

In 1935 Cary was to make one more picture for Paramount, *The Last Outpost*, already announced, in which he played a rather foolish British officer in the northwest frontier, who is rescued by Claude Rains as another British officer working behind the Indian lines. When the film was released in October 1935, *Variety* tartly noted, "Due to the Italo-Ethiopian squabble, the general run of picturegoer may not relish watching hordes of archaically equipped blacks being mowed down by machine guns."

Grant's rescue from Paramount finally came through Howard Hughes, who, since his own divorce from his wife, Ella, in December 1929, had become another of the most public bachelors in Hollywood. The gossip columns speculated about his relationships with the actresses Billie Dove, Ida Lupino and Marian Marsh, but in 1935 he met an angular and uncompromising actress who was to put all those in the shade.

Tall, bony and independent, Katharine Hepburn had been involved with her agent, Leland Hayward, until he had suddenly married the high-strung actress Margaret Sullavan. Hepburn then became fascinated by Hughes, a millionaire since the age of nineteen. As a couple they had a great deal in common. Both were neurotically shy of publicity and shared a liking for swimming, golf, tennis and airplanes. As Hughes was to say in a rare interview later, "She was brilliant, kind, devoid of sham and pretense and a woman who couldn't give a damn for convention." It was inevitable he would talk to her about his friend Cary Grant.

Several years later Grant also would recall his own fascination on meeting her. "She was this slip of a woman, skinny, and I never liked skinny women. But she had this thing, this air, you might call it, the most totally magnetic woman I'd ever seen, and probably have ever seen since. You had to look at her, you had to listen to her, there was no escaping her.

"But it wasn't just the beauty, it was the style. She's incredibly down to earth. She can see right through the nonsense in life. She cares, but about things that really matter."

Hepburn, who had been tempted to go to Hollywood from the New York stage when David O. Selznick, then in charge of production at RKO, offered her a contract worth $1,500 a week, had achieved remarkable success in her first four films under his guidance. *A Bill of Divorcement*, *Christopher Strong*, *Morning Glory* and *Little Women* all had been box-office hits, and she had won an Oscar for *Morning Glory* when she was only twenty-six.

But after Selznick's departure to MGM to join his father-in-law, Louis B. Mayer, her career had faltered. She had made three terrible films at RKO, and the disastrous run had been stopped only with the help of a new director, George Stevens, and the film *Alice Adams*. Her choice of this story, about an awkward girl who wants to make her way in the world but feels she lacks the poise to do it, encouraged RKO to let her pick her own films in the future. For her next venture she selected an adaptation of Compton Mackenzie's 1918 novel, *The Early Life and Adventures of Sylvia Scarlett,* and Cary Grant was to play opposite her.

Loosely based on a real murder case, the story told of the escape from France to England of an embezzler, accompanied by his daughter, who wears men's clothes to avoid detection. George Cukor, a former Broadway director who had also been hired by Selznick at RKO, had wanted to make the film for several years. At least one major studio had already turned it down, but Hepburn, who was Cukor's close friend, was enthusiastic and so, therefore, was RKO. Hopes ran so high that Cukor even suggested that the young Evelyn Waugh should be hired to write the script, and he paid the great English actress Mrs. Patrick Campbell a fee of $2,500 for playing a small part. But Waugh was not hired and Mrs. Campbell was never used.

Cary Grant was introduced to Pandro S. Berman, the producer of the film, in June 1935. Berman had already borrowed Randolph Scott from Paramount for another film, and he did not believe he would encounter much opposition when he asked to borrow Grant. As Berman explained later, "He had no chance at Paramount. He was a failure there. I gave him a part because I'd seen him do things which were excellent, and Hepburn wanted him too."

Grant was to be paid $15,000 for the six weeks of filming, considerably more than his regular Paramount contract but much less than Hepburn's $50,000.

When filming got under way in the late summer of 1935 on the coast north of Malibu, Howard Hughes flew to the location in his private plane. He arrived for lunch and left shortly afterward, and, according to actor Brian Aherne, everyone thought the sudden appearance of the remote, awkward and slightly deaf Hughes something of a joke. But the effect of Cukor's direction on Grant was remarkable. He seemed to blossom. His public cockiness deepened into true confidence in front of the camera. With Cukor's help, for the first time he began to use his natural intelligence to create a character. Instead of constantly fussing as he had so often before, he relaxed.

"For once they didn't see me as a pleasant young man with black hair, white teeth and a heart of gold," Cary Grant said later. And as Cukor was to remember, "It was the first time he felt that an audience could like him. He had an awfully good part (he'd had a lot of experience but he'd never arrived) and he suddenly felt on firm ground with his knowledge of the whole milieu. I think he gave a remarkable performance and that started him." Hepburn maintained that "George brought the Archie Leach out in Cary Grant."

He was to be virtually the only success in *Sylvia Scarlett*. Berman now calls it "probably the worst picture ever made." After the first audience preview, Berman went to Cukor's Hollywood home to attack him for making the film in the first place. "The audience didn't know what it was about," he told the director, "and not one person understood a word of those English accents."

"Now don't worry," Hepburn broke in, "because we're going to make it up to you for this. We're going to make another picture for you for free!"

"Oh my God, no," Berman replied. "Anything but that. I don't want either of you ever to work for me again."

Cukor was never to make another film for RKO, but when *Sylvia Scarlett* opened at the vast sixty-two-hundred-seat Radio City Music Hall in New York on January 9, 1936, Cary Grant received his first really enthusiastic notices. A good director and a part that captured something of his wry arrogance, as well as utilizing his strutting sharpness, prompted Andre Sennwald to say in *The New York Times*, "Cary Grant, whose previous work has too often been that of a charm merchant, turns actor in the role of the unpleasant Cockney and is surprisingly good at it."

Time magazine added, *"Sylvia Scarlett* is made memorable by a role that almost steals the show from Miss Hepburn's androgyne, Cary Grant's superb depiction of the Cockney." But Grant was not in America to savor his first critical success as an actor.

In the middle of November he had sailed for England on the Cunard liner *Aquitania* to film *The Amazing Quest for Ernest Bliss* at Elstree studios. He wanted to be near his father, whose health had been failing steadily for more than a year, and Alfred Zeisler's decision to direct a new version of E. Phillip Oppenheim's light comedy about a rich young man who takes a number of lowly jobs on a bet provided the opportunity.

On December 2, 1935, a week after shooting had begun on the film, Elias Leach died in his Bristol home of what the death certificate described as "acute septicaemia" and "gangrene of the bowel." He was just sixty-three.

Cary Grant had not seen his father again, but he was there to mourn the man he called "my first hero," and to bury him in the local churchyard. "He was a wise and kindly man and I loved him very much," was his son's moving epitaph.

CHAPTER 6

Yet, despite his appearance, he was really a
very complicated young man with a whole
set of personalities, one inside the other like
a nest of Chinese boxes.

Nathanael West, *The Day of the Locust*

Elsie Leach still turned her head away when Cary bent down
to kiss her, exposing only her cheek for his lips to brush against.
Stiff-backed, with her shawl drawn around her shoulders and
her fingers turning the small gold locket at the throat, she
looked exactly as he remembered her.

After his father's funeral, he brought her to London with
him while he continued filming *The Amazing Quest of Ernest
Bliss.* In the evenings he would try to get to know the tiny
woman who sat opposite him, an upright fifty-eight-year-old
with her hands clasped in her lap, looking straight ahead of
her. His task was not easy.

He would ask her if she would like to go to California and
hear her reply, "Never lived anywhere but Bristol. Don't want
to, only place I know! I'm too old to go gallivanting off thousands of miles."

Although he would never admit it, even to himself, her answer was a relief. The mask he had so readily put on in Hollywood had to be preserved. The tall, carefree Cary Grant would
never have had a tiny elderly woman sharing his house. His
mother was part of his life that had best remain in the past.
Elsie Leach was the mother of the insecure Archie Leach. But
the only parents of the dazzling Cary Grant were the movie
screen and the audience. He was their true creation.

When he wasn't trying to talk to his mother, Grant sought
out the company of his co-star on *Ernest Bliss,* Mary Brian. Unlike most of his girls, she was brown-haired and almost as small

as his mother. A former beauty contest winner, she had acted in small parts in Hollywood over the years and had appeared briefly in Howard Hughes's 1931 version of *The Front Page*. Although she had worked regularly at the studios, few executives thought she would ever be a star. Grant, knowing she was already filming in England, had suggested her for the part in *Ernest Bliss*.

She was captivated by his gallant manners, and inevitably it was only a matter of weeks before one London evening paper was reporting that they had fallen in love. When any journalist asked Cary about his relationship with Mary, he would answer, "Well, don't you think Mary is an awfully nice girl?"—just the sort of pleasantly flip remark that Cary Grant might have made on the screen.

By the time filming was finished at the end of January, it was clear that *Ernest Bliss* was not going to be a success. The script was written by John Balderston, who had worked on *The Lives of a Bengal Lancer*, but Alfred Zeisler's direction had not suited the comedy. When the movie finally opened, the verdict of most of the critics was that the silent version of the story, made fifteen years before with Henry Edwards, was far superior.

Grant settled his mother into a house in Bristol near enough to her brothers for them to be able to look after her. He also made a sensible arrangement with the local newspaper whereby, in return for their agreement not to bother her, he promised to give them an exclusive interview every time he visited her. He then sailed gratefully back to the United States, settling himself in his first-class stateroom with a quiet sigh of relief.

For his mother had now become simply a statue from his past, an embodiment of a life he wanted to forget. Separated completely for more than two decades and by a distance of six thousand miles, the two of them had moved into totally different worlds. Sometimes a messenger boy would knock at Elsie's door, "Got another cable from Hollywood for you, Mrs. Leach!" But Elsie would sit unmoving in her kitchen, and only after the messenger had gone would she walk down the hall and pick up the message from the mat. As the evening wore on, she would walk around the house bolting every outside door and then locking each of the doors inside until she finally felt her sturdy stone, terraced house was safe. Once in her bedroom, she would lock herself in and push the dressing table across the door to act as a barricade. Only then would she read the message from this man who called himself her son. But she took to saying to no one in particular, "I am a virgin."

On the surface, life in Hollywood had hardly changed for Cary Grant. He and Randolph Scott still lived together on West Live Oak Drive and worked for Paramount. But an upheaval was pending.

Randolph Scott had decided to marry a woman he had known since they were both children in Virginia. She was Mariana du Pont, of the millionaire Du Pont family. Certainly not the most beautiful woman in the world, she had been married once before, had left her first husband in 1925 and returned to Virginia. She now made it clear that she would not move to California, and Randolph made it equally clear that he would not move back to the South. The match was a strange one for an actor who was making his name playing buckskinned cowboys, and he waited five months after signing the marriage certificate in Charlotte, Virginia, in March 1936, before announcing the news in Hollywood.

As Louella Parsons was to remark some years later, "Scott's marriage to the Du Pont heiress was always a mystery. She was years older than Scott and completely uninterested in the theater. From the beginning the disparity in their tastes and years was so marked that Randy's closest friends never understood why he, a successful movie star, had married this very rich woman, who had been his neighbor in Virginia."

What Parsons did not point out was that the marriage would make no difference to the actor's life in Hollywood. He and Cary Grant continued to share their house. When the new Mrs. Scott came to Hollywood, she stayed with them, but that happened so infrequently that the routine of life on West Live Oak Drive was hardly affected.

The two men were even considering moving to a new home on the beach. Built by producer Joseph Schenck and his actress wife, Norma Talmadge, the house they had in mind had seven bedrooms, a swimming pool and an uninterrupted view of the Pacific Ocean. It had another advantage. The beach at Santa Monica was becoming one of the most fashionable areas of Los Angeles. William Randolph Hearst had built Marion Davies a substantial home there, and Irving Thalberg had built a house there as well. Norma Talmadge had told Scott and Grant that she was prepared to sell the property, and they had agreed between themselves that the first to marry should have the right to buy out the other.

Randolph Scott had no intention of exercising his right. Within two years he was to announce that he and his wife were parting on friendly terms, adding, "It's a case of being separated too much, which did not prove compatible with marriage." In the meantime Cary Grant had been perfectly content to sit in the soft sunshine outside their new house at the beach, deepening his suntan.

The closeness of the two men's relationship led to some unkind gossip, but they remained indifferent. Scott had inherited his friend's role as Mae West's foil in her latest film, *Go West, Young Man,* and the studio was talking about using Scott and Grant together again in a new film about the Arctic, *Spawn of the North,* with Carole Lombard as the leading lady. Before the project got underway, however, the studio changed its mind and gave their parts to Henry Fonda and George Raft.

The suggestion that both men were what was politely known as born bachelors was scotched by the belated announcement of Randolph's marriage and by speculation that Cary Grant might be marrying Mary Brian. Cary, however, denied the possibility. "Mary is a lovely person," he told *Photoplay.* "We get along together and I'm terribly fond of her, but there's no engagement. There hasn't even been any talk of marriage at all. It'll be five years before I'm ready for that."

Meanwhile, the relationship of both men with Paramount was breaking down. Scott would depart soon, but the studio was prepared to cooperate with Cary by letting him play a detective in *Big Brown Eyes,* his first film for them in 1936. The movie was not a success, and Cary seemed uncertain in the role of a wisecracking private detective who was occasionally forced into fist fights. Nor did relations improve when the eighth Academy Awards ceremony was held at the Biltmore Hotel in Hollywood in March. *Mutiny on the Bounty,* the film Zukor had refused to release him to MGM to appear in, not only won the Oscar as best picture but also saw its three male stars, Clark Gable, Charles Laughton and Franchot Tone (in the part Grant would have had) nominated for the best actor award— though none of them won it. Few Paramount films had even been nominated, and only the scriptwriters, Ben Hecht and Charles MacArthur, won an Oscar for the studio with their original story for *The Scoundrel.*

As it happened, at the moment when the Oscars were being awarded, Cary Grant was making his first film for MGM. The fact that Paramount had, at this sensitive moment, agreed to lend him to Louis B. Mayer only increased his bad humor. The film was *Suzy,* with George Fitzmaurice as its director. Grant was a flying ace in love with Jean Harlow, Howard Hughes's discovery and now one of MGM's biggest stars, who was playing an American show girl.

Grant had not been anxious to appear in this film. He knew the script had been worked on by Horace Jackson, Alan Campbell and Dorothy Parker, and he now discovered that it had been given to Lenore Coffee to rescue. He was persuaded to make it only after the studio promised it would be tailored to foster his image. In the end, the flying sequences, reused from Hughes's *Hell's Angels* to save money, and a memorable song, "Did I Remember," which Grant sang and which was later successfully released as a record, were the film's only redeeming features. Harlow's sexuality was wasted on an innocent role and, in spite of the endless amendments to the script, Grant did not look or feel at ease.

Back at Paramount he was once again cast opposite his co-star from *Big Brown Eyes,* Joan Bennett, in Paul Gallico's newspaper story, *Wedding Present.* Once again his displeasure at the role was reflected in his performance, and the *New York Herald Tribune* called his playing "lackadaisical."

His depression deepened. So did the studio's, some of whose executives were saying privately that they doubted whether he would ever find a part that satisfied him—"He's such a perfectionist, how could he?"—while others doubted whether he could tell a good script in the first place—"He's never had any judgment." These criticisms of him would be repeated many times in the future, and they did nothing to alleviate his misery.

In the autumn of 1936 Grant decided that *Wedding Present* would be his last film for the studio. Offers from anywhere else would be preferable. In five years at Paramount Cary Grant had made twenty-one films without ever feeling appreciated.

Publicly, he contented himself with remarking that "they had a lot of leading men with dark hair and a set of teeth like mine, and they couldn't be buying stories for all of us," but the statement only concealed the anger he felt at the studio's assumption that he could never be more than a matinee idol. In the future he would try to make sure that at least two studios were always interested in him and that any contract he signed would give him a choice of scripts, the correct billing and, of course, the right salary.

Paramount no longer cared whether he stayed or not. They had already offered him an increase to $2,500 a week, which, in their view, was extremely generous, but they had refused his demand to choose his own films. Only Mae West, Gary Cooper and Marlene Dietrich had this right; it was not a privilege to extend to an actor who had not proved himself.

While the negotiations were going on, they agreed to his suggestion that they lend him to Harry Cohn at Columbia to star in a musical, originally to be called *Interlude* but later retitled *When You're in Love,* with the opera singer Grace Moore. The new film was based on a script by Robert Riskin, who had written Frank Capra's two award-winning comedies, *It Happened One Night* and *Mr. Deeds Goes to Town.* But if Cary Grant had hopes that it would do for him what the other two had done for Clark Gable and Gary Cooper, he was due for a disappointment. Cohn had agreed that Riskin could direct the film himself; and, alas, Riskin was not Capra. The film flopped. Once again Cary Grant had failed to prove that he could choose a box-office hit.

So, when RKO asked to borrow him for a film biography of

the Wall Street pioneer Jim Fisk, the studio accepted gratefully. Edward Arnold, on loan from B. P. Schulberg's own production company, was to play Fisk, while Grant and Frances
Farmer were to have the two roles which RKO had toyed with
giving to William Powell and Ginger Rogers. Burdened by a
script that amalgamated two different books and had been
worked on by six different writers, *The Toast of New York* turned
out to be the biggest financial disaster of the year for RKO,
losing more than $500,000.

But by the time it opened in 1937, Cary Grant had already
signed his first contract after leaving Paramount.

At this point in his career, Cary Grant privately admitted, "I
suddenly became aware that I wasn't sure what or who I was
on the screen. As an actor I had a thin veneer of sophistication,
carefully copied from Noel Coward. I'd casually put my hand
in my pocket and it would get stuck there with perspiration."
Yet he was anxious to protect that image, for it reassured him
that he knew who he was. The insecure boy from Bristol clung
to it like the wreckage of a sinking ship, and this attachment
made his reaction to any change of role distinctly ambivalent.
He wanted to prove he could act—and he had enjoyed playing
in *Sylvia Scarlett;* but he was also afraid to let go of the only existence he felt he had, that of the slightly flashy, good-looking
young man of *Blonde Venus.*

"I don't think any non-actor can ever know how horrifying it
is to hear your voice, see yourself, see how you walk," was how
he put it. The well-dressed young player whose suits were tailored at Howes and Curtis in London, who whistled when he
was nervous and who was edgy in the company of strangers was
determined to cultivate the appearance of confidence and cer-
tainty, even if it concealed an almost paralyzing awkwardness
and insecurity. As Frances Farmer, his co-star in *The Toast of
New York,* would eventually write, "He was an aloof, remote
person, intent on being Cary Grant, playing Cary Grant playing Cary Grant. . . . He remained polite but impersonal."

If anyone he did not know and trust penetrated the facade
he wanted to present to the world, he became threatened. As
Julie Lang Hunt put it in *Photoplay* in 1935, "Only a handful of

his closest friends had discovered this superfastidious streak that makes him cringe from any public revealment with a self-consciousness that is torture. . . . I have seen Cary look appalled and liverish for days following the publication of what most players would consider an innocuous enough interview."

His need for privacy was one reason why he had been so keen to move to the Talmadge house on the beach in Santa Monica. "I like the ocean because no one can build a house in front of me or plant a high hedge or put up a billboard," he said. When he and Randolph Scott had moved in, he had collected all the photographs taken of him in the previous five years in Hollywood and put them in his own bathroom. He thought that was an appropriately private place for them.

As 1936 drew to a close, Cary Grant's luck was to change. In the past two years talking pictures had come out of their own depression. In the United States an estimated eighty-one million people were now going each week to one of 18,200 theaters, and in 1937 Hollywood was to produce 778 feature films, more than in any year since 1928.

This optimism was reflected in the kind of films being made. In the new Hollywood disasters could always be overcome, no one needed to be downhearted all the time and even a fool could marry the daughter of a millionaire if he had a mind to. All that was necessary for survival was to laugh. The film critic Pauline Kael later described the change by saying, "Comedy became the new romance, and trading wisecracks was the new courtship rite. The cheerful whacked-out heroes and heroines had abandoned sanity, they were a little crazy, and that's what they liked in each other."

Heroines were no longer aimless, lovelorn girls yearning after unattainable men. They were independent, good arguers and looked on members of the opposite sex not so much as protectors as prey. Marriage for them could be a cheerful sporting match on the pattern of *The Thin Man* with William Powell and Myrna Loy, and courtship the saucy affair that Clark Gable and Claudette Colbert had made it in *It Happened One Night.*

Fast and *feminine* were the words for Hollywood comedy by the end of 1936, with the verbal wit of Broadway increasingly leavened with farce and slapstick. All the emphasis was on speed, and the directors who emerged to capture the new style came from the traditions of the old two-reel comedies. When farce was mixed with drawing-room comedy, it was no longer vulgar, it was "screwball." Improvisations became the name of the game. As Kael put it, "No longer so script bound, movies regained some of the creative energy and exuberance, and the joy in horseplay too, that had been lost in the early years of talkies."

For Cary Grant that strain of comedy was to provide the perfect medium for the personality he wished to project. He became the man every women wanted to pursue but was never quite able to catch. Elusive and attractive at the same moment, the natural bachelor who was always divorcing his wife, he was charming, witty and alluring yet superficial—an image which perfectly suited both Grant and his audience.

As he looked out across the sand toward the Pacific from the patio of his new house in Santa Monica during the first weeks of 1937, Cary Grant was relaxed. His new agent, Frank Vincent, had agreed to pay Zukor $11,800 to buy out his contract with Paramount, and he had negotiated a four-picture deal with Harry Cohn at Columbia that would guarantee $50,000 each for the first two films and $75,000 each for the next two. As long as Grant made at least two films in the coming year (and in 1936 he had made five), he would be certain to earn at least $100,000, not a bad sum for an actor who had started in Hollywood at $450 a week and who had not appeared in any list of top box-office attractions. By careful steering, he had turned his own financial corner. Within a few weeks his contract with Columbia was signed. It was to start in May 1937, and it was to make him a star at last.

Beside their new pool, Grant and Scott entertained. One regular visitor was the small blond girl who had become one of RKO's biggest stars, Ginger Rogers. She had been friendly with Howard Hughes, who called her "a delight to be with," but Grant had become keen on her himself. Another persistent caller was the comedy producer Hal Roach, who lived next door and who had taken to dropping in at lunchtime for a swim. Pompous and given to belligerence, especially if anyone suggested that he might not be the sole reason for the success of Harold Lloyd, Our Gang and Laurel and Hardy, Roach had just bought the film rights to Thorne Smith's *Topper*. Hollywood had recently developed a taste for stories with ghosts, particularly stories that had a comic element, after the acclaim heaped on producer Alexander Korda and actor Robert Donat for *The Ghost Goes West* and Noel Coward's success in *The Scoundrel.*

Lying beside the swimming pool one lunchtime, Roach and Grant played a game of casting leading roles. Roach thought W. C. Fields should be Topper, while Grant suggested Jean Harlow as the ideal Mrs. Kirby.

"And I wish you'd play the husband," Roach told him.

"You can't afford me. I know I can get fifty thousand dollars for a picture at Columbia."

But Roach did not give up. For days he badgered Grant, until finally he persuaded him to make the film.

"Oh, what the hell. I'll do it. If it makes dough, you can pay me my price," Grant told him.

It was a risk, but only a small one. Columbia did not want him to start filming until May 1, and in the meantime he thought he could finish *Topper* quickly. If a major studio picked up Roach's production, he was certain to get paid, and it was only a few weeks' work.

Roland Young was signed to play Topper, and Constance Bennett was to play Grant's ghostly wife, Marion Kirby. Roach persuaded Grant to allow Bennett top billing, which he did reluctantly. Grant also raised a string of objections in his best fussy manner when the film's director, Norman Z. McLeod, with whom he had worked on *Alice in Wonderland*, suggested to him a change in the way he played his part.

"I had had another idea," Roach said later. "When the Kirbys go off together to do their good deed, Grant tells Bennett to watch her step, and she asks why. He tells her, 'After all, you're my wife.' But she protests. 'Oh no, the contract says "till death us do part." ' " The vision I had was that Grant would be trying to make love to and court his own wife.

"Out of the clear blue sky Grant refused and said, 'I'm not going to run after Constance Bennett.'

"I talked to him but he was adamant. He was not too keen on Bennett and, I think, the real story was that at that particular time he was in love with Ginger Rogers and he didn't feel like making love to anyone else." Nothing Roach could do would persuade Grant to change his mind.

When the film was released by MGM in July 1937, *The New York Times* called it "rather a heavy consignment of whimsy to be shipping from the printed page to the screen." But Cary Grant did not care. He had lost interest. He had been paid his fee and had started work on his first film at Columbia with the gifted but decidedly eccentric director Leo McCarey, who was to carry him to success.

Amiable, shrewd and unrepentantly individualistic, McCarey looked remarkably like the man he was now to direct. He was a little shorter and slightly fuller in the face, but he had the same brown eyes and slightly wistful expression that could turn into a smile. The son of one of California's best-known boxing promoters, he had started in movies as soon as he had finished law school, beginning as a third assistant director to Tod Browning. It was McCarey who had put together a thin, worried-looking comedian called Stanley Jefferson with a chubby, cheerful extra whom he nicknamed "Babe" in 1924 and seen them triumph as Laurel and Hardy, and by the 1930's his reputation was established. In 1933 he joined Paramount, where his many films included the Marx Brothers in *Duck Soup*, but the studio was never happy with him. He liked directing without a fixed script, improvising scenes as he went along and playing the piano on the side of the set whenever he needed inspiration. It was not a style to which Zukor and Paramount warmed.

Late in 1936 McCarey and Grant met on the corner of Vine Street and Melrose Avenue, not far from the newly opened Hollywood branch of the Brown Derby Restaurant. "Paramount let me go; I'm on the streets," was Grant's opening remark, to which McCarey replied, "And what do you think I'm doing? Paramount kicked me out too." Unknown to each other, they were both negotiating with Columbia, but neither let that information drop.

When Columbia finally hired McCarey early in 1937, they gave him an uninspiring project to start with, a script by Dwight Taylor based on Arthur Richman's 1922 play *The Awful Truth*, which had been filmed twice before. Undismayed, McCarey tore up the script and started writing another with Viña Delmar. The two of them would sit in McCarey's car outside the studio on Hollywood Boulevard working out ideas. Neither Cohn nor McCarey knew exactly whom to cast in the film, but since Cary Grant had just joined the studio and Irene Dunne, who was already under contract there, had just been nominated for an Academy Award as best actress for her comic role in *Theodora Goes Wild*, they decided to put the two stars together.

When shooting began in early June 1937, Cary Grant behaved as neurotically as he had at the start of *Topper*, and McCarey's habit of arriving on the set in the morning bearing bits of script on scraps of brown wrapping paper did nothing to reassure him. Within a day Grant was asking Harry Cohn if he could change his part to the smaller one being played by Ralph Bellamy, and finally, in desperation, he offered Cohn $5,000 to release him from the picture entirely.

Shortly before his death in 1969, McCarey was asked why Grant wanted to get out of the picture.

"He had no sound judgment."

"How did you convince him to stay in?"

"The studio had to convince him. I was so mad at him I wouldn't talk to him."

Indeed, McCarey was so angry when he heard about the $5,000 that he said to Cohn, "Well, if that isn't enough, I'll put in five myself and make it up to ten."

Cohn told them to get on with the picture, but McCarey's view of his star actor did not change. Even thirty years later he still described him as nervous, uncertain and insecure.

"Cary Grant was impossible," he said. And Irene Dunne remembered, "Cary used to be very apprehensive about nearly everything in those days. So apprehensive in fact he would almost get physically sick. If the script, the director, an actor or a particular scene displeased him, he would be greatly upset."

Yet McCarey's improvisation was to transform Grant's career, creating a nervous tension in the actor that inspired his performance. McCarey's technique was simple. In one scene he told Dunne to open the door of her apartment, discover Grant standing there and say with surprise, "Well, if it isn't my ex." He did not tell Grant what to reply, but the actor ad-libbed one of the film's best-remembered lines, "The judge says this is my day to see the dog."

The story of a man who divorces his wife but then wants her back again had echoes of his own marriage to Virginia Cherrill, as did many of his lines. "Trouble with most marriages, people act as if they were in prison. They exaggerate every little trifle, and the first thing you know they're in the divorce court." At another point he put in, "You can't have a happy married life if you're always suspicious. There can't be any doubts in marriage . . . marriage is based on faith, and when you've lost that you've lost everything." Just as Cukor had discovered the sly cockiness of Archie Leach in Cary Grant, so McCarey now revealed the agitation behind his aloofness.

With the wirehaired fox terrier Asta from *The Thin Man* series now playing the Warriners' dog, Mr. Smith, and Ralph Bellamy splendidly cast as Dunne's hapless suitor, the comedy opened to great acclaim in October 1937. Divorce had never before been considered a subject for film comedy. Otis Ferguson, critic of the *New Republic,* described *The Awful Truth* as "a foolishness that doesn't go wrong or strained." *The New York Times* said "its unapologetic return to the fundamentals of comedy seems original and daring," and *Variety* called the film "Cary Grant's best fast light comedy performance to date."

The success immediately sent Harry Cohn searching for a new script for Grant and Dunne, but almost two years would pass before they would play together again. Soon after *The Awful Truth* had finished shooting, Cary Grant had agreed to make three films for RKO to be spread over the next two years. He was to be guaranteed an initial fee of $50,000 against a percentage of the profits of each picture.

In April 1937, as the first film made under the new contract, RKO decided to adapt a short story from *Collier's* magazine, to be written by studio scriptwriter Hagar Wilde and directed by Howard Hawks. A slightly mysterious figure in Hollywood, Hawks had started in comedy but had gone on to make dramas, including *Scarface* for Howard Hughes. Articulate, with sharp features and a precise determination, he preferred telling good stories to making intellectual points in his movies. Impeccably dressed and "a-purr with melodrama," as his friend Ben Hecht said of him, he had joined RKO in 1936 as a producer and director.

When the *Collier's* story of a shy paleontologist whose life is turned upside down by a fey New England heiress was first discussed, RKO and Hawks knew they wanted to use Katharine Hepburn, who was still under contract to the studio but whose career had hardly recovered since *Sylvia Scarlett.* She had since made three more flops for RKO, and some executives had begun to ask why she was still under contract. Gregory La Cava's *Stage Door,* in which she had played opposite a sarcastic Ginger Rogers, had restored some of her confidence, but commercially the film had not been a success. Depressed, she still relied on the encouragement of Howard Hughes, who had followed her recent tour in a stage version of *Jane Eyre* in his private plane.

RKO was uncertain whom to cast opposite her as the paleontologist. Sam Briskin, the production chief, had talked about Ray Milland, but a loan from Paramount could not be arranged. Fredric March had been mentioned and so had Leslie Howard and Robert Montgomery. But after the success of *The Awful Truth,* Briskin and Pandro Berman decided to use Cary Grant.

When Hawks went to talk to Grant about the role of the paleontologist, Grant replied, "I won't know how to do a thing like that. I wouldn't know how to tackle it. I'm not an intellectual type."

"You've seen Harold Lloyd, haven't you?" riposted Hawks. Grant nodded.

"That gave him a clue, the innocent abroad," Hawks later recalled. "Hepburn, by contrast, was fascinated with her part.

She had not been trained in comedy at all, but she wanted to play comedy."

As the heiress with a pet leopard called Baby who could only be subdued by the song "I can't give you anything but love, Baby," Hepburn dragged Grant through the film at a frantic pace. RKO was worried about its unromantic tone. The script called for Grant to wear glasses, and they didn't like that. They were aware that his fan mail had increased from two hundred to fourteen hundred letters a week since *The Awful Truth*, and they wanted to see it continue to grow. They were also anxious that Hepburn's hair not look too unruly. They wanted the comedy to be gentle and glamorous rather than slapstick.

When *Bringing Up Baby*, which cost more than a million dollars to make and for which Grant was finally paid more than $120,000, opened, it was greeted warmly, but not rapturously. Frank Nugent in *The New York Times* said, "Miss Hepburn has a role which calls for her to be breathless, senseless and terribly, terribly fatiguing. She succeeds, and we can be callous enough to hint it is not entirely a matter of performance." *Time* magazine added that its "slapstick was irrational, rough and tumble, undignified, obviously devised with the idea that the movie audience will enjoy (as it does) seeing actress Hepburn get a proper mussing up."

Before it opened, however, Howard Hughes had had to come to its financial rescue. He had bought it from the studio in a job lot of ten films and sold it to the Loews' chain, but this shrewd act did nothing to alleviate the dissatisfaction of the trade toward Hepburn. As the filming of *Baby* finished, shortly before Christmas 1937, the Independent Theater Owners Association was compiling a list of performers who were "box-office poison." Katharine Hepburn was their very first name, followed by Joan Crawford, Greta Garbo and Marlene Dietrich. The film, although destined to become a classic, failed to win the hearts of the audience and lost the studio $365,000, prompting RKO to give up its last hopes that Hepburn would succeed.

In contrast, *The Awful Truth* had established itself as a box-office success and a favorite in the movie business. When the 1937 Oscar nominations were announced in February 1938, it appeared in five categories, including that of best picture. Irene Dunne and Ralph Bellamy were both nominated for individual awards, and Leo McCarey was nominated as best director.

Significantly, the only one of its stars not nominated was Cary Grant. Unfair perhaps, yet in the industry his reputation for being a moody, financially demanding perfectionist was gathering force.

Nevertheless, Columbia remained eager to follow up its success with another Dunne and Grant comedy. They wanted to remake Philip Barry's Broadway hit of 1928, *Holiday*, which had been first filmed in 1930 with Ann Harding, Robert Ames and Mary Astor. They had asked George Cukor, who had just left MGM after making *Camille* for Irving Thalberg, to direct it.

Cukor, however, had his own ideas. Katharine Hepburn had understudied Hope Williams in the original Broadway run of *Holiday*, and she had even used the part for her first Hollywood screen test. He urged the studio to give Hepburn the part of Linda Seaton. When Harry Cohn asked RKO if they could borrow her, the studio agreed. It was the first time they had ever loaned out Hepburn, but the disgruntled theater owners and the poor showing of *Bringing Up Baby* had convinced them that her value was waning. As a result, the aristocratic, gentle Irene Dunne, who had won Oscar nominations in each of the past two years, lost the part she had wanted desperately. As she recalled later, "When I heard about it, I cried the entire weekend."

With a script by Donald Ogden Stewart, a friend of Barry's who had even appeared in the play himself, and Sidney Buchman, *Holiday* was an examination of the wealthy Seaton family of New York through the eyes of Johnny Case, a young man engaged to their spoiled daughter, Julia, but more attracted to their other daughter, Linda. In 1928, the play's message of enjoying life instead of making money had been startlingly impudent. A decade later, after a depression that had seen thousands ruined, it seemed curiously irrelevant.

Cukor asked Grant to capitalize on his vaudeville training and play his part as the idealistic and romantic Case almost straight. Instead of appearing frenzied as he had for Hawks,

Cary looked as confident and in control as he had appeared in *The Awful Truth*. The resulting underplayed performance showed him what he was capable of and convinced him that he was most at home in light comedy.

As *The New York Times* remarked when *Holiday* opened at the Radio City Music Hall in June 1938, "Mr. Grant's Mr. Case is really the best role, although it is quite possible that neither Mr. Barry or Columbia saw it that way." But Hepburn's performance as his foil did not endear itself to everyone. *The Times* commented, "We cannot get over our feeling that her intensity is apt to grate on a man, even on so sanguine a temperament as Cary Grant's Johnny Case."

Holiday did not turn out to be the triumph that Columbia had hoped for. It was overshadowed by some of the year's other films, notably *Alexander's Ragtime Band* with Tyrone Power, Walt Disney's unforgettable cartoon *Snow White*, *The Adventures of Robin Hood* with Errol Flynn and *Boys Town* with Spencer Tracy. Indeed, neither of the pictures Cary Grant made in 1938 had proved financially successful for his two new studios. Nevertheless, after earning $175,000 in 1937 and on his way to making more than that in 1938, he felt himself established. He had always measured his success by the financial returns on his films rather than by the critical reaction to them, and he always would. When the filming was over and the reviews were printing, he would remember only the grosses. As a result, he realized that his next film needed to be a big box-office hit.

For years Pandro S. Berman at RKO had nursed the idea of making a film from Rudyard Kipling's poem "Gunga Din." Ben Hecht and Charles MacArthur had prepared a script in 1936 and Howard Hawks had been brought in to produce and direct. Hawks felt Ronald Colman or Robert Donat would be ideal for the movie, with Spencer Tracy as the second male lead. Colman had been approached, but without success. Early in 1937 Ray Milland and Franchot Tone had been talked about, but again nothing had been settled, and the project had been put off when Hawks started on *Bringing Up Baby*.

But Berman, as he himself was to explain, took Hawks off *Gunga Din* after he'd spent too much money on *Bringing Up*

Baby, and replaced him with George Stevens, who had already made a series of films for RKO, including *Alice Adams* with Hepburn and *Swing Time* with Fred Astaire and Ginger Rogers. A former cameraman with Roach, Stevens had worked with McCarey on Laurel and Hardy films and had a reputation for being sensible and easy to get along with.

Grant was to play the lead as Ballantine, the sergeant determined to give up the army and marry; Douglas Fairbanks, Jr., would be his friend Cutter; and Victor McLaglen, who had won an Oscar in 1935 for his role as Gypo Nolan in John Ford's elegant film *The Informer* at RKO, was cast as MacChesney, the third member of the trio. Once again, no sooner had the film begun than Cary Grant became nervous. He went to Berman and asked if he could play Cutter instead of Ballantine. "I think it's going to make a wonderful part, and I want the part Doug is supposed to have," he explained.

Slightly mystified that Grant should want the second lead, Berman nevertheless agreed to the change, and he also agreed to call the character Archibald Cutter. Since he was paying Grant $125,000 for his part compared to $117,000 for Fairbanks and $62,000 for McLaglen, Berman had no compunction about giving the actor what he wanted and making the switch, which was a wise one. Far from being quick and cheap, the film took 104 days to complete, 75 of them on location, and, at a cost of more than $1.9 million, became the most expensive film RKO had ever made.

In spite of this, *Gunga Din* proved to be one of RKO's biggest box-office successes, earning more than $3.8 million, even though a foreign release was severely hampered by the impending war in Europe. It was not to reach England until after World War II. *Jesse James,* starring Tyrone Power, Henry Fonda and Randolph Scott, was the only movie to earn more money domestically in 1939.

Stevens later said *Gunga Din* was so simplistic that, "if I'd experienced another year, I'd have been too smart to make it." Nevertheless, the flag-waving story of three friendly sergeants caught in the midst of a Thuggee rebellion in India took in more money at the box office that year than Judy Garland's

Wizard of Oz, Greta Garbo's *Ninotchka* or Robert Donat's *Good-bye, Mr. Chips.*

With *Gunga Din*, which he would later call one of his two favorite films, Cary Grant enhanced his reputation as an actor who could draw an audience into the theater. In just under two years, he had been transformed from a promising young leading man into a star.

Star or not, in the evening silence of his house on the beach at Santa Monica, Cary Grant sat alone on the enormous eight-foot-wide bed Howard Hughes had given him, looking through his press clippings and listening to the distant rumble of the Pacific breakers. The Cary Grant that Archie Leach had gratefully become in just six years was now recognized by millions of moviegoers throughout the world and earned a quarter of a million dollars a year at a time when the average weekly wage in America was less than a hundred dollars. Such status enabled him to choose his studios, directors and co-stars. But he was also a man who had difficulty in sleeping and eating regularly. The stiffness and uncertainty he had always felt with strangers had not vanished, nor had his shyness with women. On the screen he had developed confidence, even daring, but off it he was still the superficially agreeable, privately morose man who had left Paramount in a huff. Some called him the new Prince Charming. In reality he was nearer The Man in the Iron Mask, trapped in it even if its expression was perpetually smiling.

Once Upon a Honeymoon, the film he was to make with Ginger Rogers, had to be postponed when both she and the director, Leo McCarey, fell ill. On a personal level Grant's feelings for her had gradually evaporated, but the break had in no way affected his public image. He was as popular with Hollywood's many beautiful young actresses as he had always been, and seemed to be constantly pursued by them, even if he still preferred to retire to the solitude of 1018 Ocean Front Avenue and the companionship of Randolph Scott.

One of the few women whom he was prepared to see regularly was Phyllis Brooks, a five-foot five-inch blonde from Boise, Idaho, with something of the waiflike look of Virginia Cherrill.

She had been under contract to both Fox and Universal, but her career had never quite taken off. When she had been on location at Lone Pine with Grant while he was working on *Gunga Din*, he had treated her as he had once treated Virginia Cherrill, one moment showering her with presents and flowers and the next virtually ignoring her. In short, he was as cagey as ever.

Even as a member of the large British community in Hollywood, he remained a distant outsider rather than an active participant. As Joan Fontaine, who was then still married to Brian Aherne, recalled later, "The Beverly Hills British colony was a tight little island" whose self-appointed king, in her view, was Ronald Colman, "while the self-appointed queen was Basil Rathbone's wife." Among the other members were Sir Cedric Hardwicke, David Niven, Merle Oberon, Christopher Isherwood, Ray Milland, Sir C. Aubrey Smith, Boris Karloff and Cary Grant.

Most British visitors ended up seeing Grant. Hedda Hopper reported in the middle of 1938, "Noel Coward and Cary Grant took up where they left off about a month ago, I mean Noel was Cary's houseguest."

Like many other Hollywood columnists, Hopper was suspicious of Grant. *Photoplay* had already called him "zany, like a fox," and had written that the RKO press office had warned everyone not to inquire about his private life. As a result, most of what was printed about his private life was speculation. Columnist Ruth Waterbury pointed out, "The moment you touch on heavy things, the moment you query him about his faith or his life or his ambitions, he turns the subject aside with a deft insinuation that another cocktail would help and that the weather of Southern California is really tremendous."

Still, he genuinely liked Phyllis Brooks. After his trip to England at the end of 1938, he telephoned her from the liner *Normandie* to tell her he hoped she would meet him in New York. He was going to stay with Bert Taylor, whose sister Dorothy was one of Hollywood's most famous hostesses, the Countess di Frasso. When Phyllis arrived, he was openly pleased to see her. "I think we'll probably get married, but I'm not sure," he told one reporter who had come to the boat. "We may get married tomorrow or we may have a quarrel and never speak to one another again. I will not live my life for a lot of journalists. I'm not going to marry a girl to make some newspaper a good headline." And he stalked off to a waiting car. As he did so, another woman with whom he had had dinner on the voyage quietly disembarked. She was Barbara Hutton, heiress to the F. W. Woolworth fortune.

Even though he was paying income tax at the rate of eighty-one cents on the dollar, Cary Grant had not lost his appetite for work. Before *Gunga Din* had opened to long lines in New York in January 1939, its star had already returned to Columbia to make another film with Howard Hawks. But this time, he insisted, he was going to play a truly serious role. "You've got to show 'em you're versatile in this business or you're licked," he declared, and he chose another role that showed him primarily in the company of men.

Insofar as women were featured in "Plane Number Four," as the project was first called, they were there merely as observers of the masculine world. In Hawks's story of a small South American town where Grant was in charge of a tiny airline flying mail across the Andes, he seemed more relaxed than ever before. The film, later retitled *Only Angels Have Wings,* allowed Hawks to experiment with the tough, wisecracking female character who was to appear in so many of his later films. Jean Arthur, playing the show girl who ends up falling for Grant, was the prototype of Lauren Bacall in *To Have and Have Not* and *The Big Sleep.* And the atmosphere of male camaraderie Hawks created in the film was to emerge again a decade later in his film *Red River.* Men in Hawks's world were professionals who played down the dangers of their lives. Grant caught the mood and gave one of his finest performances. Of the film itself, *Newsweek* was to say that it "outranked most of its plane-crashing, sky spectacular predecessors" at the "tail end of an overworked screen cycle."

It was not released until May 1939, but in the interval Grant had resisted all suggestions that he should appear in another comedy. Instead he had gone back to RKO to make a love

story, to be directed by John Cromwell, who had made his reputation in 1934 with a brilliant version of W. Somerset
Maugham's *Of Human Bondage.* The new film, about a loveless
marriage in which the husband is driven into the arms of a
neighboring widow, was melodrama, but good melodrama.
Even so, Grant started complaining before shooting had even
begun and was miserable during the making. He was so unhappy that, after the film was finished and he had gone on a
visit to England, RKO's president George Schaeffer was provoked to send him a telegram. DEAR CARY, it ran, YOU SURE
PAID A TERRIBLE PRICE WITH ALL YOUR WORRIES AND FEARS.
YOU CAN COME HOME NOW. THE PICTURE IS REALLY A HIT.

The critics concurred. *Time,* more guarded than most, said,
"In Name Only will puzzle moviegoers who thought they knew
just what high jinks to expect when screwball Cary Grant falls
in love with screwball Carole Lombard," but Graham Greene,
then writing about film in *The Spectator,* added, "This is a well-
made depressing little picture of unhappy marriage. It is often
sentimental, but the general picture which remains is quite an
authentic one, a glossy photographic likeness of gloom."

Grant himself was gloomy about his own prospects of marriage. He had agreed with Phyllis Brooks that they should announce their engagement, but then he told her that he felt he
could not go through with it. She broke down, he relented, the
news of their disagreement leaked out. Within two months
their engagement was officially broken.

Afterward Brooks told columnist Louella Parsons, "We
talked it over. He has his career, in which he is deeply interested, and I have just now had a contract offered to me." The
contract was in England. RKO did not seem sorry to see her
leave their star alone, and Cary Grant did not allow the loss to
worry him unduly. He was too busy working on his third film
with Howard Hawks, a remake of Ben Hecht and Charles
MacArthur's 1928 stage hit *The Front Page,* which first had been
filmed in 1931 by Howard Hughes, from whom Columbia had
now bought the rights. Hawks had got the idea for remaking
the film at a dinner party. He had asked a woman guest to read
the part of Hildy Johnson, the reporter who wants to leave the

paper, while he had read the part of Walter Burns, the editor who doesn't want him to go.

Hawks had tried to get a series of actresses to take on the part of Johnson. He had approached Ginger Rogers, Irene Dunne and Jean Arthur, but all three had turned him down. Dunne had also turned down his offer of Jean Arthur's part in *Only Angels Have Wings*. Finally, Harry Cohn suggested that he consider Rosalind Russell, then under contract to MGM and fresh from her success in George Cukor's film *The Women*.

A trial lawyer's daughter from Connecticut and a devout Catholic, Rosalind Russell was to become one of Cary Grant's few very close women friends. Articulate and engaging, she was also determined. As soon as she saw the script of *His Girl Friday*, as the film was retitled, and saw that it gave all the funniest lines to her co-star, she hired an advertising copywriter to improve her part.

Grant, who was already being encouraged by Hawks to ad-lib whenever he wanted to, met his match in Russell. As she put it later, "He'd be standing there, leaning over, practically parallel to the ground, eyes flashing, extemporizing as he went, but he was in with another ad-libber. I enjoyed working that way too." At one point Grant was so taken aback by one of her replies that he looked across at Hawks behind the camera and asked, "Is she going to do that?" The director so enjoyed his pained expression that he left the remark in the film, just as he left in some of Russell's additions to the script, including her magnificent response when Grant, playing Burns, says, "Someday that guy's going to marry that girl and make her happy." "Sure," she replies, "slaphappy."

Russell said later, "Cary was terrific to work with because he's a true comic, in the sense that comedy is in the mind, the brain, the cortex."

But she knew he was lonely. "He was between girls then. . . . During the making he used to call up and ask if I would like to go jigging," which is what he called dancing. There was never any suggestion of romance between them; Grant simply felt comfortable in her company.

Just before Christmas 1939, the London agent Freddie Brisson, who had become one of Grant's friends in England, came to California to stay with him in Santa Monica. Because Brisson wanted to meet Rosalind Russell, Grant invited her for Christmas and the New Year but she never turned up, leaving the two men to celebrate the holidays on their own. Every time Grant asked Russell, "Do you know Freddie Brisson?" she would answer, "No, what is it, a sandwich?" Until one evening, when she arrived at the house to collect her co-star to go dancing, he introduced them. Within two years Grant was best man at their wedding.

The chemistry between Grant and Russell in *His Girl Friday*, helped by Hawks's use of rapid dialogue in which the words were allowed to overlap one another, produced his most memorable performance. If he had been a little too anxious opposite Dunne and a little too frenzied opposite Hepburn, here he relaxed and allowed his natural arrogance to provide the perfect film version of a man who seemed to share his own secret desire to manipulate women. When the film was released in January 1940, Frank Nugent commented in *The New York Times*, "Cary Grant's Walter Burns is splendid, except when he is being consciously cute." *Variety* described him as doing his role "to a turn."

In the course of the picture, Grant had ad-libbed angrily, "The last person who said that to me was Archie Leach, just a week before he cut his throat." The remark was hardly a joke. Cary Grant had begun to wonder whether he might not cut Archie Leach's throat. Getting back to England was becoming increasingly difficult. War had been declared between Great Britain and Germany in September; and Cary was considering, as he had been for some time, the possibility of becoming an American citizen.

CHAPTER 7

That's the way films got made in
Hollywood: back the hot crapshooter who
had rolled four sevens in a row.

Frank Capra

Between 1935 and 1939, Cary Grant had organized his career
as meticulously as he had emptied the ashtrays in his house.
The details of the financial arrangements for each picture occupied his attention every bit as much as the quality of the
script; the size and position of his billing were as important to
him as the choice of his co-stars. He did not see himself primarily as an actor but as a "star" whom the audience could
recognize. He was determined not to sacrifice his place in their
affections by straying too far from the personality they knew
and admired.

In private, however, he saw no reason to keep up the conventional Hollywood star facades. The house on the beach,
which he still shared with Randolph Scott, was large, certainly,
with seven bedrooms and a game room, but it was not nearly so
opulent as the vast estates of John Barrymore or W. C. Fields.
Unlike Marion Davies and Cecil B. De Mille, he did not have a
library that could be transformed into a screening room; and
he and Scott had only two servants, far fewer than the number
of Louis B. Mayer's household only a few hundred yards away.

Nor did Grant need expensive cars as badges of his success.
He did not own a Duesenberg like Clark Gable, nor a Kissel
convertible like Clara Bow, who had it painted the same color
as her hair. He bought himself a new Cord convertible, but
then sold it. Randolph Scott said later, "It drew too much attention to him, and he didn't like that."

In many ways he was as elusive and enigmatic as Howard
Hughes. He spent money carefully and unostentatiously. He

had no chauffeur, no string of secretaries, not even a personal masseur. He ate in restaurants, but not as regularly as some, and he favored Dave Chasen's shack on Beverly Boulevard, which had opened in 1936, over the more expensive Beverly Hills Hotel, the Brown Derby or the Vendome. He would go to the Trocadero on Saturday evening, as many other actors liked to do after the week's work, but his appearance would be brief.

Far from searching out crowds, he would remain at home, telling his friends, "If people want to find out about me, they can look at me on the screen." One reason he liked Chasen's was that the proprietor kept out autograph hunters. The whole idea of being besieged by people asking him to autograph a book or a piece of paper appalled him.

As he told Louella Parsons, "This autograph evil, and I do think it is an evil, has got entirely out of hand. Originally, it was charming; every player is grateful for admiration. To scrawl your name on a piece of paper, by way of expressing thanks, doesn't seem a thing. I can think of nothing more inconsequential than any actor's autograph. But to be torn apart, and insulted while you're writing it, several hundred times wherever you go, then it becomes intolerable. It's got so that no movie star can move outside of Los Angeles and Beverly Hills where people are used to us."

On the few occasions when he had to meet strangers, he would introduce himself to them as though he were unknown. "Hello, I'm Cary Grant," he would say. His name, like his career, was something he had created, and he did not feel confident enough to expose his creation to the pressures of ordinary life.

In the late spring of 1940, as the "phony war" in Europe was coming to an end and the British Expeditionary Force was retreating toward Dunkirk, *His Girl Friday* established beyond question Grant's position as one of Hollywood's new stars. But his life did not change.

A new film, *My Favorite Wife,* was conceived by McCarey as a sequel to *The Awful Truth,* and he had signed Grant to appear again with Irene Dunne. As usual, McCarey had no intention of following the script, this time written by Bella and Samuel

Spewack, the authors of the successful play and film *Boy Meets Girl*. The idea for *My Favorite Wife* came from a Tennyson poem. Just before shooting started, however, McCarey was badly hurt in a car accident.

With McCarey now in the hospital, Columbia appointed a new director. Dunne was costing them $150,000 for the ten weeks of shooting, while Grant was guaranteed $112,500 plus a percentage of the producer's revenue. In desperation, the studio, which could not afford to wait, picked the young Garson Kanin, who had just finished making a film with Ginger Rogers.

The plot had Grant, a supposed widower, on the verge of re-marrying when the wife he believed has drowned at sea reappears, having spent seven years on a desert island with a handsome scientist. Grant and McCarey had decided that Randolph Scott would be ideal as the scientist.

The confident Kanin, then twenty-eight years old, was not at all worried about taking over a McCarey film, but McCarey was definitely worried about Kanin. As soon as he was able to leave the hospital, he started visiting the set to see what was happening, and what he saw did not please him. He held what he later called "lots of conferences." He even shot a section of the film again. As he put it, "We shot about a reel that replaced two or three."

In spite of his personal reservations about Grant, whom he had taken to calling "the Happy Worrier" because of his behavior during *The Awful Truth,* McCarey recognized that his star's ability to appear surprised and yet fascinated on the screen had been honed to a fine art. As *Time* pointed out when the film opened in May, "At times *My Favorite Wife* tends to get bedroomatic and limp, but it pulls itself together in scenes like those in which Cary Grant scampers between his wives' hotel rooms pursued by the distrustful but admiring clerk, or gets caught in his wife's hat and dress by a suspicious psychologist, or tears around in Gail Patrick's leopard skin dressing gown."

Even in McCarey's semiabsence, the film captured something of his instincts about Grant. At one point in the script he had Dunne say of her co-star, "He was the sweetest boy you ever saw. But faithless!" In view of the speculation about the star's private life, it was a delicate joke.

The New York Times critic Bosley Crowther described the film as "a frankly fanciful farce, a rondo of refined ribaldries and an altogether delightful picture with Cary Grant and Irene Dunne chasing each other around most charmingly in it." This view was shared by audiences, and the movie was one of RKO's greatest successes in 1940, netting more than half a million dollars and extending the run of box-office successes that Cary Grant had begun with *Gunga Din.*

If the film failed to lift him onto the *Motion Picture Herald*'s list of the top ten box-office attractions for the year, beside Mickey Rooney, Spencer Tracy, Clark Gable and Gene Autry, it did confirm his place as one of Hollywood's "new aristocracy," a group attracting the attention of another elite, America's aristocracy of wealth. To some people's surprise, actors were now acceptable escorts for the Huttons, Vanderbilts and Du Ponts. For heiresses, as one American newspaper put it, this development marked the end of America's "quaint old social custom that forbade them to choose their boyfriends from the theatrical profession."

Unable to go to England after the shooting of *My Favorite Wife,* Grant set off for a visit to New York. Katharine Hepburn and Howard Hughes had helped to finance a Broadway production of Philip Barry's play *The Philadelphia Story,* which the author had written especially for Hepburn. Now Hughes was trying to sell the film rights in Hollywood, so far without success. Hepburn's reputation as bad news at the box office continued to haunt her.

The hope was that Grant would play the role of C. K. Dexter Haven, Hepburn's divorced husband, when the film was finally made. (Joseph Cotten was playing it on Broadway.) But first Grant had to make another film for Columbia. *The Howards of Virginia* was based on Elizabeth Page's 1939 best seller *The Tree of Liberty* and was the story of a Virginia backwoodsman who marries the daughter of an aristocratic family. Harry Cohn thought it might broaden Cary's appeal by showing that he could be more than an elegant, witty comedian, but it did not prove a success and ended Grant's string of winners. He felt uncomfortable in the blue and buff uniform the plot required him to wear, nor did he enjoy his long ponytail hairpiece. Ultimately, he found it impossible to obliterate the character he had spent so much time and trouble creating.

Even Frank Lloyd, the Scottish-born former actor turned director who had succeeded so triumphantly with the Laughton-Gable version of *Mutiny on the Bounty,* was unable to save the day. *Newsweek* was to say that the film came to life "all too infrequently" and that Cary Grant was "obviously miscast." As Bosley Crowther pointed out in *The New York Times,* "There is a familiar comic archness about his style which is disquieting in his present serious role, and distinctly annoying."

The experience convinced Grant that he should refuse character parts and concentrate on the personality he had already created. In the future he was to reject several attempts to get him to play in costume drama again, accepting only once and bitterly regretting even that decision.

He gratefully went back to work with Hepburn and Cukor, this time at MGM. Hepburn and Howard Hughes had succeeded at last in selling the film rights of *The Philadelphia Story.* The buyer was Louis B. Mayer of MGM, who paid $175,000; Cukor was to direct it. RKO and Columbia had agreed to release Grant for the film. James Stewart was the film's third star. The immensely tall, Indiana-born actor, who had a degree from Princeton, had started in the theater in New York and was sharing an apartment with Henry Fonda and Joshua Logan, had just made two excellent films, *Mr. Smith Goes to Washington* with Jean Arthur and *Destry Rides Again* with Marlene Dietrich.

Another Hollywood bachelor, Stewart had established a uniquely American presence on the screen. He had made it seem that he was never being anything but himself, an honest, down-to-earth American, and he had taken considerable pains to prevent his extensive intelligence and technique from showing through in his performance.

Barry's friend Donald Ogden Stewart was commissioned to write the script and was provided with a tape recording of the

Broadway performance as an aid. He was later to say, "So, as the writer, I had to hear that goddamned tape recorder and then make sure those laughs were in the film play, too, whether or not they belonged there."

Filming began in July 1940. Grant's performance as the slyly confident Haven, opposite Hepburn's tough but sensitive Tracy Lord, saw him very much in character. His Dexter Haven resembled his Walter Burns, who had in turn resembled his Jerry Warriner, all three of them clever, witty men of the world who knew what they wanted but were not always able to get it. Romantic and elusive, commanding the affections of every woman except the one they really desired, they emerged as both victor and victim.

Many years later James Stewart recalled that Grant "seemed very relaxed and he was very good. . . . George Cukor had told us we could pretty much do what we wanted, and I'd kind of worked out what I was going to do."

In the scene toward the end of the film when Stewart and Grant meet in the library, Stewart had decided that if he was to be drunk, as the script required, he "wasn't going to be too drunk, not slobbering, just a little. I'd decided I would have the hiccups, but I wouldn't tell anyone about it, just sort of try it out, we could always do a retake. Well, we did it, I hiccuped, and Cary said, 'Excuse me,' all of a sudden, and I said, 'I have the hiccups,' and it made the scene."

Grant's ad-lib of "Excuse me," delivered with his eye cocked and his head slightly to one side, was the perfect expression of his new confidence. As Stewart put it, "He has such humor. Kind of like a legitimate actor doing comedy rather than a comedian." He might have added that Grant was a straight man from the vaudeville days redeploying an old skill.

Billed first for the first time ever, above Hepburn, and guaranteed more than $100,000 for his services, Grant felt he need not be concerned about the film's critical success. All the same, when the picture finally opened in New York just after Christmas 1940, the response was overwhelming. Bosley Crowther described it as "having just about everything that a blue-chip comedy should have, a witty romantic script derived by Donald Ogden Stewart out of Philip Barry's successful play, the flavor of high society elegance, in which the patrons inevitably luxuriate, and a splendid cast of performers." *The Hollywood Reporter* said, "It's the type of entertainment which will set a box office on fire. It has youth, and beauty, romance and SEX and oh what sex!" *Variety* reported, "The picture is highly sophisticated and gets a champagne sparkle, jewel polish job of direction by George Cukor."

At the Radio City Music Hall in New York, where it played for an unprecedented six weeks, the film broke the theater's attendance record set by Walt Disney's *Snow White and the Seven Dwarfs* in 1937. It grossed nearly $600,000 in that theater alone, more than half the revenue from Hepburn's entire Broadway run in a year, and it went on to become one of the year's biggest box-office hits, surpassed only by *Sergeant York,* the World War I story starring Gary Cooper. It also reestablished Hepburn as an actress Hollywood was prepared to accept.

Yet Grant and Hepburn would never make another movie together. Although neither realized it at the time, the period of high romantic comedy that had helped create Cary Grant was coming to an end. The "screwball" comedies of the late 1930's were being overtaken by a world at war that had little interest in giggling high jinks and clever, brittle dialogue. As the critic Pauline Kael put it later, "After 1940 Grant didn't seem to have any place to go; there were no longer Cary Grant pictures."

Grant himself had been wondering what to do next, not only about his films but about the war. He had already taken the first steps necessary for becoming an American citizen, but in the meantime he was anxious to help the war effort, especially because of the suggestions in the English press that he and others like him were cowering away from the fighting.

Just before *The Philadelphia Story* started filming, Grant and Sir Cedric Hardwicke, another stalwart of the British colony in Hollywood, had flown to Washington to see the British ambassador, Lord Lothian. Before he left Hollywood, the thirty-six-year-old Grant told one reporter, "You feel so damned helpless here." Both he and Hardwicke were anxious to hear how Lord Lothian thought they could be of use.

"Stay put and carry on doing what you do best," was the intelligent reply. Naturally, such advice did not prove acceptable to the more jingoistic sections of the British press, which continued its attacks, but it did assuage Grant's conscience. Lothian helped a little more by adding, "It is quite unfair to condemn older actors who are obeying this ruling as deserters."

Uncertain and a little sheepish, Cary Grant returned to work. By the end of 1940 he had proved the genuineness of his concern by donating his $125,000 fee for *The Philadelphia Story* to the British war effort. His next film was to be for Columbia under the contract first signed nearly four years before and regularly amended and renewed since. The producer and director was to be George Stevens, who had left RKO in spite of the success of *Gunga Din*. Grant was again to star opposite Irene Dunne, who was billed above him for the third time, but *Penny Serenade* was not to be a comedy, which is what he would have preferred, but an old-fashioned melodramatic tearjerker. Morrie Ryskind, whose successes had included *My Man Godfrey* for Carole Lombard and William Powell and *A Night at the Opera* for the Marx Brothers, wrote the script. The plot, adapted from a *McCall's* short story by Martha Cheavens, was about a childless couple who look back over their marriage to the strains of old phonograph records, remembering their efforts to adopt a child and the tragic consequences. As Dunne said later, "Cary thought it was much too serious."

Once again he tried to persuade Harry Cohn to let him out of the picture, and once again Cohn refused. Unhappy and peeved, he returned to the filming, certain it would turn out badly. Dunne told him, "If you really stick with this and give it everything you have, I think you'll get an Academy Award nomination." She was right: Grant's performance was admirable, and Harry Cohn was delighted with him. After seeing a preview, he wired, THIS IS YOUR FINEST PICTURE, AND A NEWER AND GREATER GRANT. LET'S CONTINUE TO DISAGREE AND MAKE MORE JUST LIKE IT. The actor had earned $100,000 for the ten weeks of filming.

But now, artistically a galling disappointment was in store for him. He had hardly finished filming *Penny Serenade* when the nominations for the Academy Awards for 1940 were announced. To his utter despair, every member of *The Philadelphia Story* except him seemed to have been nominated for an Oscar: the film itself for best picture of the year; Cukor as best director; James Stewart as best actor; Hepburn as best actress; and Donald Ogden Stewart as author of the best screenplay.

At the annual banquet at the Biltmore Hotel on February 27, 1941, addressed by President Roosevelt on a radio link, James Stewart won the Oscar as best actor of the year, beating Charlie Chaplin in *The Great Dictator,* Henry Fonda in *The Grapes of Wrath* and Laurence Olivier in *Rebecca.* Stewart's victory was an ironic one for Cary Grant since he had originally thought about playing Jimmy Stewart's Macauley Connor but had chosen Dexter Haven instead.

Try as he might, he found it impossible to overlook the fact that for the second time in four years his peers in Hollywood had snubbed him. Although he still presented the confident smiling face of Cary Grant to anyone who met him, the omission deepened his inveterate sense of being an outsider and forced him further back into himself, confirming both his suspicions about the film community and his decision to remain slightly aloof from it.

One person who shared his sense of isolation from the community and, indeed, from most of the rest of the world, was the small woman who, over the past few months, had come to play an increasingly important part in his life, Barbara Hutton.

To anyone who met her for the first time, Barbara Hutton looked as if she might break in two. With clear blue eyes set in pale cheeks and fringed with wisps of blond hair, she reminded people of a tiny Dresden doll, wistful, vulnerable and sad. At the age of five she had inherited more than $20 million from her grandfather, Frank W. Woolworth, and it seemed as though the weight of all those riches might crush her.

Yet though she weighed only a little over eighty-four pounds and was less than five feet two inches in height, she was more than capable of defending herself and of making up her own mind. Married for the first time at the age of twenty to Prince Alexis Mdivani, who came from Georgia in Russia, she had divorced him after three years in May 1935, and within twenty-four hours was walking up to the altar again, this time with a German who had become a Danish citizen, Count Haugwitz-Reventlow. She bore him a son, Lance, in London in February 1936, but before the child reached the age of two she had legally separated from his father and returned to the United States.

Those who did not know her thought of her as spoiled, but that opinion was less than fair. She had simply known no life other than the one she had led, surrounded by servants and advisers, protected by well-meaning friends and bodyguards, swamped in affluence. Delicate and often lonely, she would tell her friends in America, "You know my money has never brought me happiness. You can't buy love with money."

On Barbara Hutton's first visit to California she was en route to Honolulu for a holiday with Dorothy di Frasso, the Hollywood hostess, whose current lover was the mobster Bugsy Siegel. Just before the two women left for Hawaii, Di Frasso reintroduced her to Cary Grant, whom she had last encountered on the ship from England in 1938. When they got back, Di Frasso arranged a series of dinner parties at which both Hutton and Grant were guests.

Appropriately enough, *The Philadelphia Story* itself concerned the romantic whims of an heiress. As filming continued at the MGM studios, the timid real-life heiress and the sometimes frightened star, in spite of their widely different upbringings, were instinctively drawn together. Both were uncomfortable in the presence of strangers, nervous about committing themselves and yet given to sudden childish impulses.

Gradually, almost without noticing it, Cary Grant fell in love with Barbara Hutton, and for her part she thought she might love him. Nervous about the publicity her relationship with a film star might attract, she concealed her feelings for several months. She and her six-year-old son, Lance, moved into Buster Keaton's former house in Beverly Hills, and she surrounded it with security guards because of a series of threats to kidnap the boy at a time when memories of the Lindbergh case were still strong.

When she went out with Grant they avoided restaurants or

nightclubs, went only to dinner parties with friends whom they knew well and were never photographed together. In spite of their efforts at secrecy, by November 1940 the news of their friendship had begun to leak out. *Photoplay* magazine was calling it "the most hushed up love story in Hollywood" and speculated that the couple would be married within a year. Neither Grant nor Hutton had any intention of admitting anything.

Their friends were equally discreet. Douglas Fairbanks, Jr., and his wife, Mary Lee, Ricardo Cortez, Noel Coward when he was in Los Angeles, even Elsa Maxwell, who regularly wrote about Hollywood society, remained studiously silent. Hutton usually went home to bed by eleven P.M. and she refused to visit Cary on the set. Instead, she would go to his Santa Monica house after lunch for a swim. In the evenings he would sometimes take her north along the Pacific Coast Highway in his convertible, stopping to buy hot dogs from a roadside stand for the woman who could afford everything.

The relationship did not make him more popular in Hollywood. Before long the town's less generous commentators were calling Hutton and Grant, "Cash and Cary," a sobriquet that was to rankle them both for years—and justifiably so. For, hard though it was for Hollywood cynics to accept, Cary Grant had fallen in love.

He was never to describe to anyone, even his closest friends, how he felt that summer. Some would say later that his happiness came through in the filming of *The Philadelphia Story,* so close was the parallel with his own life. No one missed the fact that he took to disappearing from the set as soon as Cukor would release him in order to return to Santa Monica to prepare for his evening rendezvous.

This man who had decided never to let his defenses slip had succumbed to a simple romantic emotion. Barbara Hutton was a woman he could protect, not a small fierce mother to argue with but someone who relied on him. He had never experienced such feelings before, even when he first met Virginia Cherrill. This time he really did seem to be the most important person in somebody else's life, and the thought delighted him.

While he fretted over *Penny Serenade,* the relationship between Grant and Hutton deepened. The division between the two halves of his life, the public one played out in front of the camera and the private one confined to the seclusion of his home, had never been more marked. But he saw no problem in that. By the time George Stevens had finished shooting the film, Irene Dunne had worked on it for seventy-four days with hardly a break and had lost eight pounds in weight. As a result, her doctor ordered her to leave Hollywood to recuperate. Grant, in contrast, felt in no need of a rest.

He had already agreed to return to RKO for his next film under their contract. This time he was to be directed by the English-born Alfred Hitchcock, whose first movie in Hollywood, *Rebecca,* had just been nominated for an Academy Award. Hitchcock, under contract to the independent producer David O. Selznick, had been loaned to RKO and had started work on a story the studio had bought six years earlier. Based on the novel *Before the Fact* by the English thriller writer Frances Iles, it was about a woman who comes to believe that her husband is planning to kill her.

There was, however, a considerable snag. Neither RKO nor Grant was prepared to accept his playing a murderer. The weepy melodrama of *Penny Serenade* was one thing, but Grant as a coldhearted villain was quite another. Finally, Hitchcock agreed to shoot the film as though Joan Fontaine, who was to play the frightened wife, was only imagining her husband to be a murderer. He wanted to call the film "Fright," but after a survey conducted for the studio by George Gallup, RKO settled for the title *Suspicion.* In the first weeks of 1941 the film began shooting, with its star receiving $112,500 and Fontaine nearly $70,000.

Hitchcock said later, "The real ending I had for the film was that Grant brings his wife the fatal glass of milk to kill her. She knows she is going to be killed so she writes a letter to her mother saying, 'I'm in love with him, I don't want to live anymore, he's going to kill me, society should be protected.' Folding up the letter, she leaves it by the bed and says to him, 'Would you mind mailing it for me?' She drinks the milk, he watches her die. In the last shot of the picture, Cary Grant, whistling very cheerfully, goes to the mailbox and pops in the letter." But, as Hitchcock dryly admitted, "It was heresy to do that to Cary Grant in those days."

The confusion over the central premise of the film remained throughout the shooting. Fontaine, already somewhat intimidated by Hitchcock after her experience with him in *Rebecca,* and with her marriage to Brian Aherne about to break up, found her co-star's aloofness slightly distressing and his niggling worries about tiny details irritating.

Was or was not Grant going to be shown as a murderer? While Hitchcock was away in New York, RKO deleted those sections of the film that indicated that Grant was actually going to murder his wife, but on the director's return they relented and allowed him to reinstate them. But there still remained the bitter debate between director and studio about whether the film should end with Grant's suspicious actions explained away or whether the audience should be left to make up its own mind about his guilt or innocence. Two alternative endings were shot and then tested in front of audiences. When the reactions were invariably in favor of a happy ending, this became the version that was finally used.

The professional relationship between Hitchcock and Grant was to continue for decades. Different though they appeared, the elegant actor with the deceptively smiling facade and the restrained director with the conventional suit and tie were, in fact, similar. Neither was naturally relaxed; both were deeply suspicious of strangers, cautious about their careers, capable of being frightened by women, unhappy in crowds and on occasion distressingly aloof.

What Hitchcock realized was that Grant's sleek charm disguised a darker and more brooding side, that a chill, potentially manipulative quality lay behind the comic timing and the dark, heavy handsomeness. He extended the image the audience was used to by revealing what it might conceal, but he and he alone was permitted by Cary Grant to do so. With other directors, Grant restricted himself to his familiar image of the man in the smiling mask.

146

By the time the filming of *Suspicion* was finished in May 1941, Grant had made five films in fifteen months, working almost without a break. He decided the time had come to take a rest and consider the future. The reviews of *Penny Serenade,* which had just appeared, convinced him that he could handle melodrama without frightening away his audience. *Variety* had called it "sound human comedy drama," and the New York *Daily Mirror* had rated it "even better than *The Awful Truth.*" He may not have been among the top ticket-selling stars—that list was still headed by Mickey Rooney and Clark Gable—but he had earned more than $200,000 in the year, from which he had made the $125,000 donation to the British war effort.

In the next year Cary Grant was to make only two films, but he was to worry over two highly significant decisions, whether to become an American citizen and whether to marry Barbara Hutton.

The mischievous alchemy worked on his screen image by the portly and crafty Hitchcock transformed Cary Grant's reputation as an actor. As *The New Yorker*'s critic John Mosher put it when *Suspicion* opened in New York on the Thanksgiving weekend 1941, "Cary Grant finds a new field for himself, the field of crime, the smiling villain, without heart or conscience. Crime lends color to his amiability." *Variety* agreed. "Grant puts compelling conviction into his unsympathetic but arresting role," it declared, and went on to compliment Hitchcock: "The story has the same dark glitter and portentous drama as *Rebecca,* which Hitchcock also directed and in which Joan Fontaine came to her high estate as an actress."

Yet Grant and the studio's conception of what sort of role he should play had weakened the movie. *The Hollywood Reporter* commented, "If this sop of a happy ending was dragged in by the heels, as it appears, it serves only to spoil a great picture."

Even so, Grant's defense of his familiar image turned out to be justified at the box office. Whatever the critics' reservations, *Suspicion* made RKO more than $400,000 and became the studio's most profitable picture of the year, although it was not as successful as either *The Philadelphia Story* or *Penny Serenade.*

After spending the summer quietly with Barbara Hutton,

Grant began to look around for his next film. The producer Hal Wallis had just bought for Warner Brothers the rights to the Broadway hit comedy by Joseph Kesselring, *Arsenic and Old Lace,* and Frank Capra wanted to direct it. But there was not much time because Capra had decided to enlist in the Army Signal Corps as a major, even though he was forty-four, and even though the terms of Wallis's deal for the play were that the film could not be released until after the Broadway run had ended.

Jack Warner had considered offering the role of Mortimer Brewster, the only sane member of the eccentric Brewster family, to Bob Hope, but Capra wanted Cary Grant for the part. When Capra approached him, Grant told him he might be interested but that his fee would be high.

Frank Vincent, as Grant's agent, began negotiations with Warner Brothers on the basis that Grant would accept $50,000 for the picture if Warner donated a further $100,000 to three charities that Grant would specify. Vincent explained that Grant wanted $25,000 to be given to the United Service Organizations, $25,000 to the American Red Cross and $50,000 to the British War Relief Association, whose chairman in Hollywood was Ronald Colman. Warner Brothers was familiar with the suggestion. Not long before, Edward G. Robinson, another of Vincent's clients, had donated a fee of $100,000 to the United Service Organizations.

While the negotiations dragged on, Grant spent more and more time with Barbara Hutton. She would still come over in the afternoon to swim, and he would go back to her house for dinner, even though the large number of guests she collected there on most evenings and her passion for the company of European aristocrats displeased him. He wished to spend quiet evenings with her alone; but "the Princess," as her staff called her, liked to entertain regally.

Early in September 1941, Grant asked Warners to send him to New York so that he could see *Arsenic and Old Lace* on Broadway, but the ever-wary Jack Warner warned Capra in a cable that Grant "should sign the contract before coming here or he may want to stall after seeing the show." Grant signed and did not stall. However, he did request that the part of Mortimer

Brewster, played on stage by Allyn Joslyn, be expanded. Both he and Capra agreed that as originally written the role was too insignificant to warrant his appearing in it.

His co-stars included three of the principals from the Broadway production, Josephine Hull and Jean Adair as the Brewster aunts who killed elderly gentlemen boarders and John Alexander as their likable brother who was convinced he was President Teddy Roosevelt. Because Warners could not reach an agreement with Boris Karloff to play the evil brother, Jonathan, they cast Raymond Massey in his place and made him up to look like Karloff. Grant's new wife was to be played by Priscilla Lane. A chirpy blonde, she had once written to Grant asking him for an autographed photograph. "But I never got one," she told the disheartened publicity man as the film started.

After building a huge set on Warners' vast Number 7 sound stage, which was thirty-five feet higher than any other stage in Hollywood, the company started work on October 20, 1941. The set, which consisted of a reconstruction of the Brewster family home and included a scale replica of the Brooklyn Bridge, featured a graveyard in which a prop man had carved the name Archibald Leach on one of the gravestones.

Things, as usual, did not go according to plan. After the first few days Capra and Grant were struggling. The director's decision to shoot the film in sequence, as though it were a stage play, terrified the unit manager, Eric Stacey. Grant, moreover, was fussing around, obsessed by detail and discussing every scene until the director's fiery Sicilian temperament was barely under control. In addition, his enthusiasm was having a bad effect on Grant. Instead of playing his part with the restraint that a McCarey or a Hitchcock knew how to draw from him, he found himself overacting, forcing the role for its comic qualities rather than simply playing it along.

Then on Sunday, December 7, 1941, the Japanese bombed the American fleet at Pearl Harbor and America was drawn into the war, and five days later Grant left Warners, his role complete. But not until after the liberation of Paris in September 1944 would Americans see the final version of the film, for the play stayed on Broadway for three and a half years, taking in more than $4 million at the box office.

Grant went back to Columbia for his third film with George Stevens. The success of *Penny Serenade* had convinced Harry Cohn that Stevens and Grant were a profitable combination. *Penny Serenade* had been the thirty-six-year-old director's first film for Columbia after leaving RKO, and the new project, under the working title of "Mr. Twilight," was to be the second. Before long the title was changed to "The Gentleman Misbehaves," then "Three's a Crowd" and finally *The Talk of the Town.*

For this story of a small-town schoolteacher who has to choose between marrying a law professor who hopes to be appointed to the Supreme Court of the United States and a mill hand whom she hides after he has been falsely charged with arson and murder, Columbia had wanted Irene Dunne but settled for Jean Arthur. They had also considered Melvyn Douglas for the part of Professor Lightcap that in the end went to Ronald Colman. The courteous, careful Colman, who had been a star since the 1920's, naturally expected first male billing, but he had caculated without Grant's sensitivity to his own position. After some delicate negotiation, Columbia agreed to give Grant first male billing over Colman, just as MGM had given him billing over Hepburn in *The Philadelphia Story.* The decision may have surprised those outside Hollywood, but the picture business was now only too well aware that Grant was a star who could not only deliver an audience but who could be difficult to deal with if he did not get precisely what he felt he deserved.

Stevens, who had just finished directing Hepburn and Spencer Tracy in *Woman of the Year,* their first film together, recalled later that there was comparatively little rivalry beween the stars of *The Talk of the Town.* He recalls, "The only time I saw any sensitivity between the three of them about who was doing what was at the very end. Cary became very uneasy about walking down that long Supreme Court corridor with Jean following. I don't know what even got into his head, but he figured she was upstaging him, doing all kinds of witty things that must be fantastically interesting because people were laughing around the set . . . but there never was a moment that Cary worked with Ronnie when that happened."

In February 1942, for the second year running, Grant was overlooked at the Academy Awards dinner, and this time it was an even more wounding neglect than it had been the year before. He was nominated for best actor for his performance in *Penny Serenade,* while Joan Fontaine was nominated for her performance in *Suspicion,* in which, of course, she had played as his co-star. When the awards were announced, he had to watch Fontaine accept the award as best actress and smile graciously as he lost as best actor to his old rival at Paramount, Gary Cooper, honored for his performance in *Sergeant York.* Miserably, he went back to work on *The Talk of the Town.*

One person who did appear to appreciate him, however, was Barbara Hutton. They were closer than ever and had talked more and more about marriage. She was still troubled by the publicity that would ensue, while he did not wish to be cast in the role of gold-digging Lothario. On this particular occasion the cynical gossip was wrong. Certainly Grant was careful with his own money, and his reputation for driving a hard bargain was well deserved, but he also had his pride. If he married Barbara Hutton, one of the richest women in the world, he would not touch a cent of her money and he would waive any rights he might have to a share of it should they divorce. He had no intention of accepting the $1.5 million that Hutton had given her last husband when they married. He just wanted to make her his wife.

There was also the delicate question of his citizenship. Hutton had considerable resources in dollar reserves in a London bank vault. Were she to marry an Englishman, those dollars would be frozen there. If she were to marry an American citizen, however, the money would be allowed across the Atlantic and she would be able to donate some of it to one of the charities nearest to her heart, the American Red Cross. As a result, the question of Cary's citizenship became vitally important to both of them, and they agreed not to go ahead with their wedding until it had been settled.

The decision was an agonizing one for Grant. He had told his friends that he wanted to become an American. "I've lived in this country for more than twenty years. It gave me a chance." But he could not forget some of the hostile comments in the English press, and even the normally affectionate magazine *Picturegoer* had remarked, "To most of us the voluntary renunciation of our nationality is an unbelievable thing. Patriotism, despite the modern fashion of decrying it, is still a warm blood emotion to you and me, we cannot understand the renegade, we can only detest him." Although counterbalancing these extremely harsh remarks, it had added, "Grant is sincere in believing that he ought to be an American."

In the end, he applied for his final papers soon after Pearl Harbor, but they were not fully processed until June 1942. On June 26, together with more than three hundred others, Archibald Alec Leach took the oath of allegiance from Senior Federal Judge Paul J. McCormick in Los Angeles, and on the same day he officially changed his name to Cary Grant.

Ten days later he arranged to have lunch with the head of publicity for RKO and told him that he and Barbara Hutton intended to get married.

"Barbara wants to invite her friends, and she doesn't want to elope," he told him. "We thought the best time to do it would be in two days' time. I have a day off."

He was shooting his third film with Leo McCarey, this time co-starring with his old friend Ginger Rogers. McCarey had told him he could be spared for one day and that he could be an hour later the next morning. "But that's all."

The following day Barbara Hutton, her friend Madeleine Hazeltine and some of the eleven members of her personal staff drove from her home in Beverly Hills to Frank Vincent's house in the beautiful countryside near Lake Arrowhead. On that same evening, July 7, they were followed to the house by the studio's head of publicity, a press agent, a cameraman and a laboratory expert to send the photograph back to Los Angeles.

On the sunny morning July 8, 1942, Cary and his secretary, Frank Horn, left the Santa Monica house and started on the two-hour drive to Lake Arrowhead, stopping en route at a Beverly Hills florist. No one had wanted to give the newspapers even a hint of the impending marriage by ordering flowers. As the best man, Vincent had arranged the marriage license but had left the names blank, and even now Horn told the florist that he was buying the orchids, carnations and bridal bouquet for his sister's wedding in Long Beach. The woman behind the counter was not convinced, especially when she saw Grant sitting outside in the car.

At 12:30 that afternoon, Barbara Hutton, wearing a simple blue suit and a cyclamen-colored blouse, and Cary Grant, dressed in a blue-gray suit and a dark tie, were married in the shade under an oak tree in Frank Vincent's garden. The ceremony, conducted by the Reverend H. Paul Romeis, pastor of the San Bernadino English Lutheran Church, took just six minutes. The marriage license gave the groom's age as thirty-eight and the bride's as thirty.

Hollywood's most spectacular marriage since Fairbanks and Pickford had taken place in front of a handful of witnesses and very few friends. Randolph Scott was not there, nor was Dorothy di Frasso—only Madeleine Hazeltine; Germaine Tocquet, Hutton's former governess; and Frank Horn. Grant had not forgotten the mad scenes outside Caxton Hall eight years before, and Hutton did not want to repeat the vast ceremony of her first marriage to Prince Mdivani. The most famous newlyweds in the world believed their marriage was of no concern to anyone but themselves.

That night, as they drove back to Hutton's house in Beverly Hills on which he had arranged to take over the lease, Cary Grant murmured to his new wife, "I can't understand why someone like you would marry me."

He had said it to her before, and she had always just squeezed his hand. This time was no different.

The following morning at ten o'clock Cary Grant went back to RKO to continue shooting the film he was making with Leo McCarey. It was called *Once Upon a Honeymoon,* but there was no time for him to take one.

CHAPTER 8

Life was pretending to be someone else.
Otherwise it was rather dull.
      Daphne du Maurier, *The Matinee Idol*

The quiet dinners together, the late-night telephone calls, the flowers and the soft searching glances as they drove up the beautiful Pacific Coast Highway in the moonlight were what Cary Grant and Barbara Hutton remembered. But the reality of their life together was quite different.

He may have insisted to his friends, "If she wants to buy diamond overshoes, that's her privilege, but all routine items, such as rent and groceries, will be strictly on me," but he could never have conceived of exactly what that would mean. The household he had taken over was nothing like the one that he and Randolph Scott had shared. In addition to her son, Lance, Barbara Hutton lived with her own companion, Germaine Tocquet, who had been with her for almost twenty years; a secretary; a valet; a chauffeur and half a dozen other servants, including a cook. She needed them all, she would tell her husband, to entertain her guests.

She had been accustomed to entertaining at home since she was a girl. Timid with strangers and hating to be photographed or asked for her autograph, she had survived by surrounding herself with people she believed to be her friends, particularly minor members of the European aristocracies. Hollywood had become a popular refuge for such exiles, many of them chased out of their native lands by the invading German armies, and Hutton was fascinated by them.

"It's bedlam," Grant would mutter. "The servants have so many shifts to feed at mealtimes that my wife and I are lucky to get a hamburger."

He preferred, as he had always done, the courtship of a

woman to her company every day. No matter how hard he tried to suppress it, he could never escape a desire to be by himself. Although he treated the small blond heiress, whom he always called Barbara, never Babs, with the kindness, courtesy and charm she had come to expect of him, her decision to live in a vast house filled with people left him feeling trapped.

He had thought that they would live in his house on the beach and had bought Randolph Scott's share in it before his wife said it would be "rather too small for the staff we will need." Reluctantly, he had sold it back to his friend.

Instead, Barbara Hutton decided they should move into a house a little farther north, in Pacific Palisades, which had once belonged to one of his leading ladies, Elissa Landi, and more recently to Douglas Fairbanks, Jr. Called Westridge, it boasted a vast terrace looking out toward the Pacific, a large swimming pool and a tennis court, and would have quite enough space for guests and the servants. Husband and wife would have separate bedrooms. Hers would have an open fire, overstuffed soft pillows and some of her paintings. His would have a view of the Pacific, its own fireplace and a place on the wall for the Boudin seascape she had given him as a present. She hoped he might collect more works by this painter over the next few years to hang beside his three Canalettos.

In the late summer of 1942 life at Pacific Palisades got under way. Grant stayed at home with his wife almost every evening. When they were not entertaining, they would play gin rummy together—he would usually win—but he avoided bridge, which many of her friends preferred. Hutton told Hedda Hopper, "When Lance is home we go to the beach to swim or ride in the afternoon, and in the evening I like nothing better than to curl up with a good book. I play tennis every morning."

Grant would play tennis with his stepson whenever he got the opportunity. To Louella Parsons he said, "I just don't want Lance to be lonely. As a child I was terribly lonely, and I don't want him to have that kind of childhood. Children should not be alone."

By the autumn, however, the endless string of visitors and the formal dinner parties were beginning to take their toll.

Grant remarked later, "I liked Sunday evening when that army of servants was away and just Barbara and I were there. She is an excellent cook and she would go into the kitchen and cook for the two of us." Those private moments harking back to their courtship were becoming all too rare. Barbara Hutton had never been used to living that way, and she saw no reason to start now. When her husband would stalk into his bedroom and firmly shut the door, she would call him "grouchy."

Meanwhile, Selznick had invited him to appear in a film he was planning of the play *Claudia,* but the deal had fallen through because Grant refused to budge from his fee of $100,000 and a percentage of the profits. But *Once Upon a Honeymoon* was progressing satisfactorily. If Leo McCarey seemed a little abstracted and the plot was hardly the full-blooded comedy that Grant had expected, he knew his director had discarded all the other stories he had been working on to do this one because the State Department wanted Hollywood to make an anti-Nazi film.

There was one cloud on the horizon. The ever-determined Ginger Rogers, who was being paid $175,000 for her performance, would not agree to give Grant billing above her as Hepburn and Ronald Colman had done in the past two years. For his part, he was not prepared to forgo top billing again, even though he was being guaranteed only $112,000, although that was an advance against a share of the profits. Finally, after a lengthy negotiation, RKO agreed that for half the film's advertising the top billing would be his and for the other half hers.

Cinema audiences were growing rapidly as the war took hold, and studio profits were rising. *Yankee Doodle Dandy* and *Mrs. Miniver* were doing spectacularly well at the box office, as were *Casablanca* and Orson Welles's new film *The Magnificent Ambersons.* But when *The Talk of the Town* was released in August 1942, it disappointed Columbia's hopes. *Variety* called it "one of the season's more important entries," but it never caught the audience's imagination.

Neither did *Once Upon a Honeymoon* when it was released late in October of the same year. *The New York Times* noted sadly that McCarey had made the mistake of "trying to mix romantic comedy with tragedy too stark and real," so that "the two are completely repellant when brought together so glibly in one film." And some people were wondering whether Cary Grant's appeal at the box office was beginning to wane.

To his friends in the autumn of 1942 Cary Grant appeared even more isolated than when he and Randolph Scott had lived together in Santa Monica. He was famous, certainly, married to one of the richest women in the world, a prince in the Hollywood aristocracy. But he seemed uncertain and unsettled to those who knew him well, uncomfortable with the fame that he had so obviously wanted to achieve.

At the Beverly Hills Tennis Club he would appear from time to time, as superficially charming as ever to anyone who spoke to him. The tennis professional there, Milton Holmes, one day caught him as he was climbing into his convertible and told him an idea he had had for a film. Holmes had never written a screenplay or indeed a story before, but in the best traditions of Hollywood Grant told him "it sounded a swell idea" for RKO. Besides, he had thought up a good commercial title. The picture would be called *Mr. Lucky,* a nice twist—for that was how many people saw him.

So in November 1942 Grant started to work on the movie at RKO, starring opposite the beautiful Laraine Day, whom the studio had borrowed from MGM. In the daily rushes Grant looked more handsome than ever. The fleshiness of his face had thinned, making his sharp jaw clearer, and he looked younger than his thirty-eight years. Also, there was none of the exaggerated comedy that had marred some of his earlier roles. He was expected to look like a scoundrel, and he did. He even seemed to relish the thought of breaking away from his image. Since his marriage to Hutton he had begun taking more risks. His part was as a handsome gambler with a neat line who decides to fleece the American War Relief Society.

Laraine Day remembers him as "constantly telling jokes" on the set. "He was a professional. He always knew where the camera was, what he needed to do, and he worked very hard. He had managed to teach himself a lot of tricks, like the double take, and he used them and taught them to other people. It was a treat to work with him."

Yet in the evenings he was utterly transformed. "We used to go to director Hank Potter's house for dinner, and he would come with Barbara Hutton. Then he wasn't the bright cheerful person he had been on the set all day, he was subdued, completely different. It was astonishing."

Hutton's dislike of the film business was clear, and the strain of trying to keep her happy in the company of his professional colleagues was showing through. "He used to look after everyone on the set, and then in the evenings he seemed to be looking after her as well, although in a different way."

Indeed, the fierce contradictions between his professional life and his position as the heiress's husband were taking their toll. Early in 1943, even *Photoplay* noticed that "he gets sudden periods of depression," and in the evenings when he got home he started retiring to his own room to eat alone, study the next day's script or look through his press clippings.

As Hedda Hopper was to remark, "Cary was upstairs cramming twelve solid pages of script into his head. Up at six for a studio call, home late dead tired, and was not amused by the upper-crust goings on around his place. Yet he was kind, tolerant and considerate of the spoiled girl he'd married."

No matter how difficult life had so quickly become, Grant was still in love with the frail heiress. Both he and his wife would have liked to have had children, and in the first months of their married life there were persistent reports of miscarriages. In fact, two years after they were married Hutton was telling Hopper, "If only Cary and I could have a baby someday. We'd like to have at least three. We're praying, both of us. Maybe our dreams will come true."

Perhaps if they had managed to have a child the isolation they felt from each other might have disappeared, but their dreams were not to be fulfilled. Barbara Hutton would never bear another child after Lance, and it was to be twenty-four years before Cary Grant was to become a father.

After the shooting of *Mr. Lucky* had been completed in the first week of 1943, Cary Grant decided to stop making films for

158

a time. He owed it to his wife, and to their life together, to take a rest. He would do some War Bond tours and entertain the troops, but most of all he would try to create a life they could live together rather than apart. He wanted to know as much about art and music as she did so that he would not be the only ignorant guest in his own house.

As he sat beside the pool in the mornings, he comforted himself with the thought that the risk he had run in playing *Mr. Lucky* had paid off at the box office. When it opened in May 1943, *Newsweek* decribed it as having "its bright moments, the overall theme of redemption is as realistic as Hans Christian Andersen and occasionally several times as arch," but in spite of this cautious note it became one of RKO's biggest hits of the year, making a profit of more than $1.6 million. Grant's canny attention to his career had once more paid dividends.

Mr. Lucky was to remain one of his favorite films, confirming the fact, as he was to remark many many years later, that he had rather more depth than some of his earlier roles had shown. "The film is memorable to me because the character I played was more like the real Cary Grant than any before. Mr. Lucky was seemingly a happy-go-lucky guy, but that was the cover for a sensitive soul."

At home the actor struggled against his feelings of incompatability. He tried to understand more about his wife, and she tried to settle into the routine he wanted of a quieter life with fewer visitors. It was a transformation that neither could manage. Gradually, the envious tittle-tattle surfaced more openly. They were "million-dollar recluses" who "never go anywhere to see any Hollywood people" and who "dine formally every night on silver plate for family and gold plate for company."

When the Academy Awards were announced in March, none of Grant's work was honored, although *The Talk of the Town* received four nominations. *Mrs. Miniver*, the box-office sensation of 1942, took most of the principal Oscars, with James Cagney triumphing as best actor as the irrepressible George M. Cohan in *Yankee Doodle Dandy*.

In the next few months Grant toured army camps while Hutton remained in Hollywood. He had abandoned the effort to change himself, realizing it would never work. In despair he went back to making films. He did not know what else to do.

At Warner Brothers, Delmer Daves, who had started as a propman, worked up a story based on an article in *Liberty* magazine about an American submarine's trip to Tokyo Bay and back. While Grant was on a War Bond tour in May 1943, Jack Warner suggested he make his first war film. Grant was willing but said Warner would have to be quick, because he had just signed a new agreement with Columbia and needed to be at the studio by the beginning of August.

Jack Warner wanted to film the first "realistic portrait" of United States submarines in action. Part propaganda, part melodrama, the film would allow Grant to capitalize on his role in *Mr. Lucky* by playing the submarine's commander. Warners had enjoyed some success with *Air Force*, a dramatization of the life of the Flying Fortress aircrews which Howard Hawks had directed for them, and in this new picture they intended to use John Garfield and Faye Emerson, who had both appeared in that earlier film. Despite his lack of experience, Delmer Daves was asked if he would like to direct it himself. The studio had recently allowed John Huston his first directorial opportunity with *The Maltese Falcon,* and they saw no reason why Daves should not do equally well. For his part, the thirty-nine-year-old writer said later, "I didn't know what the hell I was letting myself in for."

With Grant's approval Daves began work on *Destination Tokyo.* Jack Warner sent the script to Washington for clearance and received special approval from the Navy Department after agreeing to a request from President Roosevelt that there should be no reference to radar or to military electronics.

Grant, as usual, fretted about the details of his uniform and the correct way of saluting, but he seemed pleased to be once more breaking away from his old stereotype. There was to be none of the frenzied comedy of *Gunga Din* in Daves's film. Grant was to be a commander who did not joke with his men. Strong, silent, handsome and perhaps a little sad, he was to epitomize the stoic strength of the armed forces. The task of portraying suffering and concern did not prove difficult for him.

Mrs. Leach's only child, Archie: the lonely boy from Bristol who was to be separated from his mother for more than twenty years from the age of ten. (EXPRESS NEWSPAPERS PLC)

Bob Pender's troupe of Knockabout Comedians: as they were when Archie Leach ran away to join them in the English music hall. (THE RAYMOND MANDER AND JOE MITCHENSON THEATRE COLLECTION)

Matinee Idol: the
newly named Cary
Grant in the house
he shared with his
friend Randolph
Scott, where Archie
Leach survived only
as the name of his
pet terrier.

The first Mrs.
Grant: one happy
moment in the brief
marriage of Cary
Grant and Virginia
Cherrill in 1934.
They were to
separate after only
eight months.
(POPPER FOTO)

"Why don't you come up sometime, see me?"; Mae West's unforgettable invitation to Grant helped to make *She Done Him Wrong* one of the biggest hits of 1934. (UNIVERSAL PICTURES; COURTESY OF THE NATIONAL FILM ARCHIVE; STILLS, POSTERS AND DESIGNS)

Marlene Dietrich: together with the director Josef von Sternberg, she helped to establish that Cary Grant was more than just a handsome face in their 1932 film together, *Blonde Venus*. (UNIVERSAL PICTURES; COURTESY OF THE NATIONAL FILM ARCHIVE; STILLS, POSTERS AND DESIGNS)

Movie Star: his performance opposite Irene Dunne in Leo McCarey's *The Awful Truth* in 1937 confirmed Cary Grant as one of Hollywood's new stars. (COLUMBIA PICTURES; COURTESY OF THE NATIONAL FILM ARCHIVE; STILLS, POSTERS AND DESIGNS)

The inimitable Katharine Hepburn: her effect on Cary Grant was rarely less than dramatic in their four films together, and seldom more so than in Howard Hawks's *Bringing Up Baby* in 1938. (PARAMOUNT PICTURES; COURTESY OF THE NATIONAL FILM ARCHIVE; STILLS, POSTERS AND DESIGNS)

The Happy Worrier: Leo McCarey was the first director to unearth the full range of Grant's comic ability, which he exploited in four films, here with Ginger Rogers in *Once Upon a Honeymoon* in 1942.

Poor little rich girl? Barbara Hutton described him as "the husband I really loved," even though their marriage in 1942 was destined to last barely three years. (R. R. STUART COLLECTION)

Notorious: Alfred Hitchcock discovered the threatening manner which could lie beneath the smooth charm of Cary Grant and revealed it brilliantly in his 1946 film *Notorious* with Ingrid Bergman. (THE SELZNICK RELEASING ORGANIZATION; COURTESY OF THE NATIONAL FILM ARCHIVE; STILLS, POSTERS AND DESIGNS)

The third Mrs. Grant: the actress Betsy Drake, who met her husband on board the *Queen Elizabeth* and who subsequently traveled the world with him after his first retirement, remained his wife longer than any of her predecessors. (PARAMOUNT PICTURES)

Even thick glasses could not put off the attentions of Marilyn Monroe in Howard Hawks's 1952 film *Monkey Business*. (20TH CENTURY-FOX; COURTESY OF THE NATIONAL FILM ARCHIVE; STILLS, POSTERS AND DESIGNS)

Four films together: Alfred Hitchcock helped to sustain Cary Grant's enormous success at the box office, and here they celebrate Hitch's eightieth birthday together. (REX FEATURES)

"Here, hold them . . . they're the most beautiful thing in the world, and the one thing you can't resist": Grace Kelly was referring to her jewels in the 1955 film *To Catch a Thief,* but there were millions of moviegoers who did not believe her. (PARAMOUNT PICTURES; COURTESY OF AQUARIUS)

The bride that might have been: Sophia Loren and Cary Grant may have considered marriage, but they actually did it only on the screen in their 1957 film *Houseboat.* (PARAMOUNT PICTURES; COURTESY OF THE NATIONAL FILM ARCHIVE; STILLS, POSTERS AND DESIGNS)

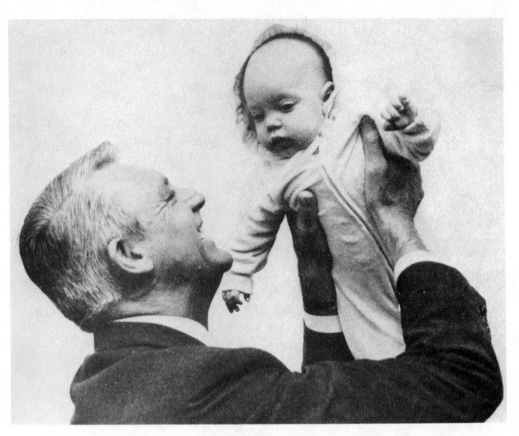

Proud parent or not, it took a long and painful series of court battles to establish his right to see his daughter after Grant separated from her mother. (EXPRESS NEWSPAPERS PLC)

Fatherhood: actress Dyan Cannon became the fourth Mrs. Grant in 1965 and presented Grant with his first child, a daughter, Jennifer, in February 1966. He was sixty-two years old. (EXPRESS NEWSPAPERS PLC)

"I think of us as the same age": Barbara Harris, who is almost half a century younger than Cary Grant, whom she married in April 1981, remains at his side. (EXPRESS NEWSPAPERS PLC)

At seventeen, as striking and handsome as her father was at her age, Jennifer Grant is close to her father and her stepmother and appears with them regularly. (MICHAELSON/TRANSWORLD FEATURES)

Although he has made no public performances to speak of since 1966, Cary Grant still keeps a piano in his home in Beverly Hills. (EXPRESS NEWSPAPERS PLC)

On the set Grant told the young Robert Hutton, whose first film this was, that stardom did not guarantee happiness. "Does it bring you happiness? Yeh, for a couple of days. And then what happens? You begin to find out that your life is not your own anymore, and that you're on show every time you step out on the street."

The misery and contradictions of his own success came pouring out. "Your eyes are weak and you wear dark glasses to protect them from the sun. 'Look at that show-off trying to disguise himself,' you'll hear people say. You buy a new suit because you need it. 'Look at that guy spending all his money on clothes, trying to be another Adolphe Menjou,' you'll hear them say. You dodge some autograph hunters because you're shy, you hate to make a spectacle of yourself. 'Huh, big shot, hasn't got time for the common people now,' they go on." To the young actor's astonishment, Grant suggested Hutton might be better off with a job in the Lockheed aircraft factory.

In the six weeks that Daves had at his disposal, he did all he could with the cast and with the submarine that had been specially constructed on the Warners sound stage on Sunset Boulevard. But shooting was not quite complete by the time Grant was due to start work at Columbia in the first week of August. To get the film finished, he had to work with Daves at night after he had left Columbia. Cary Grant was quite important enough to justify the expense of paying extra money to an entire cast and crew, especially if he could deliver a hit at the box office at Christmas.

Needless to say, Barbara Hutton was not pleased that her husband was now spending both day and night in film studios, but he had decided his work came first. At Columbia Louis B. Edelman was producing a film that had started as a radio sketch. Heavy with echoes of *Bringing Up Baby,* it called for Grant to play a Broadway producer who discovers a nine-year-old boy who has trained his pet caterpillar to dance when he plays the song "Yes, Sir, That's My Baby" on his mouth organ. Grant, as the producer, was to start out as a villainous type and then be shown to have redeeming features.

Filming finished just before Christmas 1943. While Grant and Hutton prepared to entertain forty guests over the holiday at Pacific Palisades, the actor's bitterness and resentment overflowed. He didn't want to live like this, but he loved his wife. The more he thought about it the less there seemed to be any resolution to their personal differences. Inexorably, he slipped into deep depression, convinced that he could never sustain a relationship with a woman.

Destination Tokyo opened to enthusiastic reviews in New York just after Christmas. *The New York Times* called it "a pippin of a picture." *Newsweek* gave its verdict that Grant had turned in "one of the soundest performances of his career." But the lines forming outside the theaters did not seem to alleviate his emptiness. He was aware of his own vanity, of his obsessive perfectionism, his irritability and depressions, yet he felt that his wife should have been more understanding of him and his weaknesses.

The effort to be the relaxed and charming man that his public expected overwhelmed him, leaving him desperate to shrink into an isolated cocoon. He had dreamed of a life with a woman who was as timid and reserved as he was, but the seclusion that they were supposed to have retired to had proved illusory.

Yet there was much that he and Hutton still shared, including a sense of the ridiculous. She used the word *ig* to describe something she felt lacked taste. Once, they visited a house in which a huge apricot-colored bar dominated one corner of its main living room. When the owner said to Grant, "Don't you just love the bar," and Grant told him, "Yes, it's so wonderfully ig," his wife had burst into such a fit of hysterical laughter that they were forced to leave.

But such moments were not enough. By the time the New Year's celebrations for 1944 were over, Grant was forced to acknowledge that his marriage to Barbara Hutton was on the brink of collapse. She was distant and withdrawn, and their only real contact was through Lance, who had taken to calling him General. Lance, now not quite eight years old, was all that was keeping them together. The boy missed him whenever he was out of the house, and Grant was determined not to abandon Barbara's son as his own mother had abandoned him.

The film about the caterpillar had not amused Grant, and he did not particularly want to go back to Columbia if that was all they could think up for him. His goal was to continue to extend his range as an actor, to capitalize on the success of *Mr. Lucky* and *Destination Tokyo.*

Charles Koerner, RKO's general manager, who had been looking for the right project for Grant, had heard about a new novel by Richard Llewellyn, author of the best-selling *How Green Was My Valley,* the movie version of which had won the Oscar as best picture in 1941. Llewellyn's new novel, *None but the Lonely Heart,* was set in London rather than in the mining valleys of Wales, and with Cary Grant in mind RKO had bought the film rights for $60,000.

Although Koerner did not realize it, Llewellyn's story bore similarities to Grant's own upbringing. The central character, Ernie Mott, lived with his mother, a secondhand furniture dealer who was dying of cancer. Grant was enthusiastic and Koerner, delighted but slightly surprised, instructed one of the studio's producers, David Hempstead, to make the film.

Hempstead approached the left-wing playwright Clifford Odets to write the screenplay. Intellectual, ferocious and happier in New York than Hollywood, Odets had reservations. He was even more apprehensive when, after a few evasions, Hempstead told him that the studio was casting Grant for the title role of Mott.

"Cary Grant?" he exclaimed in astonishment. "Do you realize that Ernie Mott is nineteen years old?"

"Of course," Hempstead told him. "It'll be just fine."

With Cary Grant's clearly established screen persona firmly in mind in place of the novel's original central character, Odets set to work. It was the sharp, shrewd slyness which Cary Grant had refined over the years that finally emerged in Odets's screen version, and the effort did not displease the playwright. He knew RKO was anxious to win an Oscar for their star and for themselves, and they wanted a script good enough to do it. He thought he had managed to write one. The next difficulty was to find an actress to play Grant's mother. The obvious choice was Ethel Barrymore, even though she had not set foot on a sound stage since making *Rasputin and the Empress* for Irving Thalberg at MGM in 1932.

When RKO asked about her returning to Hollywood, she turned the idea down flat on the grounds that she was too busy touring with *The Corn Is Green,* in which she was the star. Undeterred, RKO sent her the script and offered to pay $66,000 in salaries to the company of *The Corn Is Green* for the six weeks Barrymore would be needed on the set. The sum was in addition to the $50,000 they were offering her. After reading Odets's script, she agreed, but with hesitation. Her elder brother, John, had died of alcoholism in Hollywood just eighteen months before, and the story of Ernie Mott and his dying mother was painfully close to the bone.

Grant, who had the right of approving the director, had enjoyed working with Delmer Daves and suggested that Odets himself might be given the chance of directing the new film. Once again Odets was astonished. He had considerable experience on Broadway, but his rebellious attitudes and opinions had made some studios suspicious of him. Grant saw him, however, as someone who would listen and be faithful to the part that he had in mind. Although the stylish professional actor seemed utterly unlike the intellectual playwright, the two men were to become friends as a result of the film. Grant, the star, was anxious to learn from the playwright, and the playwright was flattered by the star's interest.

Odets quickly realized that Grant was not at all what he appeared to be. "His simplicity covers up one of the most complex men I've ever met," he was to say years later. "I sometimes feel I really don't know him at all."

It was a view Leo McCarey shared: "I still don't know what makes him tick. Of the sixteen hours a day when he's awake I don't think there are twenty minutes when he's not complaining. I've never seen a man more constantly in turmoil."

Directing *None but the Lonely Heart* was an unforgettable experience for Odets. Like many other directors before him, the playwright soon realized that his star's compulsive perfectionism made him endlessly question everything on the set, every piece of furniture, every accent, every line of dialogue. On more than one occasion Grant stopped the filming and told Odets that the dialogue, as it was written, was "not the way a Cockney would say it." Then his co-star, June Duprez, who had also been born in England and had started her film career there, would also interrupt to say she didn't think her co-star was right either. A weary but fascinated Odets struggled to keep the film going.

But none knew better than Cary Grant how important *None but the Lonely Heart* was to his career. After the reviews of Columbia's caterpillar film, *Once Upon a Time,* he was aware that his performance with Odets had to convince the critics that he deserved to be taken seriously.

The influential James Agee had noted in *The Nation,* "The story of a dancing caterpillar which becomes an international personality, a political and religious symbol, and a baby Armageddon for science and commercialism, and what is popularly thought of as innocence and idealism, might, with great skill, imagination and avoidance of whimsy, become wonderful. But *Once upon a Time* is not wonderful."

Even worse, as far as Grant was concerned, at the Academy Awards ceremony in March, Gary Cooper had again been nominated for an Oscar as best actor, this time for his performance in the film version of Ernest Hemingway's novel *For Whom the Bell Tolls,* which had outgrossed both *Mr. Lucky* and *Destination Tokyo* at the box office. As the filming of *None but the Lonely Heart* proceeded, he became more and more determined to try to win an Oscar himself.

The impending return to the house in Pacific Palisades of his stepson, Lance, who had been visiting his father, cheered him up. "Strange how the little chap has gotten under my skin," Grant told his friend Elsa Maxwell. "When he's away from us I can never get him out of my mind."

Lance had spent almost six months with Count Kurt Haugwitz-Reventlow, who had recently married New York socialite Margaret Astor Drayton. On the day before his expected arrival, Reventlow's attorney phoned to tell Barbara Hutton that his client had no intention of sending her son back. Before the shock had fully sunk in, Reventlow instituted a suit alleging that Barbara Hutton had "used coarse and vulgar language in the boy's presence," and had "sought to undermine his affection for his father." He also demanded that the boy not be allowed to speak to Cary Grant.

Devastated, Hutton and Grant decided to fight the action. They went to meetings with lawyers and California district attorneys, and at every turn Grant was forced to tell reporters, "Yes, I am happily married to Miss Hutton."

Yet nothing had really changed. Grant was still inclined to stay in his room in the evenings, worrying about the next day's shooting. The household was every bit as large as it had been before, and Mademoiselle Germaine Tocquet, his wife's companion, was still fearsomely in evidence. The custody action brought the husband and wife closer than they had been for several months, but its effect did not last. As it became clear that the legal battle would drag on, their unity in the face of Reventlow began to break down, and the separation they had talked about for so long took place.

In the first week of August 1944 Cary Grant disconsolately packed a few of his own belongings and moved into an apartment in Beverly Hills.

Within four days he was back, trying to persuade his wife to begin their marriage again. But Barbara Hutton was not convinced. "I think it's better for both of us if we part now," she told him in her soft voice. "You aren't happy, and you've only stayed here because of the difficulties with Lance."

With that she left the house and went for a drive with her favorite cousin, Jimmy Donahue. When they returned, they discovered that Cary Grant had moved back.

"We've got to try again," he told her. "There's no reason why we can't."

In tears the heiress packed her own clothes and moved out.

The following day Barbara Hutton told Louella Parsons, "There is no chance for reconciliation, and I think it's unfair and dishonest to take advantage of the name of my husband and to seek his protection because I am fighting to hold my child."

Parsons herself added, "The last time they were together was at a party, at which time Cary told me that Barbara was so sweet and gentle that she didn't deserve all the trouble she had had. He said he was going to aid her in her fight for the child."

The separation could not have come at a more difficult time. Jack Warner had negotiated with Harry Cohn to take over the last of the eight films Grant was obliged to make for Columbia under the terms of his original 1938 contract. He wanted to film a biography of Cole Porter, who was a close friend of Grant's, and the composer was insisting that Grant should portray him.

Michael Curtiz, whose *Casablanca,* also produced by Warners, had just won the Oscar for best picture, was to direct, and Warner had even offered to allow Humphrey Bogart to make a film for Columbia if they would release Grant to play Porter.

But Jack Warner had not considered the possible effects of the separation. Grant did not want to think about making any more movies. His life, he said, was in ruins. In Pacific Palisades he took to moping around, refusing even to pick up the telephone unless it was to plead to speak to his wife.

Warner was in a difficult position. He assured Grant that he did not want to press him into working too soon, but he could not stop the work that had already started. So he told his production chief, Steve Trilling, to talk to Frank Vincent, Grant's agent, and see when they could go ahead. The discussion was not encouraging. In a memo on September 26 Trilling told Warner, "In Vincent's opinion, because of Grant's mental condition he possibly would not be ready to make a picture for an indefinite time—certainly not by November 1 or 15. Might be a few months from now, or might be six months from now."

Trilling added gloomily, "Vincent suggests we might look in other directions to cast Porter."

Two days later, after talking to Frank Vincent again, Trilling reported that Grant believed "in his present frame of mind he could not give a good performance—it is something much more important than making a picture with his whole life's happiness at stake." Vincent, in fact, had sensibly been advising his client to keep active rather than sit miserably at home, but as Trilling put it, "Grant seems to be so low that he cannot get straightened out."

That weekend, six weeks after their initial separation, Cary Grant decided to make one final effort to get his wife back. Knowing she was staying in San Francisco with her friend Mrs. Oleg Cassini, the actress Gene Tierney, he drove the four hundred miles north along the California coast to see her. He wanted to persuade her to go dancing with him just once more.

To his surprise, she agreed. She went out with her husband that weekend and admitted that, perhaps, there was some way they could live together again. He told her how much the servants had upset him and how he had felt that they were never alone. Smiling as they swept around the dance floor together, she replied that she wanted him to be happy with her.

"You so seldom seem happy," she told him softly. When the weekend was over, he drove back to Los Angeles, and by the middle of the week she too was on her way back, to a house she had bought in the exclusive Bel Air Estates in Beverly Hills. An English-looking house in what the real-estate agent called Cotswold style, it looked out across the fourth tee of the Bel Air golf course. Large though it was, however, it could not accommodate all the staff. They would remain in Pacific Palisades.

A delighted Cary Grant told the RKO publicity department to issue a brief statement to the press. It said simply, "Yes, it is true, we have effected a reconciliation. The truth of our misunderstanding and eventual reunion, despite all gossip and conjecture, is known only to us, and we feel sure that the press and public will respect it as being our affair." But before the statement was released, husband and wife had already left Hollywood. They had no wish to discuss their marriage with the newspapers.

In fact, the only gossip to circulate recently had concerned Grant's relationship with a young blond actress named Betty Hensel. Some people believed she had been the cause of the marital estrangement, but Betty herself tried to scotch the idea by announcing her engagement to Lieutenant Henry William Dodge, Jr., of the Army Medical Corps.

The reconcilation was no help to Warner Brothers. Frank

Vincent told Steve Trilling only a few days later that Cary Grant was not prepared to start work on the Cole Porter picture until at least April 1, 1945, and probably not until May 1, 1945. But for what it was worth, he was prepared to assure them that Grant would not make any other picture before working on it.

In their new house on Bellagio Road Grant spent most of his time with his wife. He looked after her, stayed with her, amused her as well as he could. There was no need to go to a film studio: all he had to do was to make his wife happy.

For a time things seemed to work. Barbara Hutton could still be flattered by the attention of one of the most publicly handsome men in the world, one who was so clearly in love with her. But the woman who had been raised an heiress, educated in Europe, married first to a prince and then to a count, knew in her heart that her third marrriage could not last. She knew her husband missed the picture business, and she knew how much he hated the dinners that she loved to organize when her guests would speak only French, just as she knew she hated the American Legion prize fights he loved. She watched as her husband's dark moods gradually returned, creeping back into their lives like an unwanted guest.

Even the reviews of *None but the Lonely Heart,* which had opened in September 1944, failed to cheer him. *Time* magazine reported, "However the film makes out financially, it is one of the best pictures of the year, a feather in the cap of all concerned in its making. In the U.S. major productions have rarely dared to tackle so wholeheartedly so harshly human a subject." Bosley Crowther in *The New York Times* called Grant's performance "an exceptional characterization of bewilderment and arrogance." *The Hollywood Reporter* described it as "the finest thing he has ever done," and *Variety* declared the movie a "class picture apparently aimed at critical approval rather than leveled for popular consumption."

It had hardly opened when *Arsenic and Old Lace* was finally released to almost equally enthusiastic reviews, although Howard Barnes in the *New York Herald Tribune* remarked, "For some reason or other, a fine actor merely mugs through the part

179

of the sane member of the Brewster clan. Since he is a star his part has been built up out of all proportion to the plot. That is not to his advantage." But the crowds for Capra's film were almost as enthusiastic as those for the Broadway play, and Grant's ability to attract a film audience was affirmed again.

But at home in Bel Air all this seemed irrelevant. Grant knew that he could perform the role of Cary Grant, star, but could he ever succeed in that of Cary Grant, husband?

Meanwhile the legal battle for Lance continued, and Reventlow was now claiming that his former wife intended to take her son to Europe as soon as the war was over. Throughout the winter Grant's efforts to keep his wife's spirits up did not prevent their arguments.

On one occasion his friends Roz Russell and the agent Freddie Brisson had to intervene to get them back together again. As Russell recalled later, "They wound up sleeping in Freddie's room at our house, and Freddie moved in with me. Next morning Freddie went back to his own room to get a pair of socks and saw Barbara alone in the bed. Then he went into his bathroom and there was Cary asleep on the floor. Stepping over him, Freddie picked up a toothbrush and came back to me. 'I think we've got trouble again,' he said."

They had. By the middle of February 1945, Cary Grant and Barbara Hutton had mutually agreed that their reconciliation had not worked out. On February 26 she moved out of the new house on Bellagio Road and back to Pacific Palisades.

This time there was no talk of getting back together. A terse statement announced, "After much thought and with great consideration we had decided we can be happier living apart. As yet no formal plans have been formed regarding a divorce."

In her column the next day Louella Parsons wrote, "In my opinion, the Hutton heiress will seek a divorce, and I believe she'll leave Hollywood, for since her reconciliation with Cary not one of her friends has seen her. Neither she nor Cary have gone to any parties. They have been in complete seclusion."

Hardly two weeks after Barbara Hutton's departure, the results of the seventeenth Academy Awards were announced. Grant had been nominated for an Oscar as best actor for his performance in *None but the Lonely Heart,* as had Ethel Barrymore as best supporting actress. But at Grauman's Chinese Theatre on the night of March 15, Grant lost to Bing Crosby, who won for his role as Father O'Malley in *Going My Way,* directed by Leo McCarey. Even Ethel Barrymore's success did not alleviate his despair.

In the next few months Cary Grant hardly set foot outside his house and started sleeping downstairs on the couch instead of going upstairs to bed. At Warner Brothers the biography of Cole Porter was still waiting for him, but he refused to consider it. For the moment he didn't care if he never made another movie in his life.

CHAPTER 9

A man may be a fool and not know it;
but not if he is married.

H. L. Mencken

Almost a year had gone by since Cary Grant had set foot on a studio sound stage, and in the bright June sunlight he blinked hard as he pushed open the soundproof door and walked into the dark set at Warner Brothers to start work on Cole Porter's film biography, *Night and Day*. He did not want to be there, but he knew he could not just sit around the house all day moping. He had to work, and he had promised Jack Warner he would make this film before he did anything else.

Smiling at the film crew, some of whom he had worked with on *Destination Tokyo*, he could not get Barbara Hutton out of his mind. There was no hope for a reconciliation, he knew that, but the knowing looks and the sidelong glances that everyone seemed to give him made him shrink back within himself, grateful for the blacked out limousine the studio had provided to bring him to the set each day. If anyone wanted to see him, they could pay at the box office. That was where he could be judged, that was where he truly existed. He did not intend to become an exhibit in the public freak show of Hollywood. When he was not actually shooting, he would stay at home in Bel Air.

Jack Warner had decided to promote the film to mark the twentieth anniversary of the first talking picture, *The Jazz Singer*, and he intended to put the full weight of the studio's publicity machine behind it. It was essential that the movie be a hit. Warner had agreed to pay Cole Porter $300,000 over ten years for the right to use thirty-five of his songs, and he had also accepted Grant's usual fee of $100,000 as an advance against a percentage of the profits. If the film did well, Cary Grant would do well.

This was Michael Curtiz's seventieth film in a career that stretched back to 1926. While he had been waiting to start on it, he had directed Joan Crawford in *Mildred Pierce*, and now he was impatient to get to work on a project that he and Jack Warner had first discussed back in 1943. He did not think it would be too difficult. Warners had some experience with musical biographies, having already filmed the life of George Gershwin, *Rhapsody in Blue*. But Curtiz had reckoned without his star.

Eric Stacey, who had worked on *Arsenic and Old Lace*, was again to be the unit manager, and his daily reports on the film's progress showed just how badly Curtiz miscalculated.

On the third day of shooting he wrote, "Cary Grant complained all day long yesterday about the dialogue—how bad it was, how poorly written—and what lousy characterization it gave him." Two weeks later things had not improved. "Cary Grant is apparently very upset at the way he looks in the picture and he claims he is being photographed too light." By day twenty-two Stacey was adding, "This is another example, as mentioned several times before, of Mr. Grant not particularly liking to do things the way the stand-ins are rehearsed."

An anguished Stacey went on to report that Curtiz and Grant were constantly battling about the changes in the script. After two months of shooting, with the picture behind schedule, Stacey explained, "Mike is just about frantic with all this rewriting (for your information it comes mostly from Cary picking at and criticizing the script). The writers are out there two or three times a day changing things around." On day sixty-nine he wrote, "They do not know how the end of this picture is going to be done. They have been writing this story for two years and still it is not on paper."

Finally, after three months of shooting, Curtiz threatened to walk off the set, claiming Grant wanted to direct the picture himself. Then Grant refused to meet Jack Warner to talk about how the film might be finished. The crew started to joke that Truman would have done better to drop the atomic bomb on Warners rather than Hiroshima, that way the war between the director and the star would have to come to an end. Finally, on

October 15, 1945, Cary Grant left the studio and walked onto the set of his next picture at RKO, aware that he would have to return for three days in November to finish his part. He had never worked with Michael Curtiz before. The day after those extra inserts were finished he said to the tiny Hungarian, "Mike, now that the last foot of this film is shot, I want you to know that if I'm chump enough ever to be caught working for you again, you'll know that I'm either broke or I've lost my mind. You may shanghai crews and cameramen to work with you, but not me, not again."

Curtiz replied, "Yes, Cary, yes, Cary," but the following morning he rang the doorbell at Grant's Bel Air house. "Cary, last night I read the most perfect script for us to do. No story could be as good for you as this one—I'll wait until 1948 or 1949. Together we can—"

Grant interrupted him. "Didn't you understand me yesterday? Let me repeat, I'll never be lunatic enough to play in another of your pictures. Now do you understand me?"

"Yes, Cary, fine, Cary. But I'll leave the script."

It was not until after the trade showing of *Night and Day* nearly nine months later, in July 1946, that Grant sent Curtiz a telegram of appreciation. As he told *Photoplay*'s Ruth Waterbury, "That's me, I raised hell all the way through the picture—I knew it was going to be a flop—so it turns out to be a top success. As for that Curtiz, there's a feverish man to work with, but I'm no dish of weak tea either."

But Cary Grant had a great deal more on his mind than Michael Curtiz during the shooting of *Night and Day*. Three weeks after he had started on the picture, Barbara Hutton had decided to go ahead with her plan to divorce him.

Meanwhile, Betty Hensel, the blond bombshell from St. Louis, had reappeared on the scene, having failed to turn up for her wedding to Lieutenant Dodge. As the Los Angeles papers reported, "Hollywood gossip simultaneously linked the bride to be's name romantically with that of actor Cary Grant." By the middle of July Louella Parsons was adding, "There had been a rumor for a time that Cary would marry pretty little Betty Hensel. When I asked him if he intended to marry her, he said, 'How can I say what I will do when Barbara and I are not divorced? At the moment I have no plans. I want to say that all the time I was married to Barbara I did not go out with any other woman. Betty is a very nice girl, but I have made no plans to marry her.' "

Hutton herself told Parsons firmly, "I am divorcing Cary because our reconciliation proved that we cannot live together as man and wife. It would be very unfair to Cary to say that a third person broke up our home. Our separation was not brought about because I was in love with another man or because Cary was tired of me and was courting another woman."

In the middle of July 1945 Hutton's lawyer filed a suit for divorce in the Los Angeles Superior Court on the grounds of mental cruelty. At the end of the month Grant legally renounced any claims that he might have had to any of his wife's $50 million fortune, and both he and Hutton agreed that neither would make any financial claims against the other.

On August 30, 1945, just as the shooting of *Night and Day* was becoming particularly turbulent, Barbara Hutton appeared in the Los Angeles court before Superior Judge Thurmond Clarke for the divorce hearing. Grant could not bring himself to witness the proceedings. Frank Vincent went in his place. Looking thin and pale, wearing a black suit with a white blouse, a sable scarf and a black straw hat on top of her head, Hutton gave her evidence in a soft voice. She had been separated from her husband for barely six months.

Standing quite still with her hands clasped calmly in front of her, the Woolworth heiress told the court that her husband had caused her great mental anguish.

"Kindly explain that to the court," said her lawyer, Jerry Giesler.

"Well, Mr. Grant and myself did not have the same friends. On more than one occasion when I gave parties he would not come downstairs but would have dinner in bed. When he did come down he obviously was not amused."

"How did this affect you?" the judge asked her.

"It made me rather nervous."

"Did you require the services of a doctor?"

"Yes, I did."

Giesler did not pursue this line of questioning. Instead, he produced the agreement signed by Hutton and Grant releasing each other from any financial claims. Then he called on Germaine Tocquet to corroborate her mistress's evidence. In less time than it took for her husband to sign one of his contracts, Barbara Hutton was awarded a divorce.

As *Time* reported afterward, "In Hollywood, where marriages wither even faster than reputations, a spoiled little rich girl named Barbara Hutton dropped husband number three last week. The whole thing took four minutes. She would have made it in three if she had not taken time out to pose for the photographers."

Yet Grant was to remain her only real love. The man of whom she had complained, "He never took me out at night when we were married. I hardly saw him. At night he was always busy with his clippings or the radio," was to become one of her few close friends. She admitted as much many times during the rest of her life, adding, "He's really very sweet and kind." For his part Cary Grant contented himself with remarking, "The trouble wasn't with her. People just can't dissociate her from her money, and they act like idiots around her. She seldom gets to know people as they really are."

He was to be her constant support when she felt lonely, and was to be the unofficial guardian of her son, Lance, who had been reunited with her just before the divorce proceedings started. She was dependent on Cary until the end of her sad life in May 1979, hardly a mile from his house in Beverly Hills.

Within six months of her divorce, however, Hutton had left America for Europe and was considering buying a house in Tangier because, she said, she had always wanted to live like an Arab.

It was to be some time before Grant would look back on the filming of *Night and Day* with any pleasure. Jack Warner was so grateful to him for having played the part that he promised to give him a projection room for his house in recognition of his services, but more than three years passed before the studio honored its pledge. Only after a strong letter from Grant's lawyers did Warners install two 16mm projectors, a screen and sound equipment in his home.

THE MATINEE IDOL

On the set of his new film at RKO Grant felt happier. For a
start the director was Alfred Hitchcock, who did not believe in
looking through the lens of the camera and acting out every
move for his actors. He simply told them what he wanted and
let them get on with it—so long as what they did worked. He
also took more interest in his leading ladies than in his leading men.

For more than a year, Hitchcock had wanted to make a film
about a man in love with a woman who, in the course of her
official duties, has to go to bed with another man and eventually to marry him. For this project Hitchcock chose Grant to
play Devlin, a United States government agent, and the
woman he was in love with was to be played by Ingrid Bergman. Hitchcock had originally prepared the project for David
Selznick, but Selznick had grown dubious about it and had
sold the whole thing early in 1945 to RKO for $800,000 and a
share in the profits.

Bergman agreed that Cary Grant's name could precede hers
above the title, although her fee was to be $175,000 while he
was still working for a percentage of the profits and his familiar
guarantee of $112,000. She and Grant had met before, and he
had introduced her to his friend Howard Hughes. Established
as one of Hollywood's most beautiful actresses, she had just
won an Oscar for her performance in *Gaslight.* She was cool,
dark-haired and had a luminous, unforgettable beauty that audiences loved. She also had a gift that Hitchcock greatly admired: she could seem sexually attractive and yet distant at the
same time.

The filming turned out to be the exact opposite of the torture
of *Night and Day.* Grant liked Bergman and admired Hitchcock.
He was even prepared to accept that the portly director knew
as much about filmmaking as he did, and accordingly he re-
duced to a minimum his customary fussing about costumes,
settings and script. He was able to concentrate on his acting;
and while he had consciously struggled to give a strong performance in *None but the Lonely Heart,* for Hitchcock he produced
even more effective results with no apparent effort.

Grant's remoteness and yet simultaneous fascination with

Bergman's beauty were most clearly captured in the scene in which they appeared to be kissing for considerably longer than the three seconds' time the American film Production Code allowed.

Bergman recalled later, "We just kissed each other and talked, leaned away and kissed each other again. Then the telephone came between us, and then we moved to the other side of the telephone. So it was a kiss which opened and closed: but the censors couldn't and didn't cut the scene because we never at any point kissed for more than three seconds. We did other things, we nibbled each other's ears, and kissed a cheek so that it looked endless, and became sensational in Hollywood."

Although Cary Grant did not feel like one of the screen's most publicly eligible bachelors, his performance in *Notorious* reestablished him as exactly that, a man who could suffer at the hands of women but who was also desired by them. The eyebrow-arching comedian of *The Philadelphia Story* had become a wiser, less frenzied but no less romantic man. Hitchcock had captured his tortured, uncertain admiration of women and turned it into a brilliant characterization.

Ingrid Bergman was intoxicated with her co-star's charm. As soon as filming was finished early in 1946 she asked whether there was any way they might work together again. He was delighted at the idea. He admired her determination, and her confidence and control reminded him of another small, dark woman he had not seen for nearly eight years and whom he was now anxious to see again.

Elsie Leach looked only a little older. The strains of bombing, fire watching, doodlebugs, rationing and powdered milk and eggs had left her pale and crotchety but basically still the same. Nearly seventy, with the sharp, dark eyes that he remembered only too well, she looked up at him awkwardly when they embraced, as if she hardly knew him.

And indeed she hardly did. He was forty-two now, handsomer than at any time in his life, his dark hair sleeker, his chin thinner and with a suntan that made him seem unnaturally healthy in a Britain where most men of his age possessed a pallor bred of the hardships and privations of the war. Beside them he looked ill at ease.

"It's been a long time since I saw him," Elsie told the local paper. "But he writes regularly, and I always see his films." She did not tell the paper, or indeed her son, whether she liked them. She said instead, "I sometimes just wish he would settle down and have a family. It would be a great relief to me."

Even though he was slightly uncomfortable with his mother, Cary Grant was convinced that he ought to spend more time with her. Now that the war was over, there was no reason why he could not work in England. His only commitments in Hollywood were to Selznick and RKO, and Sir Alexander Korda had suggested he might make movies for his London Films company in England. That might be an ideal way of catching up on time he and Elsie had lost. After all, in the thirty-two years since she had first disappeared from his life, he had seen her on barely a dozen or so occasions.

In fact, Cary Grant was one of the few actors whom Alexander Korda did not regard as boring. For his part, Grant liked the rascally Hungarian, envied him his culture and his confidence. Thanks to Barbara Hutton, Grant was no longer terrified of European arrogance. He recognized it as a style that his own upbringing had never offered, but one not to be intimidated by.

There were remarkably few friends to keep him in Hollywood. Randolph Scott had married his own heiress, Patricia Stillman, and moved into a new house in Beverly Hills. And apart from Howard Hughes, most of his other friends had ties in England. There was still Noel Coward, whom he adored, and the other English playwright whose company he would always seek out, Freddie Lonsdale, the entertaining author of *The Last of Mrs. Cheney.*

Lonsdale had spent most of the war in America, sometimes in an apartment in New York, sometimes staying with Grant in California, and it was he who had introduced him to Alexander Korda. There was some spark of similarity in the two men. Grant called the playwright "maddening but irresistible," and Lonsdale could well have described the actor in the same way. Both were given to depression, each could cheer up the other. Speaking with the assumed accent of Eton and Oxford, Lonsdale, the son of a Jersey tobacconist, was as far from his own roots as Cary Grant was from his, and the two men recognized in each other a shared loneliness and ambition. Both were happy to conceal their uncertainty in the wit and contrived jokes of drawing-room comedy.

Lady Frances Donaldson, in her biography of her father, wrote of him, "Things that pleased him one day irritated him the next, and it was impossible to predict his reaction to any event. His dearest friends of one day were his enemies of the next and vice versa." The same could well have been said of his friend Grant.

Although Grant knew he would have to return to America to make a new film for David Selznick, he expected to be back in England regularly. Even if Britain was austere under the new Labor government, he felt more affinity for the country than he had at any time since the SS *Olympic* had steamed out of Southampton Water a quarter of a century before. He began to think about making his home in England again, perhaps for part of every year.

But the success of his two films made the prospect of such trips more remote. Not only had *Night and Day* opened to long lines at the box office, but *Notorious* was breaking records at Radio City Music Hall in New York. Only *Life* magazine struck a harsh note among the critics. *Night and Day,* it said, "was a remarkably complete dossier of all that is wrong with the current musical film. . . . Monty Woolley, who plays himself, was not a professor when Porter was at college but a fellow undergraduate. Porter himself carries out a largely fictitious war career, during which he is nursed back to health by his future wife from a wound which in fact he never received and composes future hits under circumstances having no relation to the true ones. . . . It may be of no great consequence that moviegoers are misled concerning the life of a popular composer. But now, when the Hollywood vogue for musical biographies has reached a peak (Chopin, Kern, Gershwin) such disregard for fact destroys the validity of this movie formula."

190

But the critics unanimously liked *Notorious*. When it opened in New York only two weeks after *Night and Day*, Bosley Crowther in *The New York Times* described it as a "romantic melodrama which is just about as thrilling as they come—velvet smooth in dramatic action, sharp and sure in its characters and heavily charged with the intensity of warm emotional appeal. But the rare quality of the picture is in the uncommon character of the girl and in the drama of her relations with the American intelligence man. For here Mr. Hecht the scriptwriter and Mr. Hitchcock have done a forthright and daring thing. They have made the girl, played by Miss Bergman, a lady of notably loose morals."

Back in Hollywood and ready to start work again, Grant attended a Fourth of July party at Newport Beach with Howard Hughes and one or two other friends, including Twentieth Century-Fox's brand-new nineteen-year-old discovery Jean Peters, whom the studio intended to star opposite Tyrone Power in her first film. Hughes was on the verge of test-flying his company's new military aircraft, the XF-11, but the flight was not to go well. Shortly after 6:30 P.M. on Sunday, July 7, 1946, Hughes almost killed himself by crashing into the second floor of a house on North Linden Drive.

The rumor in Hollywood that night was that he was tipping his wing to Katharine Hepburn or Ginger Rogers or Jean Peters when he crashed, but the truth was more mundane. The plane had simply developed a fault. Get-well messages deluged the Good Samaritan Hospital, including one from President Harry S. Truman, but the only people Hughes consented to see in the hospital were one or two stars, including his old friend Grant. Everyone else, even the employees of his aircraft company and his two elderly aunts from Texas, was kept out. To the amazement of the hospital's surgical team, Hughes recovered; but as he was to tell some of his friends, "After the crash I never liked to see people very much again."

Under the control of Selznick's associate Dore Schary, Grant's new film was based on a Sidney Sheldon story. Originally called "Too Good to Be True" and now retitled *The Bachelor and the Bobby-Soxer*, it was intended as a vehicle for the seventeen-year-old Shirley Temple, as well as for Grant. In it, Temple pursued a fascinated but appalled Grant through a series of new teen-age rituals, including jitterbugging and drinking ice-cream sodas, while her elder sister, Myrna Loy, looked on.

Uncomplicated, lightweight and with none of Hitchcock's somber tones, the film nevertheless appealed to Grant. That did not mean, however, that he did not take his usual pains to see that it lived up to his standards. To Myrna Loy's consternation, he would discuss every detail of most scenes before shooting started.

As soon as the movie was finished in October 1946, Grant took off for New York with Howard Hughes. With a newly grown moustache concealing the scar on his lip, the Texas millionaire started flying again as soon as possible after his terrifying crash, testing his new Constellation on every available opportunity. On the flight back from New York, Hughes and Grant, who were alone, decided to take an unscheduled trip to Mexico.

Grant later remembered, "Howard doesn't like to get embroiled in crowds. So when we landed in El Paso, Howard rolled out to a dark part of the airfield, and we sat in the plane drinking coffee, waiting for clearance."

Then they took off for Guadalajara, ignoring their established flight plan. Their disappearance made headlines across the country. Two days later a reporter in Mexico spotted them and asked, "Did you fellows know you're in the headlines? You're supposed to be lost."

Grant and Hughes laughed. As Grant put it when he got back, "Being lost suited us fine. We figured that as long as nobody knew where we were we could enjoy ourselves in peace." After another two days, they returned to Hollywood. "Howard is a mighty restful person to be around," he told Hedda Hopper. "When we're together we may go for two hours without saying a word to one another."

Hopper herself added, "Cary and Howard are the closest of friends. Like Cary, Howard's a bachelor, like Grant, he's quiet in public, somewhat of a mystery man, he likes to go places and do things. He's got money, lots more than Cary, who's not exactly poor at a quarter of a million a picture. Together that pair take their fun where they can find it." What Hopper did not point out was that both men shared a weakness for bosomy young actresses and that Hughes often asked Grant for an introduction to them. That was how Hughes met Ingrid Bergman. The only time Grant and his co-star on *Notorious* ever went out together in the evening, Howard Hughes had come along, and they had all gone dancing at El Morocco in New York.

Before starting his next movie, Cary Grant decided to throw a party. One evening in Mike Romanoff's restaurant in Beverly Hills he met James Stewart, who had just finished making *It's a Wonderful Life* with Frank Capra, which RKO had originally bought as a starring vehicle for Grant. Stewart recalled, "He said to me, 'I'm glad I've seen you because I was thinking that maybe we ought to give a party for all these people who've been giving us parties.'

"For some reason it became known as the cad's party, and John McLain [a screenwriter] and Eddy Duchin [a pianist and entertainer] became involved in organizing it." Grant decided it should be held in the Clover Club, and Mike Romanoff did the catering. The room was decorated with two thousand gardenias, which Cary Grant bought at a cost of a dollar each. Stewart, at the time also a bachelor, was responsible for hiring the band.

Stewart recalled, "I took Rita Hayworth, but she was working the next day so I had to take her home at about three A.M., and she told me to go back to the party. When I got back it was very quiet. Some of the lights were out and I saw Cary. He put his fingers to his lips. In a little room off the dance floor the two hundred people who were there were crushed together. Bing Crosby was singing and Hoagy Carmichael was playing the piano. It was magical. Cary had organized that, because Bing didn't really like to do that kind of thing. In those days, there was still glamour in movies. It wasn't hard, we just had a good time."

Hitchcock came up with the idea of Grant's playing Hamlet and asked a professor at the University of California to work on a script. Grant did not like the idea. He preferred a new comedy for Sam Goldwyn, which was again to be released by RKO. By now no producer wanted to upset this star who seemed to guarantee success. Grant's last three films had all been big box-office hits. At last, he felt that he could do what he liked.

To prove it, Grant had made a spectacular deal with Goldwyn. His agent, Frank Vincent, was ill, and Grant had arranged the terms himself, receiving a guarantee of $300,000. But dissatisfied—not for the first time—with the director and the script after filming had started, he offered to give Goldwyn all his money back if he would release him from his contract. Goldwyn refused but did agree to changes, as well as guaranteeing Grant an extra $100,000 to keep him happy. It was the highest fee any star had ever received for a single film in Hollywood.

Clearly designed to appeal to the same audiences who had loved Leo McCarey's hugely successful *Going My Way* and *The Bells of St. Mary's*, the new film, *The Bishop's Wife*, cast Grant as an angel who arrives on earth to help a Protestant bishop, played by David Niven, raise money for his cathedral. Its climax takes place on Christmas Eve, and as commercially astute as ever, Goldwyn had already decided to release the film for Christmas.

But difficulty and indecision surrounded the venture. Robert E. Sherwood, who had just won an Oscar for his screenplay for Goldwyn and RKO's *The Best Years of Our Lives*, produced one version of the script. Then Goldwyn asked Leonardo Bercovici to do another because the roles of Dudley (the angel) and the bishop had been conceived the wrong way around, with Niven originally cast as the angel and Grant as the bishop. It was Grant who insisted on the change, just as he insisted on debating his role in the film with Goldwyn as they went along. William Seiter started directing, then Goldwyn replaced him with Henry Koster, who had worked on a string of Deanna Durbin pictures.

Grant's co-star Loretta Young recalled, "Each morning I would arrive on the stage in wardrobe and makeup, ready to go to work, but Cary would start discussing our next scene with Henry Koster. It made me so nervous I would go into a scene all depressed and unsure. I finally said, 'Cary, please, I don't mind your doing this because I know you're trying to get a better film, but please don't do it around me.' He apologized to me, and he never did it again—in my presence."

His other co-star, David Niven, took to describing him as "fey," but left it at that. Not everyone in Hollywood was as generous. *Photoplay* called him "as contradictory as are his Latin looks to his English blood."

While he was moodily finishing the picture for Goldwyn, *The Bachelor and the Bobby-Soxer* appeared to enthusiastic reviews. *Variety* paid tribute to Cary Grant's expert timing which, it explained, "proves a terrific lift to an occasionally awkward plot." *The New York Times* added, "Being perhaps the most accomplished looker-askance in films, not to mention fumer and frowner, Mr. Grant has his opportunities here." The film became his fourth consecutive box-office success, taking in more than $5.5 million.

It had hardly left the theaters when Sam Goldwyn released *The Bishop's Wife* to exactly the same rave reaction. The reviewers called it "fluent and beguiling," and added that Grant's playing "rescues the role from the ultimate peril of coyness." Although not quite the equal of its predecessor at the box office, the film was nevertheless nominated as one of the best films of 1947 at the Oscar ceremonies in March 1948.

The ceremonies held more than their usual share of ironies for Grant. When George Cukor and Garson Kanin had suggested that he play the tormented actor in their film *A Double Life,* he had turned down the more demanding role in favor of *The Bishop's Wife.* Just as *The Bishop's Wife* was nominated as best picture only to lose to *Gentleman's Agreement,* so Ronald Colman won an Oscar as best actor for his performance in *A Double Life.* Once again Grant's desire to preserve his image had cost him dearly in prestige, though not in cash. He knew that he was henceforth guaranteed at least $150,000 a picture, and was likely to earn considerably more than that.

Even so, when he went to the races, he still bet only two dollars on each race, and he still could not shake off the melancholia that seemed to surround him like a dark cloud. He told one interviewer, "The fulfillment of one's ambitions doesn't always lead to happiness, but when I started out I was eager to explore the idea that success means happiness. . . . Now I know that the success is not the happiness. The working is."

He had begun to take an interest in the Chinese religion of Taoism because it helped him understand that there was a natural order of events which any man had to accept and understand. "You just have to go along with the rhythm of life," he said. For a man whose career had been notable for his relentless worrying about every tiny detail, it was a remarkable statement.

After *The Bishop's Wife,* Cary Grant set off for England again, accompanied by Freddie Lonsdale. He had two months before he was to start his next picture for Selznick, and he wanted to see his mother and discuss a proposed series of films in England with Alexander Korda.

In the front parlor of her house near the Downs in Bristol, Mrs. Leach looked at her famous son and frowned. "Sometimes I'm not sure it would be good for him to marry," she would now tell people. "Archie always was restless even as a child. He never likes to feel he's tied in any way." Her son smiled distantly and patted her hand. The insecurity and lack of affection that were the legacies of his childhood were still active influences upon him, as was the unspoken fear of women they had brought with them.

The trip to England went well. Freddie Lonsdale was a marvelous companion. The two went to the new shows in London, including one called *Deep Are the Roots,* which was just completing a seven-month run and had a young American actress Betsy Drake, as its female star.

At the end of September they were to sail from Southampton on the *Queen Elizabeth.* Also on board would be such friends as Elizabeth Taylor, traveling with her formidable mother; Lady Korda—the actress Merle Oberon, who was married to Alexander Korda, and the financier and art collector Jock Whitney. Grant and Lonsdale drove down to Southampton in two Rolls-Royce, one filled just with their luggage and two hampers of food and wine for the journey.

Not long after the ship edged out into the Solent, Grant was on his way to the first-class lounge to have tea with Elizabeth Taylor. As he passed by, a short, brown-haired woman with gray-green eyes, sensible shoes and a faintly quizzical expression opened the folding doors of one of the ship's telephone booths and almost fell into his arms.

"Hey, aren't you the girl I saw in *Deep Are the Roots?*" Grant asked her.

In the years to come Betsy Drake would insist that she was so embarrassed at being thrown into Cary Grant's arms by a lurch of the ship that she was unable to reply. But he would maintain, "I swear a bit of coquetry was going on." Nevertheless, the twenty-four-year-old actress did seem dumbstruck. She blushed fiercely and disappeared in the direction of her cabin.

Next morning on deck, however, Merle Oberon went up to her and said, "I have a friend, Cary Grant, who would like to meet you. Will you have lunch with us?" Cary Grant was hiding behind a gangway a few yards away, hoping she would not refuse. He and Freddie Lonsdale had watched her at dinner the evening before, and both had agreed that she was strikingly beautiful. Grant would claim, "Had Freddie been twenty years younger I would certainly have lost her to him."

For the remaining five days of the voyage, Betsy Drake had every meal with Cary Grant. No one could separate them. He wanted to find out everything he could about the apparently gauche young actress who stammered slightly when she was nervous. She told him that her father's family, after building the famous Drake Hotel in Chicago, had been ruined by the stock market crash in 1929. She had been born in Paris in September 1923 and had two younger brothers. When she was nine her parents had divorced, and she had had what might best be called a haphazard education. After studying drama in Washington, she had lived in New York, where she had worked in an agent's office and modeled girdles before getting one or two small parts in plays. She had been offered a Hollywood contract by Hal Wallis in 1946, but after going there and sitting in a hotel room for two weeks waiting for a screen test, she had returned to New York, determined to get on with her stage career. At the suggestion of H. M. Tennent, a leading London

producer who had formed his own production company, she
had gone to London.

"She intrigued me no end," said Grant later. "She was interested in astronomy and yoga—subjects I'd never investi-
gated myself. She was bookish but charmingly so."

By the time they reached New York, Cary Grant was convinced he had met the first woman who needed him as much as
he needed her. He was determined to help her with her career
in Hollywood and to teach her everything she would need to
know to become a star. It was the greatest gift he had to offer.

"How would you like to be in my next film?" he asked her as
the liner slipped into the Hudson River. "It's called *Every Girl
Should Be Married.* The part is perfect for you."

"They'll never give it to me," she said softly, standing beside
him on the upper deck and looking at the sunlight catching the
skyscrapers.

"I'll make them."

"Oh, you can't. They'd say you were doing it because you
liked me."

Grant took her arm. "They won't say it after they've seen
you act. And maybe they'll be a little more perceptive. Maybe
they'll say—because I need you so."

The young actress glanced down at her sensible low-heeled
shoes and then up into his eyes. "Well, perhaps," she replied, a
touch uncertainly.

While Grant started work with Myrna Loy and Melvyn
Douglas on *Mr. Blandings Builds His Dream House* for David
Selznick, Betsy Drake set about finding herself a room in an
apartment hotel and seeing whether her career as an actress
really would prosper in Hollywood. Some people, she noticed,
looked at her a little strangely, or nodded at each other know-
ingly, but she ignored them. She knew that the strangely private man she had met on the *Queen Elizabeth* had always treated
her like his daughter, rather than a starlet.

The first thing Grant did when they reached Hollywood was
to introduce Betsy Drake to David Selznick and Dore Schary.
Both men were polite and encouraging, and screen tests were
arranged. Once they saw them they told her, "Yes, there is
every chance you could have a career in films."

Betsy Drake would never know whether their response was genuine or merely a reflection of the interest in her of one of their most important stars. What Selznick and Schary did not know was that Grant had carefully coached her for the screen test. She set her jaw and made up her mind that she would succeed. As she told Louella Parsons, who was to describe her as "the most completely determined young woman I've ever met," "If people say I've made good because of Cary Grant, that's bad for him and bad for me."

Nevertheless, Cary Grant certainly took pains to be sure that RKO considered her for the film he was planning after he had finished *Mr. Blandings Builds His Dream House.* Schary, RKO's new production head, agreed Betsy might be right and said that he would buy half her contract if RKO bought the other half. The studio was not anxious to upset a star who had made four successful films in a row since *Night and Day,* even if they had been thinking of using Barbara Bel Geddes for the part. Betsy Drake's future in Hollywood was settled.

Perhaps another reason why RKO was not keen to contradict its star was that his friend Howard Hughes had just taken over the studio. Early in January 1948, after telling the press he was no longer interested in the movie business, Hughes had flown off to a secret meeting with Floyd B. Odlum, the millionaire president of the $70 million Atlas Corporation which effectively controlled RKO. Because of his severe rheumatoid arthritis, Odlum conducted negotiations from the swimming pool of his nine-hundred acre estate near Palm Springs, the desert resort two hours southeast of Hollywood.

By the time shooting had started on *Every Girl Should Be Married,* with Betsy Drake as Grant's co-star, Hughes had bought RKO and had reassured Dore Schary that he wanted no part in running the studio, a decision that did not last long. Before director Don Hartman had finished the film, Hughes had started to interfere. He was even staying in Cary Grant's house to do it. Dore Schary told *The New York Times* many years later that, when he was summoned to see his new boss at the house, "there wasn't a paper, a cigarette, a flower, a match, a picture, a magazine—there was nothing except two chairs and a sofa." The only sign of life was Hughes, "who appeared from a side room in which I caught a glimpse of a woman hooking up her bra before the door closed." Grant had bought the house looking down over Beverly Hills after he sold the one on Bellagio Road, but he had yet to move in.

After an extraordinary meeting at which Hughes seemed more interested in where Schary had bought the shoes he was wearing than in the films he was making at RKO, Schary resigned as production chief. Within a month, more than three hundred people in the studio, about a third of the total work force, had been fired.

One of the few successes RKO was to release in 1948 was Cary Grant's *Every Girl Should Be Married.* It was to be the last film he would make for the studio, which, by casting him in *Sylvia Scarlett,* had proved he was more than just Paramount's potential matinee idol. Before *Every Girl Should Be Married* was released at Christmas 1948, Grant had already left America to begin his first film with Howard Hawks since *His Girl Friday.* Hawks had decided to make a film in Europe, and it would be another comedy. He had just finished making *Red River,* with John Wayne and Montgomery Clift, and wanted a change of pace; he also wanted to work with Grant again. Set in Germany after the war, the new film was based on the true story of an officer who was unable to consummate his marriage for six weeks because of army regulations. With a script by Charles Lederer, Leonard Spiegelgass and Hagar Wilde, *I Was a Male War Bride* was to be shot in three months. And the female lead would be a woman Grant and Randolph Scott had met when they first arrived in Hollywood, Ann Sheridan.

Cary Grant took Betsy Drake with him to Europe and stopped off in England on the way to Germany to introduce her to his mother. He was in a cheerful mood. It seemed as though the film would progress without difficulties, and he had always enjoyed working with Hawks. His optimism was not to last. Once shooting started, things began to go severely wrong.

First, bad weather interfered with the filming, and Ann Sheridan caught pleurisy, which turned into pneumonia. Then Randy Stuart, another member of the cast, contracted jaundice. Hawks began to think the whole film was jinxed.

By the end of November, with the film still unfinished and with the company in London, Grant himself was complaining that he did not feel at all well. Within three days he was diagnosed as having jaundice, and a British doctor told him he could do nothing except stay in bed. He was run down and in need of complete rest.

Lying in bed in London, surrounded by solicitous telegrams, Cary Grant thought for the first time about suicide. He had been depressed before, but the sense of isolation he felt at being trapped in a chilly country that was no longer his home left him desolate. Even telephone calls to all his friends did not cheer him up. He steadily lost weight, as if he were no longer interested in the world.

Betsy Drake saved his life. "She nursed me back to health," he said. Her concern convinced him that he had at last found someone who was prepared to devote herself to him, who would make his life the most important thing in her own and give him the affection that he had always craved.

In the first weeks of 1949 his depression gradually subsided, and so did his illness. The reviews of *Every Girl Should Be Married,* which had opened at Christmas in New York, cheered him up. Most critics liked Betsy. *Newsweek* said that her "frenetic charm and windblown naturalness are sometimes nerve-wracking but more often thoroughly appealing," and *The New York Times* stated, "She gives considerable promise of more formidable triumphs on the screen." Only his old enemy *Time* magazine carped, "Newcomer Betsy Drake seems to have studied, but not to have learned, the tricks and inflections of early Hepburn."

The film made more than $750,000 and became Grant's sixth consecutive hit. Since his decision not to make any more serious films after the disappointment of *None but the Lonely Heart,* he was firmly established as one of the top ten box-office stars in the United States, and his *The Bachelor and the Bobby-Soxer* had been one of the biggest grossing movies of 1948. Once more, and incontrovertibly, he could console himself with the knowledge that his films made money, even if the critics did not always like them.

With his star slowly recovering, Howard Hawks decided that there was no point in keeping the company in Europe to finish *I Was a Male War Bride*. The weather in England and Germany was too bad, and they would have to finish the picture in Hollywood. Sheridan had just about recovered, but Grant was still weak. He had lost around thirty pounds; the director felt that his appetite for making films also had vanished. The illness had apparently left him uninterested in anything except getting back to California and sitting in the sunshine.

Another three months would pass before Grant would go back to work on *I Was a Male War Bride*. By then he had been ill for almost half a year. The pressure of his life had finally caught up with him.

For his return to California, Grant decided to go home by the long sea route, which would give him a chance to recuperate and to think things over.

Before the voyage, he told Betsy Drake that he did not need to work. He had invested his money carefully and could afford to stop making films altogether.

"I would not miss it."

The green-eyed young woman looked at him quizzically—as he had watched her do many times in the past year—and asked him, "But would you really ever retire?"

"I might," he responded, "I might."

As the Holland America Line's steamship *Dalerdyck* nosed into her berth in Los Angeles harbor in the soft April air, the crowd of reporters on the dock had already asked Betsy Drake why she was there.

"To meet Mr. Grant," she told them politely.

Fewer than five minutes after the ship's bowlines had been secured and the gangplank lowered, Cary Grant walked slowly down it toward them. It took them fewer than five seconds to ask, "Have you come back to get married, Mr. Grant? Are you and Miss Drake going to get married?"

It was the only question they wanted answered. They knew how well she had looked after him in London and that she had flown back to California to prepare for his arrival.

Looking slightly unsteady and weaker than any of them had ever seen him, Cary Grant smiled.

"Well, I have asked her. Do you blame me after getting a look at her?"

As she took his arm, Betsy Drake smiled too.

"Maybe you can get an answer for me," Grant called out.

"Well, Miss Drake, are you going to get married? Everyone in Hollywood seems to think you are."

"I'm too busy concentrating on my next picture right now," she said quietly, helping the man she had nursed into his car.

"The third Mrs. Grant," one of the reporters muttered as he walked toward the telephone booth at the end of the pier to call his newspaper.

Grant still felt ill, but the worst of his depression had left him. As soon as the filming on *I Was a Male War Bride* was over, he would have a complete medical checkup. "You've got to rest," Betsy told him. "You've got to take care of yourself."

One thing he did not want to talk about was another movie. This one seemed to have lasted forever, and he could not bring himself to think about what he should do next. His agent and old friend, Frank Vincent, had died the year before, and there were few people he trusted to talk to about his work. Most of the time he now preferred to be his own agent. After all, Frank Vincent used to tell him, "If there's a better agent in Hollywood than Cary Grant, I'd like to meet him. There only ever was one better one—Myron Selznick—and he's dead."

Howard Hawks had mentioned making a film of *Don Quixote* with the Spanish comedian Cantinflas playing Sancho Panza to Grant's Don Quixote. The idea was intriguing, but Grant did not feel like talking about films at all.

After shooting the last scenes of *Male War Bride*, Grant went into the Johns Hopkins Hospital in Baltimore for a ten-day checkup, as he had promised Betsy Drake he would. When he came out, Howard Hawks invited him to the first preview of the picture.

For once he was surprised. He told *The New York Times*, "Frankly, I approach my pictures with trepidation. But I just saw a preview of the picture here and the audience laughed themselves sick. I've been in many comedies but I've never heard an audience react like this one. I honestly feel it's the best comedy I've ever done."

After waiting more than a year, Twentieth Century-Fox was impatient to get the film into the theaters. By the end of August it was released, and the reaction of Bosley Crowther of *The New York Times* was, "The flimsiness of the film's foundations and the disorder of its episodes provoke the inevitable impression that it all fell together en route." *Newsweek*, however, was far more enthusiastic: "Under Howard Hawks' direction the end product is one of the most sparklingly original comedies of the year." Whatever the critics thought, this slight story of the trials of a French officer who marries an American officer only to find that he is not allowed to sleep with her because of army regulations was a massive box-office hit. Grant had scored again.

But at this point films were not uppermost in his mind. Cary Grant wanted to marry Betsy Drake; even though Freddie Lonsdale had warned that it would be bad for her career as an actress, she seemed to want to marry him. By the time they got back to Beverly Hills in September 1949, they were talking about the matter to Louella Parsons.

Grant was unusually frank about his intentions. He told Parsons that the date of their marriage was up to Betsy. "I'm ready at any time, but she feels, and I think she is right, that she wants to have a career, and she wants to do it independently. Of course, neither of us can be sure we won't make up our minds to marry, one day, on the spur of the moment. But it looks now as if we will be married around January first."

As the columnist wrote afterward, Betsy Drake had explained, "If I should marry before I have at least two successful pictures, no matter how good I might be, I would simply be known as Mrs. Cary Grant. I hope later to make a picture with Cary, but now I have to do two alone, one a comedy, the other a drama." She had already started work on *Pretty Baby* at Warners with Edmund Gwenn and Zachary Scott.

In the end Howard Hughes decided matters for them. Drama or comedy, films or no films, on Christmas Day 1949, the tall, thin-faced Texas millionaire picked them up in Beverly Hills, took them to Glendale airport north of Hollywood, put them into one of his own planes and flew them to Phoenix,

Arizona. He had decided the time had come for them to get married, and they had agreed. For years Cary Grant would say that his friend had made it all possible.

The plane landed in Phoenix at one-thirty in the afternoon, and within an hour and a half the couple was married in the comfortable ranch house of Mr. and Mrs. Sterling Hebbard near Scottsdale, Arizona. There were just half a dozen witnesses as the twenty-six-year-old bride, wearing a black-and-white check suit, looked up at her forty-five-year-old husband while the Reverend Stanley Smith conducted the five-minute service. As Hughes, the best man, was passing the ring, he dropped it, but neither the bride nor the groom looked in the least upset.

After a tiny reception, Hughes flew the newlyweds back to Hollywood. Betsy Drake did not even know how many people had watched her get married; she had refused to wear her glasses. As she later told her father on the telephone, "What girl wants to be married wearing glasses?"

As a wedding present, her husband gave her a string of pearls with a diamond clasp and a white poodle named Suzie. The slight woman moved out of her apartment and into the strangely lonely house in Beverly Hills. As the sun settled over the Pacific, she and her husband talked about making another film together, but they also talked about retiring and sailing around the world. This time, Cary Grant said to himself, he would be happy.

There was just one more film he had to make—a new picture he had promised to do for MGM after Christmas. Its producer, Arthur Freed, most famous for his musicals, had guaranteed that it would take only thirty-six days to shoot, and Grant liked the young man whom the studio proposed to direct it, the screenwriter Richard Brooks. Betsy, for her part, had *Pretty Baby* to finish. But after that they could be together.

Brooks, who had started his career as a newspaper reporter, had been introduced to Grant at the races at Santa Anita. As he recalled later, "Cary said, 'I know that name, there's a script I like called *Crisis.*' I said, 'Yes, I wrote it, but Mr. Grant, my problem is that I want to direct it too.' "

"Well, if you can write it, you can direct it too," Grant told him. And as Brooks maintained from then on, "If it hadn't been for Cary Grant, I'd never have been a director."

Richard Brooks, who had written *Key Largo* for Humphrey Bogart in 1948, became one of Grant's staunchest supporters in Hollywood. He told the *Los Angeles Times* two decades later, "Those stories about him being stingy are far from true. . . . I bought my present house and spent all my money on it and had no furniture. One day a truck arrived and it was filled with furniture. It was from Cary. I called him and said, 'I can't take this.' He said, "Listen, I have to pay storage for it in a warehouse. You're not going to charge me storage if you keep it, are you?' "

One of Grant's co-stars on *Crisis* was José Ferrer. This versatile Puerto Rican-born actor had been nominated for an Academy Award in 1949 for his portrayal of the dauphin in the screen version of *Joan of Arc* but had lost to Walter Huston in *The Treasure of the Sierra Madre*. Ferrer was pleased about the part in *Crisis* because it was a step forward in his career. He remembers that, when the filming started, "we were all a little excited because it was Richard Brooks's first directing job and we were all rooting for him."

Ferrer recalls that Grant "had a keen sense of the comic and the ridiculous, and it made working easy and pleasant, and I also remember that he had a very clear idea of what he wanted to do and how he wanted to do it, and on at least one or two occasions quietly made his wishes known and imposed his will."

Basically a flimsy story of a respected brain surgeon who is kidnapped while on vacation in a Latin American country and forced to operate on a sick dictator, *Crisis* bore some resemblance to the British film *State Secret*. The fact that the movie would all be shot in Hollywood on just five sets appealed to Grant; and as soon as *Crisis* was finished, he returned to his house in Palm Springs, settled in with his new wife and put motion pictures out of his mind.

That did not prevent a great deal of talk about films he might make. David Selznick was considering adapting F. Scott

Fitzgerald's novel *Tender Is the Night* for Grant and Jennifer Jones, and asking George Cukor to direct; and all sorts of other scripts were delivered to the star's door every day. But he was not interested. As far as he was concerned, the only thing he wanted was to make his marriage work.

Crisis came out in June to respectful reviews, but no business. One Metro executive later told director and writer Garson Kanin, "We could've made more money if we'd cut the film up and sold it as mandolin picks." The critics were a little surprised that Grant had broken away from comedy for the first time since *Notorious,* and so, clearly, were the audiences. At the time, it mattered little that one of the young actresses he had tested for the leading role was Nancy Davis, who was later to become Nancy Reagan. Grant was to content himself with remarking that she was probably lucky she didn't get the part.

For the remainder of 1950 he and Betsy were seldom in Hollywood. There was a trip to England to see his mother, a good deal of riding in Palm Springs, some tennis and swimming, but no talk of films. Cary Grant was learning that his wife had ambitions he had not known about. She wanted to write and hoped to turn *Mr. Blandings Builds His Dream House* into a radio series. Meanwhile, Betsy was discovering that her husband was more than happy to take an interest in anything she recommended. She gave him books on natural history, discussed new and original diets with him and introduced him to new kinds of music. He made the radio series with her, and although it was not a success, he did not mind. "What does one more bad Mr. and Mrs. show on radio matter?" he asked his friends.

Had it not been for Joseph L. Mankiewicz, Cary Grant might have remained in Palm Springs. But the screenwriter turned director who had won four Oscars in the past two years for his films *A Letter to Three Wives* and *All About Eve,* wanted to make his next film with Cary Grant and had a play that he believed would guarantee success. Darryl F. Zanuck at Fox agreed.

Reluctantly, Grant considered the film. He knew that the number of television sets in American homes had doubled in

the past year—he had one himself and had grown to like it—
and that movie audiences were falling fast. He also knew that
Mankiewicz seemed to have a golden touch, which meant that
the percentage of the profits he always looked for would make
the experience of going back into the studio again more bear-
able.

All About Eve had told the story of an aging Broadway star
and an ambitious young actress. It had won George Sanders an
Oscar for his performance as the actress's husband. Now Mankiewicz wanted to turn his attention to the medical profession,
and win an Oscar for Grant. Based on the play *Dr. Praetorius* by
Curt Goetz, which had been made into a film in Germany but
had never been released in the United States, the new film was
to explore the pressures on a crusading doctor who falls in love
with a pregnant but unmarried girl who has just tried to commit suicide.

Grant liked the script, which was now called *People Will Talk*,
and he took the pains he always did to learn exactly what
would be necessary for him to know as a doctor, seeking professional guidance from a New York heart specialist, nervously
insisting that the settings be as authentic and convincing as
possible. Shot at Fox in the spring of 1951, the picture was
completed and prepared for release quickly, while Mankiewicz's Oscars were still fresh in people's minds. It was
launched at a spectacular premiere at Grauman's Chinese Theatre in Hollywood in July.

Sadly, what had worked for George Sanders did not seem to
work for Cary Grant. The film was not the compelling portrait
of *All About Eve*, and *The Hollywood Reporter* noted sadly, "The
slick production comes up with a collation of observations that
run the gamut from cynical and shocking to delightful and
plumb foolish." Even the old-fashioned movie premiere, which
was attended by Norma Shearer, Joan Crawford and Mitzi
Gaynor, as well as by Grant and his co-star Jeanne Crain, did
nothing to help it. *Newsweek* described Grant as giving "one of
the most intelligent performances in his nineteen-year Hollywood career," but the film did not capture the audience's imagination. It was Arthur Freed's musicals at MGM, pictures like

An American in Paris, The Great Caruso and *Show Boat,* that were doing that.

Disappointed, Cary Grant agreed to do another film with Betsy, this time for Warner Brothers. Howard Hawks's idea of making *Don Quixote* had fallen through, but in the meantime Warners had found a script that had a part for Cary's wife. Cary would have the special dressing room and telephone that he always asked for now, although he would not be allowed free long-distance calls. His fee was to be ten percent of the gross revenue of the picture, with a minimum guarantee of $100,000, while Betsy was to be paid $25,000. The studio also agreed he could continue to appear in the radio series of *Mr. Blandings,* and it understood that he wanted to get the picture over quickly so that he could work with Howard Hawks again.

The Warners movie was to be called *Room for One More,* a slight story about a city engineer whose wife likes to look after unwanted children. *Room for One More* seemed to echo Grant's own marriage with Drake. All Hollywood was wondering if he might at last be about to become a father.

For once he looked calm and cheerful on the set, telling anyone who asked him, "The only place we go nights is home. Domesticity is a great invention, more people should relax and enjoy it. Somebody's always asking what we do with ourselves, and I always answer, 'Enjoy life,' but that never seems to be enough. I feel sorry for people who don't take pleasure in their homes. They apparently don't understand those who do."

He even seemed pleased when his wife made 8mm home movies about the filming. She was encouraging him to learn French, and he gave her a guitar for her birthday. They both gave the five children in the picture presents. He was no longer the nervous, overwrought star that some of the crew at Warners remembered. Betsy had taken up painting as well as amateur photography, and on Sundays she and her husband would play tennis, swim and sit beside the pool at their Beverly Hills house, although, as she told one interviewer, "We don't always see as much of our friends as we should, but the truth of the matter is that we seldom entertain."

Based on a 1950 best seller about foster parents, *Room for One*

More captured the cheerfulness its stars were both feeling. *Variety* called it "happy" when it was finally released in 1952, and *The Hollywood Reporter* added, "A delightful domestic comedy." Even *Time* magazine admitted grudgingly, "The movie's handling of child behavior is unusually sound for a Hollywood film, fairly free of obvious tear jerking." But the film did not approach the success of *Every Girl Should Be Married.*

Disheartened, Cary Grant once again realized that he no longer enjoyed making films. He had promised Howard Hawks that he would work with him a fifth time, but he felt no pleasure at the prospect. Betsy was telling him that perhaps it was time to take a complete break from Hollywood, and he agreed with her.

The story Hawks had for him was simple. An absentminded scientist experimenting with chimpanzees accidentally discovers a youth drug that makes him act like a young man. The screenplay had been written by Ben Hecht and Charles Lederer with some help from I.A.L. Diamond. Originally called "Darling, I Am Getting Older," the film had its title changed by Hawks and Fox to *Monkey Business.*

Although the inspired frenzy of *Bringing Up Baby* was in some of the big scenes, all too often the new script meandered, leaving Grant feeling uncomfortable. This time there was a chimpanzee called Peggy rather than a leopard called Nissa for him to contend with, and even the presence of his old friend Ginger Rogers, playing his wife, and the new discovery, Marilyn Monroe, as the secretary with whom he rediscovers his youth on the roller-skating rink, failed to reassure him. Later Hawks admitted that perhaps the movie had gone too far: "I don't think the premise of the film was really believable, and for that reason it was not as funny as it should have been."

Bosley Crowther pointed out in *The New York Times* that it was a curiously old-fashioned picture. The conventions of screwball comedy so appropriate and timely in the Depression of the 1930's were strained and out of place in the Hollywood of the 1950's making *Death of a Salesman, Come Back, Little Sheba* and *High Noon.* Cary Grant seemed like some prehistoric monster whose way of life had been destroyed.

The experience convinced him that his career was nearing its end. But he agreed with Dore Schary at MGM that he would make just one more picture for him. With two of the year's Oscars going to Vivien Leigh and Karl Malden for *A Streetcar Named Desire,* Grant felt the time for his kind of films had come to a close. "It was the period of blue jeans, dope addicts, and Method and nobody cared about comedy at all," he said morosely.

Dore Schary wanted to re-create the success of *The Bachelor and the Bobby-Soxer,* and he got Sidney Sheldon, who had won an Oscar for the script, to work on an unpublished story called "Dream Wife." He and Grant both agreed that Sheldon should direct it. But in spite of their hopes, the chemistry of the first film could not be repeated, despite the talents of Deborah Kerr and Walter Pidgeon. Made while MGM was also filming *Mogambo* with Clark Gable and Ava Gardner and *The Band Wagon* with Fred Astaire, *Dream Wife* turned out to be an uncomfortably old-fashioned comedy, amiable and fluffy, but rather contrived. *The Hollywood Reporter* rightly called it "stretched out far beyond the value of its basic premise."

Cary Grant really did not mind. Almost exactly twenty years after he had driven into Hollywood in his Packard he decided it was time for him to retire from the movie scene. He and Betsy could travel, perhaps go around the world in a tramp steamer, forget about motion pictures and forget the character called Cary Grant. Perhaps he might even start to find out who he really was and what he wanted to become.

PART 3

The Haunted Star

If I give the impression of being a man
without a problem in the world, it is
because people with problems always try to
give that impression. We are all the opposite
of what we appear to be.

Cary Grant

CHAPTER 10

Style is self-plagiarism.
Alfred Hitchcock

There were tears in George Cukor's eyes. It was the finest performance he had ever seen Cary Grant give, but he suspected he would be the only person in the world ever to witness it.

Beside the swimming pool of Cukor's house George watched the nearly fifty-year-old actor read a part for the film he was planning, that of the middle-aged star whose career is slowly disintegrating while his new young wife's begins. George Cukor watched, hypnotized, as Cary Grant became the fading Norman Maine.

"At least think about it, Cary," Cukor said. "It's a terrific part."

But the director knew that nothing would persuade Cary Grant to appear in his new version of *A Star Is Born*. Grant had already told him he wanted to retire, and that he had no intention of changing his mind. In any case, he was far from sure that he would want to make a serious film, and he didn't know how it would work out for him to play opposite Judy Garland.

Neither man put into words the unspoken reason for Cary Grant's refusal. The plot of the film was strangely parallel to his own life. After all, *his* new young wife was just starting on her career, while his seemed to be ending with a number of films that had not had quite the success that many had hoped for. It was asking a great deal to expect Grant to live out his private fears on the screen.

When Betsy Drake discovered that her husband had been reading for Cukor, she told the director to leave him alone, and now he knew that Cary Grant would never appear. It was sad. But the film would survive. If Garland behaved, she could even win an Oscar for it; and if she did, she would deserve it.

215

On a steamer to Japan, on the first leg of their cruise around the world away from Hollywood and the picture business, Cary Grant looked at his wife and told himself how lucky he was.

"If you'd known me when I was young," he said to her, "you wouldn't have liked me, and I wouldn't have liked you."

Slightly surprised, she glanced up from her book. "Why not?"

"When I as young, I was conceited and impossible. I was so conscious of my clothes and the way I looked. I never knew there was another actor on the set. I thought only of my lines."

Betsy Drake shook her head, and her husband reached across to her.

"Now I know how completely unimportant it is to have well-fitted clothes and an ill-fitting performance! You're the most honest person I know. Simple, direct and intelligent. When I was young, I wouldn't have appreciated your qualities. I was too self-centered."

He felt as if his life had just begun, as though all he had ever wanted was to travel in the company of a woman who cared for him. People could think whatever they liked. They could say he was the meanest actor in Hollywood, the man who never entertained anyone at his home. He didn't care; Howard Hughes never entertained much either. He and Betsy would be all right. He felt free for the first time in his life. There were so many things to discover together, so many books to read, so much to see and understand. Cary Grant could not imagine why he had not retired before this.

Besides, Hollywood was changing. Everyone was suddenly accusing everyone else of being a Communist, or a Communist sympathizer. Howard Hughes was all "worked up" and had rushed off to Washington to support Senator Joe McCarthy's attacks on the Communists in the film industry. Humphrey Bogart and Lauren Bacall could protest if they wanted to; Cary Grant would not be dragged in. Although people he knew, like Donald Ogden Stewart, who had written *The Philadelphia Story*, were under fire, it was not his concern. If Howard Hughes was refusing to back Chaplin's new picture, *Limelight*, so be it.

When they got off the steamer in Tokyo, a reporter asked

Grant about Chaplin, and the question took him by surprise. After a moment's thought, he simply said, "He has given great pleasure to millions of people, and I hope he comes back to Hollywood. Personally, I don't think Mr. Chaplin is a Communist. Whatever his political views are, they are secondary to the fact that he is a great entertainer."

What had puzzled Grant was that, so far as he was aware, Howard Hughes had never had any political views in the past. Grant didn't even know whether his friend voted Democrat or Republican. So Hughes's decision to cut down production at RKO in the spring of 1952 while he "cleaned house" of the Communists in the studio had come as a shock.

Not that Cary Grant thought all that much about it. He liked the life on the steamer; it seemed simpler than being at home in Beverly Hills. Betsy's endless piles of books, perched on every chair, got on his nerves and so did the clutter of her cameras and her tripods. "I suggest you take up some hobbies that don't take up so much space," he had told her once. "I suggest from now on you learn to write on the head of a pin." She had looked hurt, but gone on in her own way. Later she was to say, "Life with Cary is not always one big laugh. When Cary goes into his den—which is his private office—he figuratively puts a Do Not Disturb sign on the door."

To the handful of passengers traveling with them, the tall, dark-haired actor and his sensible, pretty young wife seemed locked in their own private world, full of its own idiosyncracies and their own private language. It was not the baby talk of some young couples, but a strangely archaic vocabulary of their own invention. "My, you look thoughtative," he would say, before describing himself as "happily tearful."

They shared a fascination with hypnotism, as well as with faddish diets. Betsy had brought along Leslie LeCron and Jean Bordeaux's book *Hypnotism Today* and had become so fascinated with the subject she had persuaded Grant to let her try to hypnotize him into giving up smoking sixty cigarettes a day as he had for years. It worked. "She put me into a trance," Grant would tell anyone who expressed an interest, "and planted a posthypnotic suggestion that I would stop smoking. We went to sleep, and the next morning when I reached for a cigarette, just as I always did, I took one puff and instantly I felt nauseated. I didn't take another one that day and I haven't since."

They had also tried health diets together. Grant said, "I'm sick and tired of being questioned about why I look young for my age and why I keep trim. Everyone wants to keep fit—so what do they do? They poison themselves with the wrong foods, they poison their lungs with smoking, they clog their pores with greasy makeup, and drink poison liquids. What can they expect?"

"Do you know," he would say to his wife from time to time, "we might just be called those crazy people who live on a hill." He liked to stay at home watching television in the evenings. He liked his wife to consult him about her clothes and wanted those clothes to be either simple or "ethnic," as the description would be today, like the twenty Indian saris that Barbara Hutton sent Betsy for a wedding present.

If people in Hollywood maintained he was only happy when he had someone to fuss over and manipulate, he did not mind. Betsy seemed happy to be with him. Now she was with him all the time, and he wanted to do everything with her.

But one thing she could not do was to cure him of his depressions, of the misery that sometimes still hung over him like a cloud. Periodically, he became obsessed with saving every cent he could, in the belief that he would be left penniless. At other times he became prey to extraordinarily bitter envy, especially on the night of the Academy Awards.

In short, Cary Grant was the same as he had always been. His debonair manner in the company of others vanished as soon as the door to his own home closed.

The slow trip around the world on tramp steamers in 1953 did nothing to ease his problems. Even his experiments with yoga, which Betsy encouraged, did not calm him completely. On the contrary, his disconsolate, morose moods began to last longer and longer; and although he could slip into his carefree character from time to time, he would soon slip out of it again.

By the time they got back to Grant's Mexican-style house in Palm Springs, with its simple furniture and thick adobe walls to protect its occupants against the fierce desert temperatures, Betsy was wondering whether her husband actually missed making movies, no matter how often he complained about it. Certainly he was still interested in box-office returns, and each day there were telephone calls from people in the picture business, just as each day there was a little more despair.

Sadly, Betsy realized, in the midst of the long silences, that her husband's memories of the movies were too strong to be put aside. Their plans for a happy, peaceful life away from the pressures of Hollywood were steadily fading away.

Less than a month after his fiftieth birthday in January 1954, Cary Grant decided to make another film. Nearly fifteen months had passed since he had left the set of *Dream Wife*, but he was a star, and he was not ready to slip into a vague obscurity. He was no Garbo. He wanted to be alone, but he also wanted to be noticed.

Perhaps the two could be combined. Alfred Hitchcock had told him about a novel he had just bought called *To Catch a Thief*. Written by David Dodge, it was set on the French Riviera and told the story of a retired jewel thief and cat burglar who, suspected of a new wave of burglaries, sets out to clear his name. Hitchcock wanted to make the picture that summer, possibly on location in the South of France. Not even Leo McCarey or Howard Hawks could have persuaded Cary Grant to look at a script, but Grant knew the director wanted to make a spectacularly successful film and that he would let him improvise, as he had always done. In Palm Springs Cary Grant dithered. He talked to Betsy. Looking a little sad, she assured him that, if he wanted to make the picture, she didn't mind. When he told her she could come on location with him, she murmured quietly, "If you want me to."

But it was Grace Kelly who finally drew Grant back into films. As he put it later, "I didn't want to do the film. It was only when Hitch told me I'd play opposite Grace Kelly that I did accept."

Hitchcock was just finishing *Rear Window*, starring the young Grace Kelly and James Stewart, and he wanted to use her again in *To Catch a Thief*. Her apparently chill manner, as he had found in his last two films, concealed a passionate, intelligent mind that fascinated him. He had never fallen in love with her, as he had with some of his leading ladies, but he had also never been able to intimidate her as he had intimidated some of the others.

According to Robert Cummings, who played opposite her in her first Hitchcock film, *Dial M for Murder*, "She said no more than fifty words to me outside the script; the hairdressers would refer to her as the princess; she wouldn't sit and talk, she was a very private person like Ingrid Bergman." The daughter of wealthy Irish-Catholic parents from Philadelphia, Kelly had started making films in 1950, after a brief spell on Broadway and some experience in television. Although she was best known in Hollywood for her cool and aloof elegance, she had just finished an atypical film for her, *The Country Girl*, opposite Bing Crosby, in which she had played a frumpy harridan desperately encouraging her drunken husband to resume his singing career.

Grant, like Hitchcock, was fascinated by Kelly's sexual elegance. She seemed to him to be the one untouchable woman, the blond beauty who could be admired from afar but who, close up, was far more than that. Knowing that in John Michael Hayes's script he was to become the object of Kelly's affections, Cary Grant could not resist the combination of the blond actress and a summer on the French Riviera. He decided to go.

Besides, his need to reassure himself that he would never be a pauper had not diminished, nor had his need to find an identity. He still wished to prove to himself that he deserved the audience's praise; and he still had the feeling, which he had noticed in himself before, that when he was single he wanted to be married and when he was married he wanted to be single.

As he packed to leave Los Angeles for France, he convinced himself that he had finally found the kind of film he wanted to make. He told one interviewer, "I think comedy must have a certain grace, and that involves living with a certain grace, which very few people—writers or anyone else—do these days."

He certainly managed to do so in Cannes. With Grace Kelly, who at that time was rumored to be on the verge of marrying the designer Oleg Cassini, Grant and Alfred Hitchcock settled into life on the French Riviera with all the style that Paramount's generous budget allowed. Grant's contract stipulated that he could stop work by six o'clock each evening, and he firmly adhered to the rule. He may have returned to the movies, but he had no intention of returning to the slavery of the studios. Besides, as he had said, to make films with grace, one had to live with grace.

And to her co-star—to face the pun—Grace Kelly was grace personified. "She was the most beautiful woman I'd ever known," he said later. "She had the most incredible ESP about me. She could almost read my thoughts. She was cool and reserved, but then she'd say something about my own mood or attitude and it was like she was completely tuned in."

Whatever his fantasies about their relationship, however, he also said, "It seemed like the only passionate words of love I ever spoke to her were with Hitchcock staring in my face." The irony of the situation may have been in Hitchcock's mind from the start. Certainly he made every effort to make their relationship one of the most openly sexual in any of his films. The script was heavy with an innuendo still unusual in a Hollywood-financed movie that had to exist within the moral confines of the Production Code.

Kelly's sudden kiss on Grant's lips in the corridor of their hotel was unquestionably the most openly aggressive act any of his female co-stars had ever made toward him. It was capped, even more crudely, in the course of their picnic lunch, when the dialogue has her say to him, "I've never caught a jewel thief before. It's so stimulating," and then add, as she offers to help him to cold chicken, "Do you want a leg or a breast?"

He replies, "You make the choice," and she says, "Tell me, how long has it been?"

"Since what?"

"Since you were last in America." The innuendos became some of the most notorious repartee in the American cinema.

While Hitchcock grew increasingly excited about the filming, Betsy Drake found herself spending more and more time alone, uncertain what she should do next. Her husband was already talking about another new film on location either with Grace Kelly or another star of comparable beauty. Betsy Drake felt isolated and increasingly resentful.

In contrast, Cary Grant was unusually cheerful and relaxed. Hitchcock was always telling him, "The best screen actor is the man who can do nothing extremely well." The elaborate overreactions Grant had so often relied on in his earlier films were triumphantly replaced by responses infinitely more interesting. With Hitchcock's help Grant was refining his own screen character into something more sophisticated than the eyebrow-arching hero of screwball comedies. In its place stood a man still attractive to women and highly resilient.

Hitchcock himself described the effect many years later. "I've always taken the average man and got him involved in the extraordinary. That's how a man like Cary Grant has been cast, because they represent someone with whom the audience will identify and worry about."

The only thing Grant was nervous about was wearing a swimming suit. The veteran costume designer Edith Head explained later that he was very embarrassed at the idea of appearing on the screen wearing trunks. When she told him that was what Hitchcock had in mind, he looked stunned.

"Good lord," he told her, "I can't go out there looking like that. I'd feel as if I had nothing on."

After endless urging, Head persuaded him to put the trunks on. "Then he looked at himself in the mirror, and then went very red," she recalled.

When the filming was finished toward the end of the summer, Grant went to Bristol to visit his mother. She was approaching her eightieth birthday but looked as strong and as controlled as always. She still lived on her own, looked after her own needs and proudly took a walk most afternoons across the Downs toward the Clifton Bridge, just as she had when she was young. She still also looked disapprovingly at her son and turned her face when he bent down to kiss her. The habits of a lifetime were not forgotten. Yet underneath everything she was extremely proud of her boy, although she found it difficult to tell him so.

On the journey back to California Grant reflected that perhaps he would return to Palm Springs and the quiet life that he and Betsy had been leading before he left. To do so would cheer her up. If he was to be tempted to go before the camera again, it would have to be by something exceptional. Besides, Hollywood had grown so terribly serious.

With falling production and declining movie attendance, the kind of razzmatazz and showmanship that had been the industry's stock and trade for three decades was out of date. Howard Hughes had tried to recreate it by taking two hundred journalists to Florida to look at a preview of his new Jane Russell film, *Underwater,* and had provided them with aqualungs so that they could watch it twenty feet underwater themselves. But that sort of stunt was rare. The film industry was intent on making harsher, more dramatic films. Pandro S. Berman was producing *The Blackboard Jungle* with Richard Brooks as director at MGM. Susan Hayward was playing an alcoholic singer in *I'll Cry Tomorrow* for the studio, and Ernest Borgnine, writer Paddy Chayevsky and director Delbert Mann were planning to transfer their realistic television success *Marty* to the screen at United Artists.

One man in Hollywood, however, was not intimidated by the fashion for dramatic films. Mike Todd had no appetite for such things. Todd, a Broadway producer with a taste for spectacular productions, was convinced that Hollywood needed his sort of showmanship. He intended to assemble the largest collection of stars the industry had ever seen in a single film and to link them with a simple story, Jules Verne's adventure, *Around the World in Eighty Days.*

Boundlessly energetic, relentlessly persuasive and eternally optimistic, Todd, who had recently married Elizabeth Taylor, had decided that the one person who would be able to carry his film was Cary Grant. Todd saw Grant as one of the old Hollywood stars who believed films should be witty and entertaining rather than solemnly thought-provoking, and whom audiences would instantly identify with an entertaining film. So he set out to persuade Grant to be the centerpiece of his project. The ebullient producer waxed lyrical. There would be all the money they needed, they would be filming all over the world, there would be spectacular sights for the audience to see as well as the story to keep them interested, and there was no need to worry about the script. S. J. Perelman, John Farrow and James Poe were working on it.

But Cary Grant was by no means certain. From the way Todd was talking it seemed to him as though all that mattered was the fact that it was being filmed in exotic locations throughout the world. There didn't seem to be much room for him to create a character. He did not want to be just an elegant bystander, even if the magnificent offer that Todd was making meant that he would own virtually half of the film and its potential profits. So for what seemed to him entirely sensible reasons he turned down the part, which was finally offered to his old friend David Niven.

Instead of embarking on a new project, Cary Grant sat quietly at home and wondered what to do next. Betsy, although still a bit unsettled, was pleased he was not filming anymore. And he thought she would be additionally pleased that he was not about to dash off around the world with Todd. When *To Catch a Thief* opened in New York in August, the reviews were not as good as he had hoped. The *Saturday Review* called it a "little bit of a mess" and *Variety* added, "As a mystery it fails to mystify. This one won't enhance the prestige of either the stars or the producer-director." Bosley Crowther in *The New York Times* was kinder. "The film," he said, "does nothing but give out a good exciting time."

But the box-office appeal of Grant, starring in his first film in two years and his first ever on the new wide screen, had not waned. In spite of the reviews, the film became one of the year's successes, helped by the fact that, just before it was released, Grace Kelly won an Oscar for her performance in *The Country Girl*, defeating, to the considerable surprise of Hollywood, Judy Garland in *A Star Is Born*. The combination of Hollywood's newest Oscar winner and oldest hearthrob carried the film past the critics' skepticism.

But for Grant, sadly, the last year had seen the sudden deaths of two of the few people whom he regarded as his friends. In 1954 Dorothy di Frasso had died on a train from Las Vegas to Los Angeles. He and Betsy had stayed with her coffin throughout the night before her funeral because, as they explained, "She hated to be alone; we didn't want her to be tonight." Not long before that Freddie Lonsdale had collapsed and died in a London street on his way home from Claridge's. Almost the last letter he had received had been from Mrs. Cary Grant.

For the first time, Cary Grant began to experience a fear that would from then on consume him, the fear of death.

Cary Grant and Betsy did not entertain often. Grant liked to have dinner served on a tray by their butler so that they could eat in front of the television set. The habit totally astonished one noted English director who visited him in Palm Springs. For years afterward this man would tell his friends, "There we all were, the three of us—Cary, Betsy and I—sitting in black tie in front of the television set, while the butler served dinner on trays on our knees."

In the evenings Grant liked to talk to his few old friends on the telephone, especially when he could not sleep. The insomnia he had suffered for years continued to plague him; and although Betsy had helped a little with her attempts at hypnosis, his restlessness was at its worst after the half light of the California night had fallen across the desert.

In the dark hours before the dawn Cary Grant brooded over the films he should have made and the reputation he should have had. He knew he was one of Hollywood's greatest stars, yet he also knew that he had never dominated the list of top box-office draws, hugely successful though he had been. And he had never won an Academy Award. In the early hours of the morning, Grant decided to prove to Hollywood that he remained a star.

There were plenty of offers. The success of *To Catch a Thief* had unleashed a deluge of scripts from hopeful producers. Most of them he looked at briefly and laid aside. At the same time, the new television networks were asking him to appear on their shows, but he did not even put their requests aside. "No television," he told any producer that asked him, even though he had made a brief appearance on a Dave Willock and Cliff Arquette show in 1951. "Television men are a fast trading group, and I don't want to get involved with them." It was a decision he never reversed.

The picture that sounded of greatest interest was one that Sam Spiegel was producing at Columbia, a film about British prisoners of war in Burma who are forced to work on a railway and to build a bridge over the River Kwai. Spiegel and the English director David Lean had already cast Alec Guinness as the English commanding officer and wanted Grant to play one of the party sent to destroy the bridge.

It was a good part, dramatic, convincing and well written by Carl Foreman and Michael Wilson. But Grant was not altogether sure that he wanted to spend a long period on location in Ceylon. "Meanwhile," he said later, "Columbia, knowing me, had also sent a script to Bill Holden. Holden read the story, decided it was magnificent, which it was, and said he'd do it. By then of course I realized what a great part I'd lost."

Grant still saw Howard Hughes regularly, even though Hughes had sold the RKO studio to a subsidiary of the General Tire and Rubber Company. Grant had introduced Hughes to Stewart Granger and Jean Simmons, and Hughes had arranged their elopement and marriage in Arizona in December 1950 in much the same way he had arranged Betsy and Grant's. Grant enjoyed introducing beautiful women to the reclusive Hughes, and there was no denying that Hughes delighted in it.

Stewart Granger says now, "Cary Grant is exactly not what he appears to be. He isn't carefree, debonair and relaxed at all, in fact he's the opposite."

Betsy knew exactly what Granger meant. Her husband's only real pleasures seemed to come from looking at the financial returns of his films and remembering the deals he had made. Gradually she realized that their marriage was going nowhere, and decided she had better go back to work herself. Perhaps that would make their life together easier. If they would see less of each other, at least they would have more to talk about. She told Hedda Hopper nearly a decade later, "I gave up my career when I got married. I couldn't be an actress and a housewife too, and if I were married now I wouldn't be acting."

By the beginning of 1956, both Grant and Betsy knew that their marriage was not satisfying either of them. Producer Frank Tashlin at Fox was putting together a project that might appeal to Betsy, while Stanley Kramer, the forty-three-year-old producer of the Oscar-winning *High Noon* with Gary Cooper and *The Caine Mutiny* with Humphrey Bogart, wanted Grant to appear in *The Pride and the Passion,* a film based on C. S. Forester's Napoleonic story, *The Gun.*

Grant was the first person Kramer approached for the movie, which was to be shot entirely on location in Spain. "Cary had some reservations about leaving his usual pattern of roles," Kramer recalled, "and he was not entirely easy with the idea of playing an English naval officer whose hair is tied with a bun at the back." Nevertheless he agreed to make the film.

Kramer was not certain whom to cast as the woman. His first thought had been Ava Gardner, but then he switched to the rising Italian actress Sophia Loren, who at twenty-one was already famous in Europe, though she had never made a film in English. Kramer offered Carlo Ponti, Loren's forty-two-year-old lover and manager, $200,000 for her services. Ponti was happy to accept.

"Originally Cary objected to Sophia," Kramer said. "He thought she was too commercial a ploy, but I arranged a meeting and he looked at two of her films, and he changed his mind very quickly." As Loren recalled later, as soon as Grant was introduced to her, he started to tease her by calling her Miss Lolloloren and Lorengida but, she went on, "He exuded charm, and he was even more handsome and debonair than he appeared on the screen. I immediately felt at ease with him, and after a few minutes of lively banter I could tell from the look in his eyes that I had passed muster."

She had done considerably more than that. She had fascinated him.

He himself recalled, "She was halfway between stardom and

star-struck. That was half her appeal. She never had an air of
self-importance. She was a totally honest woman. Between
takes she'd eat spaghetti out of a tin plate with insatiable
gusto." When any reporter asked if Grant was in love with her,
he would reply, "Who wouldn't be? She's an adorable flirt."

Loren was perceptive about Grant. "As I got to know him,"
she wrote later, "I began to realize that he had an inner conflict
of wanting to be open and honest and direct, and yet not make
himself vulnerable. . . . And slowly as our relationship grew and
his trust in me grew, he came to realize that trust and vulnera-
bility went hand in hand, when his trust was strong enough he
no longer bothered with his mask."

After having dinner with her alone every evening on location, Cary Grant fell in love with the beautiful actress. He told
her he was prepared to give up everything for her. "We can
start a new life together," he said.

Loren was flattered, delighted and confused. She thought she
still loved Carlo Ponti, and she knew Betsy was to arrive soon.

The closeness of Grant and Loren had its effect on the film's
other principal star, Frank Sinatra. One evening in the large
mess tent the company used, Sinatra stood on his chair and
shouted across to his co-star, "Sophia, you'll get yours." The actress, who did not understand what Sinatra meant, asked the
person next to her to explain. When he did, she shouted back at
the actor, "Not from you, you Italian son of a bitch."

The filming did not go smoothly. Grant suffered sword
wounds in his back, and Sinatra was anxious to get back to
New York as quickly as possible. Disagreements broke out between Kramer and Sinatra, and Sinatra suddenly left before
the filming was completed.

Working in Hollywood, Betsy had no idea what was happening. She simply waited for her husband to ask her to visit.
"It was agony always waiting for him to call to say to come,"
she wrote later. Finally, late in June he called, and she went to
Spain, where she got her first inkling of her husband's feelings
for Loren. The contrast between the controlled, bookish Betsy
and the sensuous, instinctive Sophia could not have been more
obvious, and Grant left his wife to her own devices. She occu-

pied herself by writing an account of her visit and recording it on home movies.

Betsy never had cause to doubt her husband's generosity or concern. He had bought her more than $200,000 worth of jewels, though, unlike Barbara Hutton, she would have preferred less ostentatious tributes. Clifford Odets said, "Their marriage dissolved into a brother-sister relationship. At no point in the last few years of the marriage did I feel they were truly man and wife."

Whatever her feelings, Betsy did not interrupt her husband's work on location. She simply looked after herself. Toward the end of July she prepared to go back to Hollywood to start on the Frank Tashlin picture *Will Success Spoil Rock Hunter?* She was to sail for New York on the flagship of the Italian Line, the *Andrea Doria*.

On the night of July 25, 1956, in patchy fog less than two hundred miles off the coast of Newfoundland, the *Andrea Doria* was rammed by the Swedish liner *Stockholm*, slicing open seven of her eleven decks. After the collision, the Italian liner heeled over so quickly to starboard that barely half her lifeboats could be launched, and the 1,134 passengers on board were forced to abandon ship within half an hour. Survivors were picked up by the *Stockholm* and the French liner *Ile de France*, which had been forty-four miles away when the collision occurred. In spite of their efforts, forty-three people drowned. Although forced to leave the ship wearing only a simple dress and abandoning the $200,000 worth of jewelry she had taken with her to Spain, as well as her manuscripts and photographs, Betsy was among the survivors. She was picked up by the *Ile de France* and taken back to New York.

No sooner had she landed than she sent a cable to Grant which ended, YOUR SAFE, SOUND AND RESCUED WIFE. "I don't think I have ever loved Cary quite so much as I did the night I thought I would never live to see him again," she was to say later.

But her husband did not go back to see her right away. His infatuation with Loren was complete, and he talked more and more urgently about the possibility of their getting married.

The actress recalled, "With every passing day, he said he was more sure that we belonged together, that he had finally found in me someone to whom he could totally relate. Finally someone to whom he could commit himself and to hell with being vulnerable." "I trust you and love you and want to marry you," he said. She, for her part, testified, "I never doubted for a second that Cary loved me as much as I could hope to be loved by a man."

On the last night of their filming, just before Loren was to leave for Greece to start work on her new picture, *Boy on a Dolphin* opposite Alan Ladd, and Grant was due to return to Hollywood to begin a new film with Deborah Kerr, she told him, "I wish I weren't so mixed up and confused. But one day I am pulled one way and the next day another. I don't know what's going to happen."

Grant told her, "Why don't we just get married and discuss all this afterward?"

A trembling Sophia Loren set off for Greece the next morning, while Cary Grant began the long trip back to California and Betsy. When Betsy arrived at Los Angeles International Airport to meet him, she was wearing a polka-dot dress, a firmly set smile and her hair had been restored to its original brown color instead of the blond he preferred.

Grant had been away from Hollywood for seven months and was worried that the pompous stiffness of his dramatic role in *The Pride and the Passion* might lead some people to think that he was no longer interested in comedy. His fears proved groundless. Every studio wanted him. As he shot the last few scenes on Stanley Kramer's picture in California, using a coat hanger to speak to in place of the absent Frank Sinatra, the thought cheered him. It was not the only good news. There was also the prospect of seeing Sophia Loren again. She would be coming to Hollywood to work on the film, and he read that she was discussing a contract with Columbia.

In the meantime he decided to make another film immediately; and although it was not to be a straightforward comedy, it was to be directed by Leo McCarey. In the past few years the ebullient but accident-prone director had been struggling. His health had not been good, and his enormous successes in the 1930's and 1940's had not guaranteed him the right sort of niche in a Hollywood increasingly dominated by Method actors and message pictures. His light touch seemed out of place, and his favorite explanation of the sort of work he liked to do—"I'll let someone else photograph the ugliness of the world; it's lousy to remind people of how lousy things are and call it entertainment"—did not endear him to the new breed of producer.

However, this attitude greatly appealed to Cary Grant, espe-cially when McCarey told him that he intended to remake *Love Affair,* the film he had first directed at Columbia in 1938 with Charles Boyer and Irene Dunne. It was the story of a couple who meet on board a ship, fall in love and then part. McCarey explained, "I want to do it because of a lot of people saying it's the best love story they have ever seen—and it's my favorite love story." Grant did not disagree. He could still remember visiting the set of the original to talk to Irene Dunne and wish-ing he had been playing in it.

What truly amazed McCarey was the newfound cheerfulness of his star. The tense, haunted man of *The Awful Truth* and *Once Upon a Honeymoon* seemed to have turned into a calm, generous actor who genuinely enjoyed making the film and working with his co-star, Deborah Kerr, even if he did tell the producer, Jerry Wald, that the cabin boy's buttons he intended to use were wrong and must be changed.

According to McCarey, "The difference between *Love Affair* and *An Affair to Remember* is very simply the difference between Charles Boyer and Cary Grant. Grant could never really mask his sense of humor—which is extraordinary—and that's why the second version is funnier."

The elated director even put in a joke at his star's expense. During the shooting, he added to the script a line for a cabin boy to say to Grant: "I've heard so much about you."

When his star asked the boy what he'd heard, McCarey had him reply, "I don't know. Whenever they start to talk about you, they make me leave the room."

As McCarey explained, "That way I could tell the audience

231

the opinion people had about Grant without having to underline it—and get it from a character they liked."

In the end McCarey preferred his original version of the film and felt that Boyer had given a better performance than Grant. But the director knew well that Grant meant infinitely more to the average film audience than Boyer ever had. *To Catch a Thief* had more than made up for the unsuccessful films that had immediately preceded Grant's temporary retirement, and his presence in the new one would almost certainly guarantee its success.

There were two good reasons, unknown to McCarey and Wald, for Grant's uncharacteristically relaxed approach. One was that Sophia Loren was in Hollywood. Not only was he telephoning her every day, he was also sending bunches of flowers to the Beverly Hills Hotel, where she was staying with Carlo Ponti. But the other reason was that he had also started psychoanalysis, and the experience had begun to transform him.

At Betsy's suggestion, Grant had visited two Beverly Hills psychiatrists, Dr. Mortimer A. Hartman and Dr. Arthur Chandler, who were carrying out experiments with the hallucinogenic drug lysergic acid diethylamide (LSD), which they gave their patients to facilitate the process of psychotherapy. Betsy had tried the treatment, and she encouraged Cary to follow suit. He could hardly refuse because, as he was to admit later, "I felt I had to do something. I'd already had two unsuccessful marriages and now this one was threatened."

The Hartman and Chandler treatment was distinctly experimental. Nevertheless Cary Grant attended sessions every Saturday in the doctors' Beverly Hills consulting room. Like the other 110 patients taking part in the experiment, he would lie on a couch wearing a shield over his eyes and, with wax or cotton plugs in his ears, would take LSD and then try to relive the past. Whatever the medical establishment might think of the practice, this experience was to change Grant's life.

Hartman and Chandler did not give him the drug right away. Before they allowed any of their patients to take it, they carried out a detailed psychiatric examination; but they were convinced, as they put it in the American Medical Association's Archives of General Psychiatry in March 1960, that "certain drugs on which we have done research have the capacity to broaden the patient's spectrum of awareness. If a patient uses this enhanced capacity to look inward, he is often enabled, particularly in the case of LSD, to see and experience many effects, childhood memories, conflicts and impulse strivings which were previously blotted out by the repressive forces."

Hartman and Chandler came to the conclusion that Cary Grant would certainly benefit from the drug, and Grant was to become one of its enthusiastic supporters. He would lie in the doctors' consulting room in near darkness, with classical music playing in the background, and remember his past for up to four hours at a time.

After the session was over, he was never allowed to drive himself home and was occasionally given a sedative to calm him down. "Patients were required to write up the sessions between twenty-four and forty-eight hours later in a free associative manner," Hartman and Chandler wrote. "Occasionally a pillow will be pounded or thrown, or a magazine torn up . . . but no physical assaults or property destruction occurred."

In the next eighteen months Grant attended more than sixty Saturday sessions and took LSD every time he did so. As he was to write three years later, "I passed through changing seas of horrifying and happy thoughts, through a montage of intense love and hate, a mosaic of past impressions assembling and reassembling, through terrifying depths of dark despair replaced by heaven-like religious symbolism. Session after session. Week after week."

Before he began, he was to say later, "I was always professing a knowledge I didn't have. I was an utter fake, a know-it-all who knew very little. I was very aggressive, but without the courage to be physically aggressive. I knew I was a bad-tempered man, but I hid it. . . ."

If he had not reached those conclusions in his first few weeks of taking LSD, there was no denying his distinctly more cheerful appearance on Leo McCarey's set. Some of the crew continued to attribute his change of attitude to Sophia Loren's appearance in Hollywood, but three years later the other reason emerged.

To the average moviegoer in 1957, the knowledge that Cary

Grant was experimenting with the hallucinogenic drug LSD and undergoing radical psychotherapy would have come as a profound shock. The relaxed, handsome figure they saw on the screen, perpetually tanned, looking at least fifteen years younger than his fifty-three years, relentlessly attractive to women and never at a loss for a worldly, witty line of dialogue, seemed only to be acting himself. That was the very cornerstone of his appeal. It was to be some years before he himself would admit that the reality was quite different. In the meantime he made films in which he acted exactly as his audience expected him to.

Soon after *An Affair to Remember* was finished, *Around the World in Eighty Days,* the film Grant had turned down, became a massive hit at the box office. What he could not yet know was that both *The Pride and the Passion* and *An Affair to Remember* were to do very nearly as well. McCarey might say his judgment of a film may never have been all that good, but his appeal at the box office was stronger than ever.

Once again Cary Grant went back to work almost immediately, returning to Fox and producer Jerry Wald, this time with the thirty-three-year-old Stanley Donen as director and Fox's new contract star Jayne Mansfield as his co-star. The movie was based on Frederick Wakeman's best-selling novel *Shore Leave,* which was also turned into a play by Luther Davis, *Kiss Them for Me,* and ran for 111 performances on Broadway in 1945. The amply proportioned Miss Mansfield, whom Fox's publicity department announced had just increased the size of her chest measurement from forty to forty-one inches, had been something of an attraction to Cary Grant, as had the script by Julius Epstein, to say nothing of his familiar fee.

Before he could start on the new picture, however, Grant had a small benign tumor removed from his forehead. He had been advised in England that it might take him up to a month to recover from the operation. But, as he put it, "I couldn't spare that amount of time." He persuaded Betsy to hypnotize him so that the surgeon would need to use only a local anesthetic and he could recover more quickly.

With hardly any delay, Grant was able to start work on *Kiss Them for Me.* He liked the young Donen, whose earlier films as a

234

director had been musicals, including the uninhibited *Seven Brides for Seven Brothers* and *Pajama Game.* The filming itself was easy. Jayne Mansfield and his other co-star, model-turned-actress Suzy Parker, were amenable enough to work with, but Cary Grant's real thoughts were with Sophia Loren. He wanted to see more of her and he still wondered if they would ever get married. One thing was certain. Now that Columbia had signed her to a four-picture contract, he would do everything he could to work with her again.

In July 1957, when *An Affair to Remember* was released to unenthusiastic reviews—*The New Yorker* called it "awfully maudlin" and *Time* commented, "Only sensitive acting from Deborah and Cary saves this saccharine trifle from suffocating in its sentimental wrappings"—*Kiss Them for Me* finished shooting. But by then Cary Grant had found the film he wanted to make with Sophia. Jack Rose and Mel Shavelson, who had worked on the script for *Room for One More,* which he had made with Betsy at Warners, had come up with the script for the new woman in his life. Almost the only significant difference between the two films was that in *Room for One More* the children in the story were orphans, while in the new story, *Houseboat,* they had lost their mother but still had their father.

Rose and Shavelson described the plot of their new script simply enough. "Sophia Loren plays the misunderstood daughter of a harassed father who runs away and meets a misunderstood seven-year-old son who is running away from Cary Grant . . . because of her own experience she is able to bring father and son together, and what she learns in the meantime of Cary's problems brings her closer to her own father—and so close to Cary that marriage is the only solution the Motion Picture Production Code will accept."

It was also a solution that Cary Grant wished for in real life. *Houseboat* was virtually completed when his future with Loren was decided for him. While she and Carlo Ponti were staying in a bungalow in the Bel Air Hotel in Beverly Hills, two Mexican lawyers in Juarez, some one thousand miles south, not only finalized Ponti's divorce from his wife but also executed his marriage to Sophia Loren, even though neither Ponti nor Loren was within miles of the ceremony. Whether they realized it or not, Sophia Loren and Carlo Ponti were now legally man and wife.

Yet one more time, Grant's screen life echoed his own. Fewer than two days after Loren's actual marriage, the last sequence of *Houseboat*, the wedding scene, was to be shot. When she came on the set, Grant said to her simply, "I hope you will be very happy," and kissed her on both cheeks, but the filming was intensely difficult for both of them. "I was aware how painful it was for him to play this scene with me," Loren recalled, "and to have the minister pronounce us man and wife, to take me in his arms and kiss me."

As Mendelssohn's "Wedding March" echoed across the set at Paramount, Cary Grant knew he had to do something. He had fallen in love with a woman who had been married by proxy, and he doubted whether he could face life without her. Betsy Drake was marvelously friendly and kind, but he could not deny that he had come to regard her more as a sister than a wife. And even some of his friends had begun to notice that she did not seem happy either at work or at home with Grant.

Once again Grant decided to leave Hollywood. He wanted to see his mother, and Stanley Donen had a project that might mean he could make a film in England once he was there. Gratefully, he planned his escape.

Ingrid Bergman had not made a Hollywood movie since 1949, when the uproar that surrounded the revelation that she was pregnant by the Italian film director Roberto Rossellini while still married to her first husband forced her to leave the United States. As *The New York Times* reported years later, "Suddenly the American public that had elevated her to the point of idolatry cast her down, vilified her, and boycotted her films. She was even condemned on the floor of the United States Senate."

But Cary Grant had not forgotten her, and he had always wanted to appear with her again. In March 1957 he had promised to stand by at the twenty-ninth Academy Awards ceremony in case she won for her performance in *Anastasia*, which had been filmed in England. She did win, defeating both

Katharine Hepburn and Deborah Kerr. As he collected her gold statuette, Cary Grant declaimed to the audience in the ornate Pantages Theater on Hollywood Boulevard, "Dear Ingrid, wherever you are in the world, we, your friends, want to congratulate you, and may you be as happy as we are for you." Their friendship, which had always been close, was even more firmly cemented by this gallant speech.

Stanley Donen thought that he could persuade his friend Norman Krasna, whose light comedy *Kind Sir* had been playing on Broadway, to move the location of the film version of the story from New York to London and to adapt it for Cary Grant and Ingrid Bergman. He then suggested to Grant that they form their own company, Grandon Productions, to sell the film to Warner Brothers while guaranteeing Grant his customary fee of $300,000.

Once the deal had been made—and Grant had persuaded Jack Warner to provide him with a Rolls-Royce in London— he and Donen settled into the Connaught Hotel to prepare for the shooting. In the meantime, Ingrid Bergman's marriage to Roberto Rossellini had publicly broken up. When she arrived at Heathrow Airport, she was met by a tumultuous crowd of reporters, as well as by Cary Grant. When she was ushered into a packed press conference, she found him already there; he shouted to her, "Ingrid, wait till you hear my problems!"

Bergman recalled, "That broke the ice. Everybody burst into laughter. He held them at bay in such a nice way."

In particular he kept telling the reporters, "Come on, fellas, you can't ask a lady that. Ask me the same question and I'll give you an answer. So, you're not interested in my life? It's twice as colorful as Ingrid's."

Although no one in the room was aware of it, his life was indeed twice as colorful as his co-star's, and he was about to go through exactly the same painfully public separation from his partner as she had. But in the banter of the press conference no one suspected that Cary Grant might have been concealing his own feelings. He seemed as he always seemed, handsome, charming, cheerful and very protective of a beautiful woman.

"*Indiscreet* was a light comedy," Bergman wrote later. "I

237

played a famous wealthy actress: Cary Grant was an American diplomat protecting his bachelor status by pretending he was already married."

The line of dialogue that captured the spirit of the plot, the one in which Bergman challenged Grant by saying, "How dare you make love to me and not be a married man," had been suggested by Grant himself. He believed that that single remark made every other line in the picture funnier, and Bergman agreed with him.

"It ended happily ever after," she remembered. "And that's what I wanted to be. I was in love with Lars Schmidt, a successful Swedish theatrical producer, and we wanted to get married."

For Cary Grant, however, things were not to progress so smoothly. By the end of 1957, as the filming of *Indiscreet* was drawing to a close, the rumors about his own marriage to Betsy were growing. His wife had already spent some time in London, appearing in the play *Next to No Time* opposite Kenneth More, and she was about to make *Intent to Kill,* a film with Richard Todd, at Pinewood Studios. Her relationship with Grant seemed strained and distant.

At Christmas he took her to Monte Carlo, where they spent two days on board Aristotle Onassis's yacht the *Christina,* and had dinner with Grace Kelly and her new husband, Prince Rainier III. But even there the troubles of the past few years and the memory of Sophia Loren took their toll. On the surface Grant was the elegant, relaxed guest; but in the quiet moments when he thought no one was watching him, he was in despair.

Once again, however, he hesitated before doing anything. First he took a weekend trip to Moscow with producer Sam Spiegel and novelist Truman Capote, then returned to Bristol to see his mother on her birthday. By the time he got back to Hollywood, the previews of *Indiscreet* had shown that he almost certainly had another success on his hands. At the same time, Cary Grant was continuing to struggle to understand his attitude toward women. He knew that he could not go on with Betsy, but he did not know what to do instead.

For the first time in his life Cary Grant was publicly conscious of growing old. He had fought against the wrinkles and the folds of skin by massages, rest, a careful diet and the occasional resort to cosmetic surgery. Although he was fifty-four, he knew he looked ten years younger. Suddenly, however, it dawned on him that he could not remain one of the movies' most romantic leading men forever. After *Kiss Them for Me* had been released in November 1957, Bosley Crowther in *The New York Times* had commented tartly about Grant that "he seems somewhat overage for this assignment," and a year later had described him in *Houseboat* as "leathery" and "old enough to be the kids' grandfather." To his fragile confidence these judgments left deep wounds.

He had also seen Sophia Loren leave Hollywood married to Carlo Ponti, who was ten years his junior. He had to accept that he would not be able to continue making films if he wished to remain a romantic star. He was well aware that Gary Cooper had not done himself much good with the critics in his recent film, *Love in the Afternoon,* opposite the young Audrey Hepburn. One or two of them mentioned that he looked too old to be convincing as Hepburn's romantic attachment. Cary Grant had always tried not to commit Cooper's mistakes.

So even though he had just been voted Hollywood's most attractive man, Cary Grant began to say, "I'm getting to the stage when I have to be very careful about love scenes with young actresses."

Saying good-bye to Sophia Loren had been particularly difficult. He had persuaded Alfred Hitchcock to create a part for her in the film they were planning together, and her outright refusal to accept it upset him. He could not understand why she wanted to go back to Italy to make a film about two women, neither of whom was beautiful or seductive. "That man Ponti will ruin her career," he told his friends. "Here she could have been in a Hitchcock picture seen by millions, now she will go into that small Italian picture. It will ruin Sophia, such casting." In fact, the film she left to make, *Two Women,* won her an Oscar, the first ever to be awarded to an actress in a foreign-language film. The person who telephoned her from Hollywood with the news that she won was Cary Grant.

The part Grant had originally suggested for Loren was the

tantalizing government agent in Hitchcock's new film *North by Northwest*. The screenwriter Ernest Lehman had been working on it for months, basing it on Hitchcock's idea of a chase across America that would end inside the nose of a massive stone face of President Lincoln at Mount Rushmore, South Dakota. One of Hitchcock's first titles for the film had been "The Man in Lincoln's Nose," later amended to "In a Northerly Direction" and then to *North by Northwest,* the direction of the chase across the United States.

Hitchcock was determined to center the film around the character that Cary Grant had created over the years. The plot he and Lehman had in mind depended on the audience identifying totally with Grant as a man to whom terrible things happen but who nevertheless remains in control. Hitchcock wanted it to be the American version of his acclaimed English thriller *The Thirty-Nine Steps*.

After Loren's departure, Hitchcock and Grant agreed that the blond actress Eva Marie Saint, who had won an Oscar as best supporting actress in her first film, *On the Waterfront,* without ever having set foot in Hollywood, might be suitable for the government agent. Intelligent and superbly controlled, Saint fell very much into the Grace Kelly mold: cool, blond and intensely attractive, her restraint still giving the impression of hidden passions.

This time Grant was not particularly relaxed during the shooting. He insisted on contributing some of his own dialogue to Lehman's script, and a third of the way through the filming he told Hitchcock, "It's a terrible script, and I still can't make head or tail of it." The director ignored his star's complaints—he was used to them—though afterward he was to say that it was a relief to be working with birds. James Mason recalls that he hardly saw Grant when they weren't shooting together, and Eva Marie Saint remembered that she found him very attractive but did not see very much of him. Cary Grant had begun to retreat into himself again, wary of any invasion of his privacy.

Hitchcock knew that the role that Grant was playing on the screen was a precise parody of his own image. While the director delighted in transforming Saint from her customarily drab roles into an unexpectedly glamorous Mata Hari, he was depending on Grant to seem himself, the man the audience recognized. Hitchcock even had him tell Eva Marie Saint toward the end of the filming, "My wives divorced me. I think they said I led too dull a life."

It was a bleak commentary. The shooting had not finished when Cary Grant and Betsy Drake announced that they were separating. The marriage that Howard Hughes had arranged on Christmas Day 1949 came to an end in October 1958 with a brief statement, which Grant drafted himself. It read simply, "After careful consideration and long discussion we have decided to live apart. We have had, and shall always have, a deep love and respect for each other, but alas, our marriage has not brought us the happiness we fully expected and mutually desired. So since we have no children needful of our affection it is consequently best that we separate for a while." And it ended, "We have purposefully issued this public statement through the newspaper writers who have been so kind to us in the past in order to forestall the usual misinformed gossip and conjecture. There are no plans for divorce, and we ask only that the press respect our statement as complete and our friends to be patient with, and understanding of, our decision."

Less than a year later, Betsy Drake said, "I left Cary, but physically he'd left me long ago."

CHAPTER 11

A star is authentic: you never doubt him; he
is real—*not* an actor, not even, any longer,
someone playing himself. He simply is.
                                        Peter Bogdanovich

Outside on Wilshire Boulevard the cars were streaming from
the beach in the late-afternoon sunshine, but in a small dark
room in Beverly Hills Cary Grant was crying. The tears
had been running down his cheeks for more than an hour,
and he could not stop them. The face he had studiously kept
tanned and lean for fifty-five years was blotched, and his
mind was struggling with the effects of the LSD he had taken
that morning.

In the past three hours every fear he had ever remembered
had become a nightmare; all his memories had come to life in
the small quiet room with Mozart's music playing softly in the
background. He had been to other sessions on other Saturday
afternoons over the past year, but today had been the breakthrough. He felt as if he had actually traveled down from his
mother's womb into the chill air of that January night in 1904,
as if his whole life since then had passed in front of him. The
loneliness of childhood, the conscious search for affection as an
adolescent, the adoption of a character and the fitting of the
mask, the obsessions about money and the screen image in
middle age and the final recognition that Cary Grant, film star,
was a stranger to himself, unable to love women or, it seemed,
to be loved by them.

The four-hour session had left him dazed and exhausted, but
when he was driven home that evening in his Rolls-Royce, he
was ecstatic. At last, he felt he was beginning to understand
why he had always been so miserable and so afraid. He could
hardly wait for the next Saturday. The LSD injected into his

242

body and the quiet tones of Dr. Mortimer Hartman's voice seeping through into his mind had provided a revelation.

The following Saturday he spent almost the entire four hours talking about his parents and his attitude toward women. Once again, on the way back to his house in Beverly Hills, he wanted to shout for joy, to stop the car and tell everyone he passed on Rodeo Drive what had happened to him. It might startle his friends, but they did not know what he'd been through, they did not know he could change. Only Betsy would understand.

Ever since they had first met, Cary Grant had never stopped confiding in her. Even though they had been separated for three months, he saw no reason to stop doing so. She lived in a Spanish house on Mandeville Canyon in the hills north of Sunset Boulevard, and although she had lost patience with him during the last months of their marriage, she remained one of the few people he trusted. Her own experiences with LSD sessions, which she had since given up, would further enable her to appreciate how he felt.

He talked to her and then, cautiously, to a few of his other friends. All of them told him the same thing, "If you think you've changed, then you should tell other people about it, tell everyone what's happened."

Sitting in the small study of his house, looking through his collection of scripts and contracts, photographs and clippings, Grant resolved to do so. There were likely to be plenty of opportunities in the weeks to come. He was already working on his next film, and when the unit went on location in Florida, the set was bound to attract reporters from all over the world. He would make sure that it did.

He had never worked at Universal before, but they had approached him about making a film with Tony Curtis, and the idea had appealed to him. He had seen Curtis's spectacular impersonation of him in Billy Wilder's *Some Like It Hot,* and he had heard that when the young actor had been in the submarine service during the war, the crew had only his old film *Gunga Din* to watch. To keep themselves amused, they had trained themselves to play all the parts. Tony Curtis had always played Grant, and had perfected a fine imitation of his accent. The idea of possibly imitating Curtis now appealed to the older star.

The film, *Operation Petticoat,* was originally to star Curtis and Jeff Chandler, but neither would agree to give the other top billing. Eventually, Universal asked Curtis whom he would accept as a star over him; his reply was only Clark Gable or Cary Grant. Gable had just finished making another submarine picture, *Run Silent, Run Deep,* so the studio approached Grant who, ironically, had turned down Gable's role in the other film.

Grant liked Robert Arthur, who was to produce the new film; and he also liked the studio which, though smaller than some, was prepared to look after him. They agreed to let him have a bungalow on their lot just off the Hollywood Freeway going north, about twenty minutes from his house, and to provide him with a secretary. They originally offered him $750,000 as an advance against ten percent of the profits, but he preferred to accept $300,000 in advance and a seventy-five percent share of the profits. That way, if the picture was a hit, everyone would benefit. The script was entrusted to Stanley Shapiro, who had won an Oscar for *Pillow Talk,* with instructions to tailor it for Grant.

No matter what the benefits of Dr. Hartman's treatment of Grant in other ways, Grant on the set was the restless perfectionist he always had been. Robert Arthur remembers now that "Cary did not want new clothes made for his role as the submarine's commander. He wanted the wardrobe department to find the leather jacket he had worn for *Destination Tokyo,* because he thought that was precisely right." He was none too happy that Tony Curtis intended to have his clothes specially made and, even worse, to wear shorts in the picture. "Cary didn't think that would actually have happened, and that worried him," Arthur recalls.

The unit was to spend five weeks on location in Key West off the coast of Florida, where President Truman had had a house and where there was still a large naval base, before coming back to Hollywood. Universal wanted the whole thing wrapped up by September because they intended to make the picture their major Christmas release.

The weather in Key West was perfect, and the shooting went fairly smoothly. Robert Arthur had to intervene only now and again; and the director, Blake Edwards, then in his mid-thirties, got on well with both stars. Grant once or twice demanded changes in the script, but in general was decidedly cheerful. In fact, one of the women in the picture, Madlyn Rhue, seemed to be taking a particular interest in him.

But he was still determined to spread the good news about LSD. As the shooting continued in Key West and reporters were ushered onto the set to interview him, Grant started to talk about the changes that had come over him. In particular he told both Lionel Crane of the London *Daily Mirror* and Joe Hyams, a columnist based in Hollywood, exactly what had happened to him.

"I have been born again," he told Hyams confidentially as they sat on the deck of the pink-painted submarine that was the heart of the picture. "I have been through a psychiatric experience which has completely changed me. It was horrendous. I had to face things about myself which I never admitted, which I didn't know were there. Now I know that I hurt every woman I ever loved. I was an utter fake, a self-opinionated bore, a know-all who knew very little."

Hyams was astonished. He did not know whether or not to believe what he was hearing, or certainly whether or not he could print it. This was the star everyone in Hollywood knew *never* talked about himself, avoided the columnists and who, so the jokes ran, was "always on, and when he isn't on he's depressed."

"I found I was hiding behind all kinds of defenses, hypocrisies and vanities. I had to get rid of them layer by layer. The moment when your conscious meets your subconscious is a hell of a wrench. With me there came a day when I saw the light. I know that's a cliché, but clichés are clichés because they're true," he told Hyams.

The columnist, who had started to tape-record the conversation, said that Grant went on. "Each of us is dying for affection, but we don't know how to go about getting it. Everything we do is affected by this longing. That's why I became an actor, I was longing for affection. I wanted people to like me, but I went about it the wrong way, almost all of us do. . . .

"Every man is conceited," Grant continued, "but I know now that in my earlier days I really despised myself. It's when you admit this you're beginning to change. Now everything's changed. My attitude toward women is completely different. I don't intend to foul up any more lives."

Hyams later wrote, "It was an astonishing interview, and I was tense with excitement as I turned off the tape recorder. I was convinced by much of what he said, Cary's new frankness, compared to his old taciturnity, bespoke some profound changes in his personality."

"May I publish what you've just said?" Hyams asked him.

"Not yet, but the time's coming, and I'll let you know when I'm ready."

The two men went on to talk about other things, including Cary Grant's habit of wearing women's nylon panties because they were easy to pack and wash. It was a trick he said he picked up on location. Sitting on the submarine with a small aluminum sheet attached to his neck to catch the best of the sun's rays and increase his suntan, he looked completely relaxed and very much the new man he said he was.

He told Lionel Crane almost exactly the same things. Within a matter of days, the first public revelation that one of Hollywood's most enduring stars had experimented with LSD and had found himself a changed man appeared in England.

When Joe Hyams heard, he asked Cary Grant if he could now write up his own interview for America. One night at the Huntington Hartford Theater in Hollywood, when they sat beside each other with Betsy Drake only a little farther away and accompanied by someone else, Grant told Hyams he had no objections. "As long as you use the same quotes I approved for Lionel's article."

But the secret fears that Cary Grant had harbored for more than a quarter of a century had not disappeared in Dr. Hartman's consulting room. Grant had always wanted to become a star, and he was determined never to do anything to endanger his place as one of Hollywood's most famous names. His fear that his achievements could suddenly be taken away from him had never left him; neither had his habit of changing his mind and his mood from moment to moment.

On the day before Hyams's series of articles was due to appear in the *New York Herald Tribune,* Grant called the columnist and told him, "You can't run the articles."

"Why not?"

"Because I don't want them run in America."

When Hyams explained that they were already on press in New York, Grant simply said, "I can't help that. You better find a way to stop them or you'll be discredited. I'll tell the press I haven't seen you at all."

"But that's ridiculous and you know it," Hyams protested.

"It's your word against mine, and you know who they'll believe."

Grant hung up, and within a few minutes Hyams was telephoned by Stanley Fox, Grant's lawyer, who told him, "You'd better do something about killing the series." When Hyams repeated that there was nothing he could do, Fox went on, "You must do it. Cary tells me he hadn't seen you in two years, which means you've made the whole series up or pirated it from another source."

Hyams was unable to stop his articles, so on Monday morning, April 20, 1959, barely two months before *North by Northwest* was scheduled to open in New York, newspapers throughout America were proclaiming that Cary Grant was being treated by a psychiatrist and that he had experimented with LSD. They were also reporting that Cary Grant was firmly denying the story, saying, "I've never had an interview with Joe Hyams on any subject. The article is completely erroneous."

The denial did nothing to lessen public interest. The articles had Grant admitting, "I've just been born again. I've been through a psychiatric experience which has completely changed me. . . . Before this happened I was in a fog. Afterward I was given eyesight to see everything as it is. . . . I have been married three times, but never had a child. Now I am fit for children. I hope I will beget some . . . I am no longer lonely. I am a happy man."

Follow-up articles reported him as saying that after his psychiatric treatment he had discovered that he and Betsy Drake "loved each other more than we'd ever done before." And continuing, "Now I know that I hurt every woman I loved, and they tried to hurt me, too, but the faults were mine, always mine."

On the third morning Grant was saying in print, "I'm bored by that word *charm*. It was tacked on to me some years ago. Now I'm sick of it." And concluding, "Heaven knows I needed to change. I left it late but at least I did it. There are some people who go screaming in ignorance to their graves."

His revulsion from his own "indiscretions" was swift. Cary Grant, the star of more than sixty films, was not someone who felt he should talk about psychiatry or hallucinogenic drugs, no matter how much Archie Leach may have wanted him to. Angry and resentful, he retired again to the small, dark study of his house in Beverly Hills and tried to forget the world outside.

Within a month Joe Hyams had issued a suit for slander against Grant claiming $500,000 in damages. Shortly after that Universal sent Hyams a photograph of himself and Grant, talking to each other on the set of *Operation Petticoat* in Key West. Within four months Grant had withdrawn his denial of the interviews and had settled the slander action out of court. He had even agreed to cooperate with Hyams in the preparation of his life story.

Whatever Cary Grant's private fears, the public revelations about his experiments with psychiatry and LSD did nothing to detract from his appeal in *North by Northwest*. When the film opened at the end of July 1959, *Newsweek* said enthusiastically that it "resoundingly reaffirms the fact that Cary Grant and Alfred Hitchcock are two of the very slickest operators before and behind the Hollywood cameras. Together they can be unbeatable." *The New Yorker* called Hitchcock's film a "brilliant realization of a feat he had unintentionally been moving toward for more than a decade, a perfect parody of his own work," and *Variety* found it "the mixture as before, suspense, intrigue, comedy, humor, but seldom has the concoction been served up so delectably or in so glossy a package."

Nonetheless, rumors about Grant continued to swirl back and forth in the American newspapers. It was said that he was not going to stay in Hollywood any longer because he disliked the smog; that he had spent the entire Cannes Film Festival dancing with Kim Novak; that he had fallen in love with Sophia Loren's stand-in, a Yugoslavian actress named Luba Otesevic, who bore an uncanny resemblance to her.

There were even reports that his former chauffeur, Raymond Austin, had had an affair with Betsy Drake and would be cited in their divorce suit. Grant issued a statement to the press saying that "as far as Mrs. Grant and I can gather, the young man is denying something of which he has never been accused. So, since neither of us has any way to defend ourselves against such publicity we have decided it is best to make no other comment either upon the story or its ridiculous implications."

The reason for the interest in him was clear. At the age of fifty-five, and after one abortive attempt at retirement, he had become one of the most popular film actors in the world. But the publicity this brought him was torture. Shortly after *North by Northwest* opened, he left Hollywood for England. He was not to complete another film in America for almost two years.

But his enthusiasm for LSD had not waned. Despite his reaction to Hyams's articles, he had agreed to tell *Look* about his experiments and to allow the magazine to talk to Dr. Hartman. *Look*'s reporter, Laura Berquist, did not find the task easy. The more she talked to the actor's friends about him, the more confusing the information became.

"I discovered many baffling and contradictory Grants," Berquist wrote in September 1959. "The Lone Wolf who can't bear to be alone, the Simple Grant, happily relaxing in Levi's at 'The Dump,' his Mexican adobe retreat in Palm Springs, the Perfectionist, who drove one director to a hospital with nervous exhaustion, the Evangelist for new enthusiasms. There is also Grant the Tycoon, bargaining his six-figure earnings with a mind like an IBM machine, Grant the Tastemaker and, of course, Grant the legendary charmer."

Betsy Drake, who had never cooperated with an interviewer in the past, did nothing to eliminate the confusion. She told Berquist, "Who knows? He may come back to me, or not marry

249

at all, or marry somebody quite different from me. He's dizzy! Enormously stimulating! Younger than many young men I know."

On one point Cary Grant was clear: the benefits of psychotherapy with LSD. He told Berquist, "I know that all my life I've been going around in a fog. You're just a bunch of molecules until you know who you are. You spend all your time getting to be a big Hollywood actor. But then what? You've reached a comfortable plateau and you want to stay on it, you resist change."

"All my life I've been searching for peace of mind," he went on. "Nothing really seemed to give me what I wanted until this treatment. I'd explored yoga and hypnotism and made attempts at mysticism. Now people come to me for help. It's amazing, but young women have never been so attracted to me. All my life I've been running from what I wanted most. I've shied, for example, from women who look like my mother." He was even prepared to admit, "I used to love a woman with great passion, and we destroyed each other. Or I loved not at all, or in friendship. Now I'm ready to love on an equal level. If I can find a woman on whom I can exhaust all my thoughts, energies and emotions, and who loves me that way in return, we can live happily ever after."

By the time Berquist's article appeared in *Look,* Cary Grant had left the United States and was safely hidden from anyone who wanted to ask him where he might find a new woman. In reality he had no idea, although he was beginning to wonder whether he had already found her in Betsy, the woman he was about to divorce. In the months since they had officially announced their separation, he had spent more time with her than ever before.

Three times a week for almost a year he had sent her a spray of orchids for her bedroom, and twice a week they had had dinner together while their lawyers were discussing the details of their divorce. He discussed with her any problem he had, and he had begun to tell his friends that "we never loved each other when we were married as we do now."

One solid fact was Grant's continued appeal at the box of-

fice. Hardly had the massive lines for *North by Northwest* subsided than new ones started for *Operation Petticoat*. In spite of its
flimsy plot about a wartime submarine forced to pick up a
group of female officers, the picture opened at Radio City
Music Hall in December 1959 to good reviews and enthusiastic
audiences. *Variety* called Grant "a living lesson in getting
laughs without lines . . . it is his reaction, blank, startled, always
underplayed, that creates or releases the humor," and the Los
Angeles *Herald Examiner* suggested that he was the "motivating
keynote that held together the whole movie."

By the beginning of January 1960, he had become the first
star in the history of movies whose films had grossed more than
$10 million in a single theater, Radio City Music Hall. *Opera-
tion Petticoat* was to take in $8 million at the box office and to
bring Grant almost $3 million as his percentage of the profits,
more than he had ever made from a film before.

With his success at the box office, his urge to prove his attraction to young actresses seemed to increase, and so did the
number of his appearances in the world's press. The stories of
his reported conquests grew day by day; yet at Christmas, when
he visited his friend and former director Clifford Odets, he refused to stay because he wanted to spend the holiday with
Betsy. As Odets recalled, "He had a bag packed for a visit. Her
house wasn't a twenty-minute drive from his, but he wanted to
move in."

Not long afterward, when he flew out of Los Angeles to make
a film with Stanley Donen in London, Betsy Drake was there to
see him off.

"I wish you were coming too," he told her, looking down into
her eyes. "You will think about it, won't you?"

"Yes, I'll think about it."

As soon as he arrived, he started to telephone her every day
to persuade her to "come on over," even though the London
papers were reporting that he was spending his evenings in the
company of the singer Alma Cogan, whom he described to a reporter as "one of my closest friends."

Finally, Betsy agreed to come, and he booked a suite for
them both at the Savoy. It seemed as though they had decided

to resurrect their marriage. Certainly they acted like honeymooners. The Rolls-Royce he'd demanded as part of the fee for *Indiscreet* was still in London, and in the evenings he would take her for a drive and then they would get out and walk for a while, with the chauffeur driving discreetly behind them.

If his wife noticed that it was precisely the same maneuver he had used to entrance the beautiful Ingrid Bergman in the film, she did not mention the fact.

One person who was anxious to see Cary Grant and Betsy Drake reunited was Elsie Maria Leach. When he took his wife down to Bristol to see her, she asked her son firmly, "When are you two going to stop all this nonsense and get back together again?"

"Maybe soon, Mother, maybe soon," Grant replied.

Betsy, however, did not see any need to dispel the confusion in people's minds. "Why should we make a reconciliation announcement?" she asked one fan magazine interviewer stiffly. "We might not be together tomorrow. He might decide to go somewhere I don't want to go, or I might want to go somewhere he doesn't enjoy. But as long as we enjoy doing things together we will be together, because we are in love." In fact, Cary Grant and Betsy Drake had decided to resume living together, but not to restrict each other's freedom. The American press called it "marriage on the installment plan" and a "wildly Utopian idea," but neither Betsy nor Grant appeared in the least concerned.

The film that Grant had gone to London to make was a version of the English stage success *The Grass Is Greener*. Grant found it just the kind of light comedy that suited him best, the sort of frivolous story and elegant setting that he felt most comfortable with, filled with expensive surroundings that allowed him to look elegant and the women both stylish and beautiful.

When they had first discussed it a couple of years before, Grant and Donen had decided that Kay Kendall and her husband, Rex Harrison, would be perfect as the two other stars and that Deborah Kerr would be ideal for the fourth main part. But Kay Kendall's sudden and tragic death at the age of thirty-three had forced them to revise their plans. They had talked about asking Ingrid Bergman to take Kendall's part as the Countess of Rhyall, but when Deborah Kerr suggested that she might play it herself, Grant and Donen had gratefully agreed.

For Deborah Kerr's original part Grant wanted Jean Simmons, whose marriage to Stewart Granger was on the verge of collapse; Donen suggested that they use Robert Mitchum as the leading man. Grant's old friend Noel Coward had told Donen that he would be interested in playing the part of the literary butler when they made the film, but after some thought Donen eventually turned down his offer and decided to use the English actor Moray Watson, who had created the part on the London stage. He was to be the only member of the London stage company, which had included Celia Johnson and Joan Greenwood, to appear in the film.

As soon as shooting began, everyone on the set became aware that Cary Grant was not at ease. He was having some difficulty with his lines, and every shot seemed to be lined up so that only he would be cast in the best light. Deborah Kerr remained studiously loyal, but she told her friends privately that a change seemed to have come over him since *Dream Wife* and *An Affair to Remember*. Robert Mitchum was less diplomatic. "I had a girl at the side of the set who told me when to say 'Why? Really,' whenever Grant came to the end of a speech."

Some things had not changed, however. Grant was still obsessed by the tiniest detail of the production, but now he vacillated alarmingly between elation and depression, as if he hated the business of playing the role he had created for himself and yet was hypnotized by it.

Moray Watson remembers that when he asked Grant if he thought he would ever come back to England permanently, the actor had told him, "I doubt it. I've kind of got used to the climate in California, and besides, I can't understand your electricity system over here. Why don't you have simple plugs?"

The two men spent a lot of time together during the filming, going over their lines and talking about the past. Watson was slightly surprised when Grant talked about women. "He talked about himself as if he were an exhibit, not a man at all."

In fact, he had not lost the habit of introducing himself to anyone he met with the words "Hello, I'm Cary Grant," even though his face was one of the most familiar in the world, just as he had not lost the habit of continually looking at himself in the mirror. His unhappiness was rooted in his age. In *Sylvia Scarlett,* in 1935, Katharine Hepburn had preferred Brian Aherne, but ever since then it was Grant who had got the girl. Now he knew that that would not be the case much longer.

As if to compensate for this unpalatable realization, off the screen he desperately tried to prove he could still charm any woman he chose. By the time shooting was finished, several American newspapers had reported his appearance at Alma Cogan's birthday party. The columnist Sheilah Graham reported that they "held hands" and Cary Grant "generally looked like a man in love." Another columnist went so far as to quote him as saying that Cogan was "the sweetest girl in the world. She has brains, talent, a sense of humor and a wonderful sense of understanding." The columnist concluded, "Cary has neglected to mention whether his third wife, Betsy, thinks Alma is wonderful too."

Within a week Louella Parsons was telling her readers that Betsy Drake had suddenly left London; Sheilah Graham added that Grant was developing a crush on another actress, Agnes Laurent. In the next few months other beauties of the screen like Haya Harareet and Nancy Kovacs were also reported as being among his closest friends. But by the middle of August he was back in Hollywood with Betsy Drake. To the amazement of the press they held hands at a sneak preview of *The Grass Is Greener* and again at a party for her birthday in September. Yet when he went back to England for a little extra work on the film, Louella Parsons reported his interest in Jackie Chan, a former girl friend of the photographer Antony Armstrong-Jones, who was later to become Lord Snowdon.

In Hollywood once more, he was seen escorting another actress, Ziva Rodann; but at Christmas he traveled with Betsy Drake. Cary Grant had never appeared in the world's gossip columns so often and with so many different women.

Solely on the strength of Grant's appeal at the box office,

Radio City Music Hall had planned to make *The Grass Is Greener* their Christmas attraction. However, they changed their minds after seeing the first version of the film; and when it was shown in Hollywood, the trade press was also unimpressed. *The Hollywood Reporter* called it "pseudo-Coward," where the "stars did not glitter, or even glow," and *Variety* said that it was a "generally tedious romantic exercise."

When the film eventually opened at Christmas 1960, even harsher criticism came from *The New York Times*. Bosley Crowther said, "Mr. Grant and Mr. Mitchum try hard to create the illusion of being moved by love and passion. They both appear mechanical and bored." But *Time* magazine came closer to revealing Grant's strength and the film's weakness when it commented, "He is the only funny man in movie history who has maintained himself for close to thirty years as a ranking romantic star. He wears only one expression, the bland mask of drawing-room comedy. He plays only one plot, the well-pressed, elegantly laundered, masculine existence that finds itself splashed by love's old sweet ketchup. About that situation Grant had nothing important to say, no social or moral message to deliver. He creates in a vacuum of values, he is a technician, but he is a technician of genius."

Whenever he went out in Hollywood, Cary Grant made sure that he appeared as the star. He attended only the very best parties, the smartest openings. On these occasions he was the movie industry's perfect ambassador, elegant, charming, with a faint fey smile in his eyes, the man whom every woman in the room felt that she alone could finally make happy. As carefully and as professionally as if he were on the set, he acted the part the industry had come to expect of him.

In fact, he went out less and less. The publicity of the past few years had bruised him, and the depression that had always haunted him had not disappeared. He preferred to stay at home, rest by his pool, talk to Stanley Fox about his investments, eat carefully—drink only light white wines and well-cooked meat—and consider how much time there was left in his career. He looked a decade younger than he was, but he did not want to tarnish the end of his long career by getting a reputation as a lascivious old man unable to age with dignity and charm. No amount of cosmetic surgery finally could stop time, and he knew that movie audiences were growing younger as the older generation stayed at home to watch television. At best, only a few years were left in which these young spectators would accept him as a leading man. The curtain was falling on Cary Grant's career because he did not want to play any part other than that of his perennially suave self.

When Jack Warner asked him if he would be interested in the lead in the film version of Meredith Willson's Broadway musical *The Music Man*, Grant told him the person who should play it was Robert Preston, the actor who had starred in it on Broadway. Few of the vast pile of scripts that were sent to his bungalow at Universal appealed to him. In fact, it was to be the man who shared his bungalow, Robert Arthur, the producer of *Operation Petticoat*, who finally helped him decide what to do next.

Arthur realized that Cary Grant liked to work with people whom he knew and trusted, and that only then did he feel comfortable enough to give his best performance. Arthur had also long wanted to put him together with Universal's other major star, Doris Day, whose string of hits included *Pillow Talk* and *Lover Come Back*. Both pictures had been partly written by Stanley Shapiro, who had also written *Operation Petticoat*. Robert Arthur suggest that this time Shapiro should write a film especially for Cary Grant. The film he came up with was *That Touch of Mink*.

The blond, freckled Day, a former dance band singer now age thirty-eight, had established herself as the virginal sweetheart of America, naive and yet endlessly enthusiastic, with a girlish twinkle in her eyes. Marty Melcher, her second husband and manager, who was also the film's co-producer, demanded that for this picture his wife receive a fee of $750,000. Cary Grant was prepared to take a lower sum of $600,000 as an advance against a share of the profits.

Filming started in the summer of 1961. Day later wrote, "Of all the people I performed with I got to know Cary Grant least of all." She found him pleasant but private, professional but obsessed with detail. In the script he was to play a millionaire, and he insisted not only on changing the doorknobs Universal had designed for his office on the set but also on adorning it with paintings from his own home. He brought in some of his Boudins, which Universal had to have specially guarded to satisfy its insurance company. "If I'm meant to be a millionaire, I should look like one," Grant explained. "A hundred little details add up to an impression."

Day trusted him enough to allow him to take her to New York for a week to choose a wardrobe for the film. He wanted Norman Norell to design her clothes. There was only one major point of disagreement. Cary Grant still disliked being photographed from the right, he always had, but so did Doris Day. Finally, he allowed her the privilege, occasionally.

Day remembers him with some affection. "I trusted his judgment; he had an innate sense of what is right for a film. He's definitely a rather underrated actor. He's just himself, and that's the most difficult thing to be."

As always, Cary Grant insisted on wearing his own clothes during the filming. "He was very conscious of every detail. I'd never come across an actor like that before. He always struck me, though, as being a bit of a loner," the film's director, Delbert Mann, said. "He was always affable, jovial, professional, but I never thought I got to know him." In fact, Mann believed that "the challenge of acting seemed to have gone out of things for him. He was just playing Cary Grant, and nobody does it better than he does."

Glossy, inconsequential, rooted in farce and making few demands on the audience, *That Touch of Mink* was a recreation of a Leo McCarey story. A wealthy bachelor not interested in marriage meets a small-town girl working in New York, and after an on and off romance in the style of *The Awful Truth*, they finally marry. Although *Variety* called the film "essentially threadbare," the old screwball comedy formula still had its charm. Brendan Gill in *The New Yorker* remarked that it was "identical to Delbert Mann and Stanley Shapiro's earlier film *Lover Come Back* except that in *Lover Come Back* the Cary Grant part was played by Rock Hudson and in *That Touch of Mink* the

Cary Grant part is played by Cary Grant." The film was a huge success, taking in more than a million dollars at Radio City, the first film in movie history ever to do so in a single theater. It was to earn Grant another $3 million as a result of his share of its receipts.

Meanwhile, off the set, his relationship with Betsy Drake was still mystifying Hollywood. They saw each other regularly and were often noticed deep in conversation; but Grant's appetite for beautiful young actresses had not diminished, even if he courted them in a distinctly eccentric way. One of these women, Greta Thyssen, stated, "Cary was fifty-eight when I knew him, and yet I was never conscious of the fact that he was older than my father. He is as romantic and virile as any younger man I've ever dated and never acts or does anything to make you aware of his age. According to him, and this is a viewpoint he expressed over and over again, he has full rights to love all attractive people he meets."

A former Miss Denmark who had gone to Hollywood to take part in the Miss Universe contest, Thyssen admitted, "I knew that Cary's philosophy was only a highly refined version of many lines I had heard. Yet, all the same, I really felt he believed it and still does. At least when he says, 'I might love you today but I can make no promises if I find someone as pretty as you tomorrow,' you know how you stand and build no false hopes for the future."

Thyssen regularly visited Grant at home, where he would offer her dinner on his bed in front of the television set. The housekeeper served them on a tray, and after they had finished they would continue to watch television. If they went out together, Grant usually just took her for a long drive in his Rolls-Royce, through the Hollywood Hills toward the Pacific Ocean, much as he had done with Barbara Hutton twenty years earlier. There were hardly any candlelit dinners in expensive restaurants, and very few parties; he did not besiege her with flowers or expensive presents, "just records and stuffed animals," she said later.

Occasionally, they would visit Tony Curtis for dinner, but Grant liked to be in bed early. "On weekends he sometimes does nothing but stay in bed, resting, reading, and just taking it easy," Thyssen said, "so he is always watching his health, his youth and his rest. Sometimes he will talk to people only on the phone, but not see them for days at a time."

Thyssen also recalled that Grant disliked anyone disagreeing with him, that he "wants his domestic help to be perfect," that he would tell her which clothes to wear and ask her not to put on makeup. Although he never introduced her to LSD, there were certain other girls to whom he would extol its benefits. Once he paid for a girl to have sessions.

However, by the summer of 1962 Dr. Hartman's experiments with the hallucinogenic drug had fallen foul of the California Board of Medical Examiners. In August 1961 they placed him on ten years' probation and instructed him to take an oral examination before they would allow him to practice again. In October 1961 they formally suspended him from practicing in California after he had failed the oral examination three times. He then moved to the East Coast, but insists now, "All of the one hundred ten patients in the experiment that we ran were volunteers. We never intended it to be a particularly deep psychological examination. We were interested to see how the volunteers responded to the drug itself.

"There were always a lot of people against the drug. But I think I underestimated the power they had, because they finally banned it. I considered my experiment a success. There were never any accidents with it in our experiment, although I know there were in some others. The reason was that we were very careful."

In July 1962, at Santa Monica Supreme Court, Betsy Drake finally filed for divorce. With press reports of her husband's many attachments multiplying, she had almost no alternative. Like Barbara Hutton before her, she claimed that Cary Grant had subjected her to "grievous mental suffering" until the breakup of their marriage in 1958.

At a formal hearing a month later Betsy told Judge Edward R. Brand that her husband had "left home for long periods," that he was "apparently bored with me" and that "he preferred watching television to talking to me." Wearing a beige

silk dress trimmed in black, the thirty-nine-year-old actress testified, "He told me he didn't want to be married. He went
away for long periods of time, not in connection with his work.
He also showed no interest in any of my friends." After being
granted a divorce, Drake confided to the hubbub of reporters
waiting outside the courtroom, "I was always in love with him
and I still am."

More than fifteen years later she said to *The New York Times*,
"I divorced the whole town as well as Cary, and they divorced
me." The bookish, sometimes visionary actress's film career
evaporated, and she finally turned to studying psychotherapy
herself, becoming a teacher of psychodrama and a writer.

Hardly had the divorce been granted than Cary Grant
planned another trip to Europe with Stanley Donen. Now, at
fifty-eight, the biggest box-office star in the world, he took seventy-five percent of the profits of all his films with Universal
and was entitled to have the negatives revert to him after eight
years. As *Time* noted, "All this has made him so rich that he
could, if he chose, join NATO," and added, "He also has virtually every nickel he has ever earned."

Embittered by the rumors about his meanness and eccentric-
ity, he responded by growing even more aloof. The standoffish-
ness that had originally grown out of his shyness became the
central feature of his character. It was the audience at Radio
City that had made him and kept him a star, he told himself.
He owed his allegiance to them, not to the magazines and columnists.

On his way to Paris to meet Stanley Donen and start work
on their new film *Charade*, Grant stopped off in Philadelphia to
see a performance of the touring version of the Broadway comedy *The Fun Couple*. This detour had nothing to do with the
play. He had gone because of a young, blond actress who was
appearing in it. Her name: Dyan Cannon.

Grant had first set eyes on her while sitting alone on his bed
one evening watching a forgettable television series called *Malibu Run*, and he had been hypnotized by her. Within an hour
he had discovered who she was and had telephoned her agent,
Adeline Gould, to ask if she would be prepared to talk to him

about making a film. It was an old Hollywood ploy, the aging star asking the well-endowed young actress if she would like to make a picture with him, but Gould had taken it seriously enough to call Cannon, who was filming in Rome.

Cannon was interested but not prepared to come back to Hollywood unless Grant was willing to pay her air fare. Cary Grant was not falling for that one, and so it was not until the summer of 1962 that Gould finally ushered her client into Cary Grant's bungalow at Universal. That day they spent an hour and a half together without saying a word about a film, and the next day Cary Grant called her directly to ask for a date. Cannon made one but broke it. He asked again, and she broke it again. Indeed, she broke the next seven dates they made. Not until the ninth time he asked her did she allow Hollywood's most successful male star to take her out to lunch, and not until the tenth did she allow him to take her to dinner.

She said later, "He brought me home and then, outside the house, I asked him to kiss me good-night. I had never asked a man to kiss me. Never had to . . ."

The twenty-three-year-old actress with blond hair and hazel eyes had been born Samille Diane Friesen in Tacoma, Washington, the daughter of an insurance salesman who was a deacon in the Baptist Church and his Jewish wife. At seventeen, she had arrived in Hollywood to become engaged to a businessman, an insurance salesman like her father; although her mother had persuaded her that she was too young to get married, she had decided to stay and try her luck as an actress. Like legions of Hollywood starlets before her, she had been eternally hopeful. She had worked as a drama student, a model and a Slenderella beautician while awaiting her opportunity. Finally, a screen test offered by producer Jerry Wald led to more than two hundred television parts and some stage work.

Cannon recalls that at their first dinner together she was "enchanted by Cary, I was charmed in the true sense of the word, we talked for a couple of hours. It was a marvelous conversation. I was completely smitten with him, and with his ideas."

By the end of the summer of 1962, Dyan Cannon, who at one

time had been the girl friend of the comedian Mort Sahl, had become the most important of the young actresses with whom Cary Grant occupied his time. As always, the couple watched television at Grant's home and rarely went out. Grant suggested that Dyan wear less perfume and less makeup, and that perhaps she might consider wearing different clothes. As she put it later, theirs was a "Pygmalion relationship."

But Grant was not prepared to play Professor Higgins in public. Jack Warner had paid $5.5 million for the film rights to the Lerner and Lowe Broadway musical *My Fair Lady,* based on George Bernard Shaw's play *Pygmalion.* He wanted Grant as Higgins, whom Rex Harrison had portrayed on Broadway, with George Cukor as director, and he had pursued Grant for months about the possibility.

The studio, convinced that the film would be an enormous success, was prepared to give Grant almost any terms he wanted, including his choice of co-star. Eventually, for a fee of $1.1 million, Jack Warner signed Audrey Hepburn to play Eliza Doolittle, rather than Julie Andrews, who had starred in the part on Broadway.

To Warner's disappointment, after months of uncertainty Cary Grant turned down the part, telling him, "No matter how good I am, I'll either be compared with Rex Harrison, and I don't think I'll be better than he is, or I'll be told I'm imitating him, which isn't good for him, or for me."

His refusal was certainly not prompted by any dislike of Hepburn, who had won an Oscar for her first major Hollywood film, *Roman Holiday.* He thought she could well become the last of his great leading ladies, a successor to her namesake, Katharine Hepburn, Grace Kelly and Ingrid Bergman. Planning his next movie, *Charade,* he and Stanley Donen were convinced she would be perfect for the part of the chic but naive UNESCO translator, Reggie Lambert.

Based on an original short story by Peter Stone and Marc Behan, which the thirty-two-year-old Stone had turned into a screenplay, the film was heavy with echoes of Grant's earlier work with Hitchcock. Once again he was to be presented as every woman's desire, but someone who was probably not quite what he appeared.

Grant wanted the movie to open at Radio City at Christmas 1963, and the filming in Paris went well. Hepburn proved every bit as good as Grant had thought she would be. The only thing he disliked was the cold, which reminded him of why he would never return to England. He sent Dyan Cannon a crystal ball from the set and telephoned her regularly, and he crossed the Channel to England to celebrate his mother's eighty-sixth birthday with her in Bristol. Among the things they discussed was whether it might not be time for her to move out of her house and into a nursing home. Although Elsie Leach was never prepared to admit that she was any less in command than she had always been, she agreed that such a move might make her life a little easier. Grant told her he would keep the house if she moved, so she could always come back to it. She said to him, "Why don't you dye your hair? That gray makes you look old." He did not know what to reply.

In spite of the Parisian cold, he was not anxious to return to California. The life story that he had agreed to tell Joe Hyams was about to be published in the *Ladies' Home Journal*. He had worked on the series of three articles himself after Hyams had submitted them to him, and the columnist had agreed to remove his by-line and share his $125,000 fee with him. But Grant was still not anxious to see his past dragged into the open and his experiments with LSD publicized again.

In the end, the repercussions were not so bad as he had expected. He had restricted his reminiscences mainly to his early life, with little about his various wives, although he did say, "I've never clearly resolved why Betsy and I parted. We lived together, not as easily and contendedly as some, perhaps, yet it seemed to me, as far as one marriage can be compared with any other, compatibly happier than most. I owe a lot to Betsy."

He did launch an attack on the press for associating him with "all sorts of ladies, some I've never met, some whose names are unknown to me and some who don't even exist." The articles also gave him an excellent opportunity to defend his taking of LSD. "Orthodox psychiatrists using the slower customary methods resisted its usage," he said, "and it's unlikely that it will be reintroduced until some brave, venturesome and respected psychiatrist speaks publicly out in its favor.

Meanwhile the authorities have banned its usage, at least for therapeutic purposes. Although how men can be authorities on something they've never tried mystifies me."

When he did return to California, Grant resumed the quiet, restrained life that he preferred. There were few alterations to his daily routine of going to bed before ten o'clock in the evening, sleeping late and spending the day resting, looking at his investments and talking to his friends on the telephone.

He was surprised by a call from President John Kennedy. At first he thought that someone was playing a joke on him, but after the President persuaded him the call was real, Grant assumed he was to be invited to a White House dinner. To the contrary, the young President told him that he and his brother Bobby had "just wanted to hear his voice," and after that initial conversation they took to calling Grant regularly. Finally, in the autumn of 1963 Bobby Kennedy invited him to Washington to help launch a project to stop America's high school students from dropping out.

At the opening of *Charade,* he was still the irresistible star. As *Look* put it, "He is the tall, dark, handsome, charming, lovable, considerate, dependable, athletic day and night dream man who lurks deep in most women's fantasies . . . who has wooed a Who's Who of glamour." Yet privately he was still vulnerable. In August 1963, when Clifford Odets was dying, Grant was refused permission to see him. As Margaret Brenman-Gibson revealed in her 1981 biography of Odets, the man who had directed *None but the Lonely Heart* from his own script denounced Grant as "Mr. Hollywood" and called the bunch of carnations that he had sent to his hospital room "phony," a wounding insult from someone whose intellect Grant had so publicly admired.

Variety's assessment of Grant's fortune at more than $15 million did not please him either. There were other, richer actors, Bob Hope for example, and he took no pleasure in being compared with William Holden, Gregory Peck and Doris Day. He had worked hard for more than thirty years and had appeared in sixty-nine films. If he preferred to handle his own business deals, with the aid of his experienced adviser, Stanley Fox, that was his affair; and if he demanded control over everything that affected a film he was working on, that was simply common sense. Now he had decided to produce his next film himself. His choice was a picture based on another script by Peter Stone, and once again the studio would be Universal. Grateful to him for saving them from a slump, Universal again conceded Grant seventy-five percent of the gross receipts. The enthusiastic reception that *Charade* was receiving made them even more excited about the project.

When it opened in December 1963, *Charade* was the twenty-sixth Cary Grant picture to play Radio City Music Hall, and the fourth of his previous five films to play there at Christmas, as he had planned it would. Bosley Crowther warned his readers, "I tell you this lighthearted picture is full of . . . gruesome violence," going on, "Mr. Grant does everything from taking a shower without removing his suit to fighting with thugs, all with the blandness and the boredom of an old screwball comedy hand." *Time* was no kinder. It pointed out that Stanley Donen had let the film degenerate from a sensible idea "into a bloody awful farce, and the sort of shaggy dog story in which the customers are the real victims—they are inexorably gagged to death." But to Grant's relief, *Newsweek* called the picture "an absolute delight."

Grant knew the audience enjoyed it. He stood at the back of the theater and watched them. In its first week the film took in more than $170,000, a record for the Music Hall, and once again Cary Grant was able to cheerfully ignore the critics.

What was interesting to him now was who to choose as leading lady for his own proposed film, *Father Goose*. Audrey Hepburn was unavailable, and he was considering Leslie Caron. He had just seen her in *The L-Shaped Room* and thought she looked like Hepburn.

Caron had not enjoyed the happiest of times in Hollywood. After a brilliant start with Gene Kelly in *An American in Paris* in 1951, she had later become the town's favorite fallen woman after her second husband, the English stage director Peter Hall, named Warren Beatty as the "other man" in their divorce action in 1966. Small, slight and with her native French accent still intact, she had been nominated for an Oscar for *Lili* in 1953, but her fortunes were not restored until *The L-Shaped*

Room, for which she was being tipped as an Academy Award contender.

Grant's plan to produce the film himself did not go smoothly. David Miller, who had just completed the comedy drama *Captain Newman, M.D.,* with Gregory Peck and Tony Curtis, and whom Grant had hired as director, left the film in March 1964 not long after Grant's sixtieth birthday. Finally, Grant went back to Robert Arthur, asking him to take over the production for him. Together they agreed on a new director, the talented Ralph Nelson, whose career had begun with great distinction in television. He had directed the award-winning *Requiem for a Heavyweight* with Jack Palance.

More than anything else, what had appealed to Cary Grant in the Peter Stone script of *Father Goose* was that it allowed him to be old, unshaven, gray haired and eccentric yet still able to win the heart of his co-star at the end. For the first time in seventy feature films he was not to look impeccably groomed. He was to wear dirty jeans, a week's beard and straw sandals as the history professor who rebelled against society and escaped to a Pacific island, only to be caught up in World War II and to find himself the protector of Leslie Caron and seven children. Perhaps he also felt that his performance might win him an Oscar, just as Humphrey Bogart had won one for his disheveled river trader in John Huston's *The African Queen.* He was well aware that by April 1964 he had been nominated no more often than his young co-star, Leslie Caron. Justifiably, he resented the number of Oscars his films had won for their directors, co-stars and writers. Ironically, within a year he would see Rex Harrison win one for the part he had turned down in *My Fair Lady,* and Peter Stone win for the script of the film he was just about to make.

Once more he began to talk about giving up films, or at least retiring again for a period. "After all," he told Roderick Mann of the London *Sunday Express,* one of the few journalists he trusted, "I am quite an old fellow to some young people. But to be honest with you I don't know what I will do. Maybe I will quit. I am getting to the stage where I have to be very careful about love scenes with young actresses. The public doesn't like to see an older man making love to a younger girl. It offends them. That's why in *Charade* I insisted on putting in so many references to my age. I anticipated a lot of people's reactions."

Mann noted that Grant was still studiously having a massage every day and resting as much as he could so that he remained "lean, suave, incomparably tanned," as well as "rich and famous." The British journalist then added that the one thing Grant would miss from the filming he had just finished was the seven children who appeared in it. Cary Grant was thinking about having a child. He was sixty; Dyan Cannon was twenty-five. But he was still seeing her, and they talked about the possibility of children.

As Cannon was to explain, "Cary and I talked about having a family when we were going together. I knew somehow that if we both willed it we would have a family. I don't think he really wanted them enough to have them before. I believe that when he wanted a child he decided to have one." This view was shared by some of his other friends, who thought that until then he was too involved in the meticulous planning of his career.

Grant and Cannon had talked about marriage a month after their first meeting, but "after that," she said later, "we'd bring it up and consider it, and then it wouldn't be brought up again for months." They would occasionally drift apart, but never for very long and never because of the difference in their ages. "Neither of us was concerned about age," Cannon was to say. "I was so taken, smitten, so enamored of, so much in love with him that I didn't, couldn't see anything else. . . . He didn't want to get married because, he thought, if we did it would ruin our relationship. 'I can't be married,' he said, 'I've tried, I ought to know.' "

In January 1964 he celebrated his sixtieth birthday by flying to see Dyan perform in the touring version of the comedy *How to Succeed in Business Without Really Trying*. In the next two months he paid for her to fly back to Los Angeles on weekends, and in April she left the cast to be with him. Cary Grant's friends, like Tony Curtis and Howard Hawks, watched his attachment to the tawny-blond woman grow, and were pleased that Dyan was clearly fascinated by him.

Cannon would not accept his reluctance to marry. "I

couldn't understand that," she said, "and, of course, I wanted a child, his child. So after that he asked me three times. The first time he was so nervous he came down to my house and cracked up his car in the garage.

"I said, 'Okay, I'll marry you,' but nothing happened. So, after a while, I said, 'It doesn't look like we are getting married, so I better check out.' He didn't like that, so he asked me again. And again."

Cary Grant vacillated throughout 1964; and while *Father Goose* was prepared for its Christmas release at Radio City in New York, he was still not sure. When the film opened, Bosley Crowther in the *Times* was more complimentary than he had been about *Charade.* He wrote that it was "Mr. Grant's blustering and bristling in his filthy old clothes and scraggly beard, rising in righteous indignation and shooting barbed shafts of manly wit that make for the major personality and most pungent humor in the film." However, Brendan Gill declared in *The New Yorker,* "*Father Goose* offers us a surly, slatternly, unshaven and hard-drinking Cary Grant in a part that would have suited Humphrey Bogart to a T but suits Mr. Grant only to about a J."

Meanwhile, Grant had taken Dyan Cannon to see his mother, who had finally, at eighty-eight, left her house and moved into a nursing home. Cannon thought Elsie was "incredible," a woman "with a psyche that has the strength of a twenty-mule team." Grant was pleased by his mother's reaction to this blond actress, even though she did keep calling her Betsy. Finally, as the spring of 1965 passed into summer, Cary Grant made up his mind. He went to visit Cannon's parents, and early in July he invited them to their wedding.

This time Howard Hughes did not actually arrange the ceremony, but it did take place in Las Vegas, where the millionaire was to have his new home in less than a year. Grant had an agreement with the Dunes Hotel whereby he acted as their adviser and host from time to time. In return for his services the hotel and casino provided him with a suite when he needed it. As secretive as Hughes, he decided it would be the best place to get married without attacting the attentions of the press.

On Saturday, July 22, 1965, with Justice of the Peace James Brennan conducting exactly the same three-minute ceremony he had provided for six thousand other couples in Las Vegas that year, Cary Grant and the former Miss West Seattle, Dyan Cannon, were duly married. Brennan recalled afterward that Hollywood's most popular male star "had a quiver in his voice and a tear in his eye." Only a dozen people were present, and all of them were sworn to secrecy. The ceremony was hardly over when the new Mr. and Mrs. Cary Grant left for a honeymoon in England. Cary Grant wanted to make sure that his mother knew before anyone else in England that he had married for the fourth time.

Although the only other person in Britain whom he told was his old friend Roderick Mann, the news could not be kept secret. Grant and Dyan were were so besieged by reporters that they were forced to leave the single rooms they had booked at the Royal Hotel, Bristol, by climbing out of a back window at three o'clock in the morning and escaping to stay with friends. While he did not intend to give interviews or information about his plans, he did call Jack Garland of the *Bristol Evening Post,* a photographer with whom he had worked many times before, and asked him if he would like to come to the Bristol Zoo, where he and Dyan would pose for one or two pictures. Garland recalled, "They got out of an old Austin Cambridge like fugitives. It was very strange, but they were almost the only pictures anyone took of them on their honeymoon."

When they got back to California, they had hardly settled into his Beverly Hills house when Dyan told him she thought she was pregnant.

"You have to find out," he told her nervously, before calling the doctor in what looked to his fourth wife like a very young man's panic. "You have to go down there right now. We must know."

When she got back, her pregnancy confirmed, he took her out to celebrate. They went to a night baseball game at Dodger Stadium, and he bought her a hot dog.

PART 4

Retreat into Privacy

I have spent the greater part of my life
fluctuating between Archie Leach and Cary
Grant; unsure of either, suspecting each.
                                    Cary Grant

CHAPTER 12

It's hard for a star to take stock of himself.
There he is sixty feet tall on the screen.
Women fall in love with him; he lives in a
world of special consideration.

Richard Brooks

If Dyan Cannon had thought she could change Cary Grant,
she was soon to realize her mistake. She was, like her predecessors, the companion of a persnickety, obsessed man haunted by
the fears of his childhood, desperate to avoid poverty and to
protect his secrets. He saved the string from parcels and the
tinsel from the Christmas tree, cut the buttons off the shirts he
was about to discard in order to save them for future use,
marked the wine bottle to make sure that none was drunk
while he was not there, shouted abuse at the television set when
he saw someone he was jealous of and was capable of putting
his new, young wife over his knee and spanking her if she wore
too much makeup or too short a miniskirt. Dyan Cannon discovered what perhaps she should have known before, that her
husband's public charm was left at the parties or the dinners
they sometimes went to. It seldom accompanied him home.

She found herself living in a rented house in the San Fernando Valley with a man who liked to stay at home and watch
television and who preferred to eat sitting on his bed. When
they did go out to a baseball game or to the races, there was no
dinner afterward at one of Beverly Hills's better restaurants;
instead, they would stop at a hamburger stand or a drive-in for
a quick bite.

Some of Grant's friends wondered why he had married
a woman who was addicted to loud parties, short dresses
and elaborate makeup. True, Frank Sinatra had married Mia
Farrow, but Sinatra was different, younger, tougher, more

273

straightforward, less private. And surely, they said, Dyan must have known what her husband was like. After all, she had even laughed at his failure to give her an engagement ring. "Are you kidding?" she told Sheilah Graham when the columnist had asked to see it.

In the first few months of their marriage, however, while he was planning a new film and she was growing more and more obviously pregnant, they were both more concerned about the welfare of their future child than about going out. Grant had started to read books on childbirth and motherhood; and soon after he had announced publicly that he and Cannon were expecting a child, he began visiting maternity hospitals all over Los Angeles to check what they were like. With the same passion for detail that he brought to film sets, he looked at each hospital's delivery room and labor ward, its medical care and surgical record. He was every bit as determined as his mother had been that any child of his should survive.

He was equally determined that neither he nor the child should become public property. Universal's recent decision to run tours of its studio for members of the public had enraged him. The tour buses came past his bungalow throughout the day, and he could hear the guides say, "That's Cary Grant's bungalow," and "That's Cary Grant's car." This made him so angry that he refused to eat in the studio's restaurant, and instead ate his lunch far away on the back lot where no one could see him. "I'm not an animal in a zoo," he told Universal. He decided that his next film would be produced for Columbia.

Besides teaching Universal a lesson for allowing his privacy to be invaded by tourists, which seemed to him the equivalent of giving free performances on TV, Grant had another reason for the move. The studio owned the rights to George Stevens's 1943 hit comedy *The More the Merrier,* which had originally starred Jean Arthur, Joel McCrea and Charles Coburn and had been nominated for an Oscar as the best picture of its year. Though it lost, Coburn had won an Oscar for his performance as the older of the two men whom a kindly young girl in Washington allows to share her apartment. The studio, hoping a remake might do the same for Cary Grant, asked Sol Saks to update the original script with him in mind. In addition to changing the setting from Washington to Tokyo and from World War II to the 1964 Olympic games, there was going to be one even more significant innovation. For the first time since 1936, Cary Grant was not going to get the girl. His career as the cinema's longest lasting matinee idol had come to an end.

Originally, Grant had hoped to take Dyan Cannon with him to Tokyo, but she had decided that she should stay at home to rest, even though the child was not due until the late spring of 1966 and she seemed to be in the best of health. Being a father now mattered to him far more than his career. In Tokyo he publicly explained once again that his days as a leading man were over. He reported to Sheilah Graham what he had said half a dozen years earlier, "I honestly think that young people, who are the bulk of the moviegoing public, prefer young men to make love to young women." He also confessed, in another interview, "This may be my last film, I don't know."

Grant's co-stars in *Walk, Don't Run*, as *The More the Merrier* was now renamed, were to be the young English actress Samantha Eggar and the tall American Jim Hutton. Eggar, who had just finished filming the screen version of John Fowles's novel *The Collector,* and who also had just given birth to her first child, recalled later that Grant treated her wonderfully. "I'd only had my son three weeks before I arrived in Tokyo, and I got there with a forty-two-inch bust rather than the more normal thirty-four, and so I had to squash myself into my costume." Although she was a friend of Dyan Cannon's, Eggar had never met Grant before the filming started. "I remember he really impressed me by showing me all sorts of comedy moves for the camera. I got the impression he was involved in everything. He insisted that I had to change my hair, and chose my dress, just as he brought all his own props. He was on top of everything." But she also admits, "I didn't really get to know him. He kept himself to himself. Besides, he was being wined and dined by the head of Sony. He really didn't open up personally at all, even though I was a friend of Dyan's."

Directed by the veteran Charles Walters, who had made his name with musicals like *Easter Parade* and *High Society,* the new film was to be photographed by Harry Stradling, who had worked for Cukor on *My Fair Lady* and won an Oscar as a result. Grant had asked for him especially; Sol Siegel, who was producing the film after having gone independent from Fox, had been happy to provide him.

Overcautious though it may have appeared, Cary Grant's concern for his wife's health turned out to be justified. Hardly had he got back to Hollywood than Dyan Cannon felt the first pains of labor. At seven o'clock on the morning of Saturday, February 26, 1966, Cary Grant ushered his pregnant wife into his car for the drive to St. John's Hospital in Burbank, north of Hollywood, where he had decided their child should be born. The journey took just eighteen minutes. As they waited for Dr. Abner Moss, the obstetrician he had chosen, he held her hand.

Moss, who had delivered all three of Bing Crosby's younger children by his second wife, Kathryn, examined Dyan Cannon and told them both that the birth might well take some time. The best thing they could do was to wait; he would be back to see them regularly. While Cannon settled into her room, her husband slipped out to telephone the head of publicity at Columbia, John Flynn.

"How is she, Cary?"

"Marvelous, you've never seen a girl as brave. But you know how premature this is, there's a possibility of complications. This may not even be the day."

"Is there anything I can do?"

"Pray for us, John."

"I'm with you," Flynn told him.

"Incidentally, I've asked the hospital to refer all calls to you."

Walking nervously up and down, Grant gave a perfect performance of a new father; and when the nurses suggested he move to the hospital's Fathers' Waiting Area while his wife was taken into the delivery room, his presence amazed the men already there.

"Didn't you just come back from Japan?" one asked him.

"*Walk, Don't Run.* We shot in Tokyo."

"Yeh, yeh. With Samantha Eggar. Lotta good love scenes?"

A distracted Cary Grant smiled. "Samantha Eggar and Jim Hutton. You've probably seen me in my last picture as a romantic lead. I'm too old for that stuff."

"You look great."

"Feel great, but I'm playing my love scenes in private life."

At last, shortly after eight o'clock in the evening, Moss came into the waiting room and told him, "Mr. Grant, you're the father of a healthy four-pound eight-ounce baby girl." It was forty-two days after his sixty-second birthday, and he had been married for just seven months. Even more significantly, there was now another woman in Cary Grant's life who was destined to become as important to him as his mother: his daughter.

A jubilant Grant went to see the new baby in the incubator Moss had put her in, and then visited his wife. Within a few hours they had agreed she would be called Jennifer, just Jennifer. "If she wants another name she can add it herself," he explained. He did not want her struggling under the weight of names he had had to contend with.

When they got back to their rented house in the San Fernando Valley, Grant became even more obsessive than he had been on film sets during the past thirty years. He went to his daughter's room at seven-thirty each morning to gaze down at her; he supervised the warming of her bottle and the food she would be weaned on; he made certain that he would always be back from working on the editing of *Walk, Don't Run* in time to see her seven o'clock feeding. "I like to be part of that," he told *Look*, the first magazine to feature his new child.

He took innumerable photographs of his daughter and tape-recorded her first sounds. "She's the most winsome captivating girl I've ever known, and I've known quite a few girls," he said. "She's probably the only completely perfect baby in the world." The thing he wanted most was to show her to his mother, and he decided to take her to England as soon as she could travel. "Because I don't know how much longer I shall have a mother in my life," he told the *Los Angeles Times*.

If Cary Grant's fascination with every detail of his daughter's upbringing irritated Dyan, his ability to lose his temper suddenly and fly into an uncontrollable rage terrified her. While

277

they were watching the Academy Awards together, he had suddenly jumped up and down on their bed, screaming insults at the actors as they took their awards, his hands trembling. She also had been astonished when he had taken the keys to their three cars to stop her from going out. He had locked her into her room and threatened to spank her.

Before boarding the *Oriana* to visit his mother in England on July 1, 1966, they even argued about whether to take any special formula milk for Jennifer's bottle. No matter how she felt, though, Dyan had to smile at the photographers who had gathered at San Pedro to see them embark, the first time Grant allowed anyone to photograph Jennifer. The fact that his new film was about to be released obviously influenced his decision, but Dyan Cannon had a much more important decision to make—how long could she remain Mrs. Cary Grant.

When *Walk, Don't Run* opened, the notices were all flattering. Even the normally skeptical *New Yorker* commented, "Mr. Grant has never looked handsomer or in finer fettle," and went on to say that if it "proves anything it is that his attempted abdication as a screen dreamboat is premature and will have to be withdrawn; he is a good ten years away from playing anyone's jolly, knowing uncle, and as for lovable Mr. Fixit, he should be ready for that role in about the year 2000."

In England Grant made sure that her grandmother could see as much of Jennifer as possible. He also occupied himself with looking for the most hygienic, safe and private places to stay. He spent less time wondering why his wife was becoming steadily more and more depressed.

All Dyan Cannon knew was that her husband acted as though he wished he had never married her. He did not trust her to bring up their daughter, and he seemed pleased when she was miserable. Even in her worst moments she had never envisaged that married life would be so painful. By the time they returned to Hollywood, in October 1964, he too was facing the fact that once more he might have failed.

At Rosalind Russell and Freddie Brisson's twenty-fifth wedding anniversary celebration in Las Vegas in October, all Cary Grant could do was sit there and cry, even though he was sharing the table with his old friends Russell and Brisson, as well as with Frank Sinatra, who had got up a party specially to attend. Russell said later, "It seemed even then his marriage was on the rocks." The man who had just been voted the biggest box-office attraction in America by the Motion Picture Association remained doomed in his private life.

Cannon was to explain, "He thought that LSD would help. I was a very troubled girl, and Cary told my family that I was on the verge of having a nervous breakdown and that he hoped I would have one because the new me rebuilt through LSD would be a much healthier being. He really believed that.

"I remember my father came down from Seattle and told him, 'You mustn't,' and Cary got very upset and said, 'You're her father and I'm her husband, and I'm the one she answers to now.' My father said, 'I would tell my next-door neighbor not to take LSD, let alone my own daughter.' "

Dyan Cannon did indeed take LSD to please her husband. "When I stopped taking it, it became one of the things he became very unhappy about. But we had Jennifer, and I didn't want to admit failure, and when Cary said, 'I want a divorce,' I said, 'No, let's go to a doctor, let's go to a marriage counselor,' and we had already been to doctors and all that. And then Cary said no, and I said okay, and I moved out."

Three days after Christmas their neighbors noticed that Dyan Cannon and Jennifer had abandoned the rented house, and so had Cary Grant. A terse note had been left for the milkman telling him to "stop further deliveries until further notice." The rumor was that Grant had gone to stay with friends in Westwood while Dyan had taken Jennifer back to her parents. It was not until the end of January, almost four weeks later, that Cary Grant acknowledged officially that his fourth marriage, and the only one to bring him a child, had foundered and that he and Dyan Cannon had separated. Once again this most publicly attractive of men had to acknowledge the fact that his romantic life could not bloom beyond the warm glow of a movie studio's klieg lamps.

No sooner had Dyan Cannon left the house than her husband wanted her back again, and more particularly he wanted his daughter.

The gloomy evenings they had spent bickering about his

meanness and her desire for a more interesting and more glamorous life were forgotten. Grant telephoned anyone whom he thought might see her with messages about how much he loved her and how everything would be different from now on. He sent flowers and presents for Jennifer. He even talked to one or two newspaper columnists, so desperate was he to salvage his latest marriage.

"The thought of being separated from your child is intolerable," he told his friends Connie Moore and Johnny Maschio, with whom he was staying. "I don't want to miss a bit of her." As he said it, his head dropped down toward his chest and he produced a photograph of his baby daughter lying on the lawn in front of his house clutching a pink rabbit—a tiny, wide-eyed child too trusting and small to know what was happening to her.

He began telephoning Dyan every night, pleading with her to start again.

"Everything will be different."

"I doubt it."

"You'll see, of course it will."

But Dyan had heard that before, and she did not believe it.

"There's no point, Cary! We've been through all that." She felt she had been her husband's mother, sister, girl friend all rolled into one, but never really his wife.

"But we've got to stay together for Jennifer's sake," Grant told her.

"When there's dissension and heartache in the house, you stay apart," she said later in an interview. "Otherwise it's just a cop-out. Like you're saying, 'I don't have to make a decision; I'll let my kid be the football, and she'll take the brunt of all the anger I feel and all the anger he feels.' The child of ours would have been all mucked up."

Cannon went on to explain why the thought of returning to her husband had become intolerable. "After Jennifer was born Cary suddenly became an expert on child raising. Well, I'd never had a child either. But what makes him a better expert than I? And I at least was at home all the time. I didn't have a career to pursue as well!"

She believed she had suffered enough. She no longer trusted her husband, and she was determined to make her own way in the world again.

"Cary is a very demanding man," she said. "In a peculiar way. He's such a perfectionist and has such strong ideas of his own about everything, even about things that women are ordinarily concerned with. He meddles in what should be women's work."

But Grant was not to be put off. He offered his wife the leading role in an original script he was working on with MGM, *The Old Man and Me.* He told the studio he would do it only if they signed Dyan Cannon without a screen test. Frank Sinatra was planning to make the film *The Detective* with Mia Farrow, so there was no reason why Grant and Cannon could not appear together. But MGM was hesitant, and Dyan did not want to be given the part only because of her husband. She wanted to go back to the stage in New York where she had been offered a part in a play called *The Ninety-Day Mistress.* She had every intention of accepting it.

Grant was distraught. If the play was a success, then Jennifer would be in New York for months and he would be able to see her even less often than he did now. He had agreed to pay his wife $4,000 a month in maintenance, and in return she had given him access to their daughter for limited periods. But all that would change if Cannon went to New York. Jennifer would not be able to have the garden and the beach, the riding in Palm Springs and all the other things that he had planned for her. In despair, Grant began to plan an action for custody of his daughter. After all, he told his friends, he would be able to spend much more time at home with her than his wife would, for he did not need to work again.

Grant became more and more vehement. When Cannon took Jennifer to New York for a visit, he turned up at the airport with a seat on the same plane. When she checked into the hotel with their nanny, he booked a suite just down the corridor. When she went out to dinner with friends, he "happened" to be in the restaurant too. When she went to the theater, he would be in the same row. "Just keeping an eye on

things," he would tell her. "An eye on the baby and you."
Dyan was furious. She told him he had to move out of the hotel
and that he had to "stop bothering us." He had no intention of
doing so. His daughter was the only thing that mattered to him
now. He would be ready to fight for her when the divorce
hearings started.

They began in September 1967, barely two years after the
marriage in Las Vegas. Dyan told the Los Angeles Domestic
Relations Court that she needed "reasonable" support of
$5,470 a month for herself and Jennifer, and claimed that her
husband was worth at least $10 million with an annual income
of more than $500,000. As on three previous occasions, Cary
Grant did not go to court, nor did he make any public statement. When the respected Producers Guild of America announced in October that it had decided to give him its coveted
Milestone Award for his "historic contribution to the motion
picture industry," he was sitting disconsolately in New York
wondering how often he would be allowed to see his daughter.
The movies and the award could not have mattered less.

During the last months of 1967 Grant lived in New York
with his friend the public relations consultant Bob Taplinger,
visiting his wife when she would let him but mostly quietly
talking to his friends on the phone, watching television and
wondering how he was going to survive the rest of his life alone.
Some people told him he was a natural bachelor, pointing out
that he had spent fewer than fifteen of his sixty-three years with
his four wives, but he refused to admit the truth of this. He was
still driven by the need to be loved.

Throughout the winter the battle over how often he could
see his daughter, and whether she would ever be allowed to
stay with him overnight, raged on. Cannon was firm. Grant
could see Jennifer occasionally, but she could not stay overnight. He offered to hire a nurse to look after her when she was
with him, but his wife remained adamant. She wanted her divorce. There was nothing to talk about anymore. If her husband would not accept her decision, then she would go back to
Los Angeles and state under oath just how difficult life had
been as Mrs. Cary Grant.

The prospect of this terrified him. Yet he did not see why Dyan should be allowed to dictate his visits with his own daughter; if he had to suffer in public to get more time with her, then he would. As he set off for John F. Kennedy International Airport in March 1968, to go back to Los Angeles for the hearings, he was gloomy, though the presence of the beautiful twenty-three-year-old heiress Gratia von Fürstenberg, who was riding to the airport with him in the limousine, cheered him a little. No one would ever sympathize with him. Once again he would be portrayed as the villain in a divorce.

Grant never made the plane for Los Angeles, or the divorce court. On the Long Island Expressway two trucks traveling in the opposite direction collided and four wheels flew across the central divider and crashed into Grant's car. The next thing he knew he was in a hospital in the borough of Queens, with his nose broken and fierce pains stabbing through his chest. He had a drip leading into his arm, and he could barely move. Even so, he had been luckier than Gratia von Fürstenberg, who had a broken leg and a broken collarbone, though she too was in no real danger.

Tiny St. John's Hospital, which had never had such a famous patient, could not cope. The switchboard was jammed with telephone calls from all over the world inquiring about Grant's progress. Eighty-seven bouquets of flowers arrived on the first day, and his room was more like a funeral parlor than like a hospital. From his bed Grant asked Bob Taplinger to hire a security guard to protect him from visitors and told the hospital to put through calls only from people who asked for "Count Bezok."

As the worst of the pain subsided, Grant realized that his stay in the hospital would bring him one benefit. He would not have to travel back to Los Angeles and hear the accusations about him fly back and forth across the courtroom. Though the proceedings would be reported in the press and on television, what went on three thousand miles away never seemed quite so bad.

A week after Grant had been admitted to St. John's, Dyan Cannon walked into Santa Monica Superior Court in Los Angeles to tell Judge Robert A. Wenke and a packed courtroom that life with the world's most famous romantic film star had been a "terrifying, unromantic nightmare." As she stood in the court's pine witness stand, she looked frail and tired; but she was clearly determined that no one should be in any doubt that Cary Grant had not only beaten her up and locked her in her room but had frequently dissolved into "fits of uncontrollable temper." Smoothing her blond hair with one hand, she told the court quietly that he was "outlandish, irrational and hostile." When her lawyer, Frank Belcher, asked her why she thought her husband behaved like that, she told the court softly, "I attribute it to LSD."

"He told me he had been taking the drug for about ten years and suggested I try it," she went on, and Belcher asked her how often she had seen Grant take the drug.

"About once a week."

There was a stunned silence as she announced that he had urged her to try it and had even telephoned her after their separation and told her he was "on a trip."

"He had a habit of admitting publicly his use of LSD and suggesting that his friends try it," she said.

Then she described how, following their separation, he had sent a lawyer to suggest to her that after a divorce "they could go back to living together and announce publicly we had remarried."

The bleak list of Cary Grant's failings continued. Cannon explained to the court how "he would yell and scream and jump up and down. Sometimes all it would take would be if I said, 'Please pass the sugar.'" When they had watched the Academy Awards ceremony together, "He yelled that everyone on the awards show had their faces lifted, and he spilled wine on the bed."

Finally, she alleged that Grant had twice beaten her because she wanted to wear a miniskirt and had invited their servants to watch as he did so, that he had bolted the gates of their house and locked her in her room and that he had accused a psychiatrist that he had urged her to visit of trying to seduce her.

"I couldn't please him, no matter what I'd do or say," she

concluded. "He criticized everything I did: the way I carried the baby, the way I fed the baby, the way I dressed and the way I dressed the baby. I couldn't do anything right."

Then came the final blow. She demanded that any visits Grant might make to their daughter must be conducted in the presence of a third party, because "in my estimation he is an unfit father due to his instability."

Cannon's agent, Adeline Gould, testified that Grant had even suggested LSD to her husband as a cure for migraine. She also stated that when Cannon had called her from her room, after Grant had locked her in, the actor had picked up the phone and screamed, "Stay out of my marriage, I'm going to break her like a pony. She's not going to leave until I break her."

Another of Cannon's friends, Mary Gries, added that Grant had told her he hoped Cannon would have a nervous breakdown so he could "remake her into a new girl with the aid of psychotherapy and LSD, then she would be a wonderful person."

Grant's lawyers replied that what he had actually said was that "she was heading for a nervous breakdown and nervous breakdowns are usually self-made and that rests would be good for her." Then they got down to the main points of their client's case.

They told the court that they were not opposing the divorce, only the demand for substantial financial support and the refusal to agree to regular visiting rights. In support they called to the witness stand two psychiatrists. Dr. John Marmon of the University of California told the court that he had examined Cary Grant in September 1967. Although Grant had told him he had used LSD regularly, Marmon had "found no organic defects in Grant's brain as a result. Mr. Grant is an emotional individual, as seen in many actors," Marmon said calmly. "But there are no irrational effects to prevent him from being a loving father or to make him endanger his daughter."

The second psychiatrist was Dr. Sidney Palmer, of the University of Southern California. He also testified that he had examined the actor and concluded, "I found nothing irrational or incoherent about him, he shows a great concern for his daughter's welfare, he reveals a deep love and affection for the child. I found nothing indicating his behavior would be dangerous to the child."

In his final statement, Dyan Cannon's lawyer, Frank Belcher, told the court, "We are not dealing here with an adventuress who walked into a rich man's life, then walked out again. We have a woman who married a man because she loved him, then gave him a child, something he could not get with three previous wives. But she ultimately was driven from her home because of the conduct of her husband."

Lawyer Harry Fain's response on Cary Grant's behalf was quiet and unemotional. In soft tones he told the court, "We don't have a naive little lamb coming into marriage and not knowing about her husband. He, at the age of sixty-four, wants to devote the rest of his life to making his daughter happy."

Judge Robert Wenke then gave his decision. He granted Dyan Cannon the divorce and ordered that she receive $4,250 a month maintenance. But he saw no reason to deny Cary Grant reasonable access to his daughter, Jennifer, whatever amounts of LSD he might have taken. He concluded sternly, "Violence is a serious matter, but in this case it seems to be directed only toward the wife. This could have been due to LSD, and it may no longer be a problem. . . . The evidence shows that Mr. Grant is no longer using LSD and he appears to be a loving and devoted father. He should be entitled to visiting rights."

Wenke ruled that Grant should be allowed to see his daughter "sixty days of each year," and to keep her overnight "at reasonable times." Dyan Cannon's plan to separate her daughter from her ex-husband had failed.

In the hospital in New York Cary Grant was stunned. Although he had not appeared at the hearing, he realized that what the court had heard was a brutal condemnation of him, one of the most telling catalogs of a distinguished actor's failings ever to be made public. He watched his former wife say on television, "I'm sorry all this had to be aired." Yet he vowed he would never take revenge on her or do anything to endanger his right to see his daughter. Instead, he would do precisely what his lawyer had told the court that he intended to do. He would devote his life to Jennifer. He wanted to be for her what he had always hoped his own parents would be for him, affectionate, supportive and loving. And because of this resolution, he would never make another film.

A week later, he walked out of St. John's Hospital, a little unsteady on his legs but as relaxed and as handsome as he had ever been on the screen. He joked with the nurses on the doorstep, told every photographer who asked him that "this is the best place to be ill if you've got to be"—he was later to go back for a fund-raising benefit—and waved at everyone who had come to see him. It was a performance any actor would have been proud of.

He flew out of Kennedy Airport in a private jet owned by George Barrie, the president and founder of the successful perfume company Rayette-Fabergé. Grant and Barrie had only recently been introduced by Bob Taplinger, but they had talked about the possibility of the actor's joining the board of the company, which had sales of $124 million in 1967. Now they discussed further what Grant could do for Fabergé. "George's enthusiasm, endless curiosity and self-criticism fascinated me," Grant was to say. "He'd started out in life as a musician, spent years in show business and spoke its lingo." On the trip across the continent in the privacy of the jet, the two men were on the brink of a deal.

Short, formidably intense and given to impromptu jam sessions in the company's boardroom, Barrie believed Grant could give his company a superb image of class and style. He knew the star had always been interested in the business side of filmmaking, and he saw no reason why he should not enjoy perfume every bit as much. For his part, Barrie had launched a bid to take over Twentieth Century-Fox the year before. It had failed, but he might be tempted to try the same sort of thing again. Cary Grant could be a help if he decided to.

Fewer than seven weeks later, to the amazement of Hollywood, Grant accepted Barrie's offer to join the board of Rayette-Fabergé, and its stock rose two points on the New York Stock Exchange at the announcement. *Time* expressed mild surprise that the actor should associate himself with something as mundane as a perfume company and noted that he had not announced his actual retirement from films. "The last of the great matinee idols, he symbolized male impeccability and the kind of ageless elegance everyone dreams of attaining."

Grant maintained there was not much difference between the film business and the perfume business. "They find a fragrance as we find a story. They find a title for it that's merchandisable and salable. They find an advertising campaign for it and we do. They ship it out in cans, we ship it out in cans. They ship it to department stores. We ship it to theaters." To anyone who had seen only Cary Grant the elegant comedian, all this was quite a surprise.

When his ex-wife went back to court to ask for an increase in her maintenance payments on the grounds of his "extreme wealth," Grant turned to Barrie for support. The two men spent the summer traveling together, talking about what Grant would be doing to help Fabergé and trying to forget the miseries of the divorce.

Whatever he was doing and wherever he was, Grant now made a point of flying back to Beverly Hills to see Jennifer when he was allowed to, and he would always visit her if her mother took her away for a trip. The play Dyan had wanted to do had flopped on Broadway, but he still went to see Jennifer in New York. As the little girl started to run and play, he became prouder and prouder of what he called "my greatest production." For the first time in his life he decided he would live in only one house. He wanted to build a nursery Jennifer could stay in on the nights she was permitted to spend with him.

The house he chose was one Howard Hughes had always admired. The millionaire had once tried to swap his own for it, and both he and Katharine Hepburn had rented it at different times. It was not large, but it had a swimming pool, three bedrooms and a small set of rooms for a butler and a cook. Although there was no tennis court, the grounds were spectacular, providing a view across Los Angeles from the heights above Beverly Hills. In the evenings Cary Grant could sit on the terrace and look out across the city from one of the most expensive and select vantage points on earth. Behind him was the Spanish-style mansion that had once belonged to Charles Boyer, in front was Harold Lloyd's old villa and beyond that lay Valentino's house, Falcon's Lair. None was too close. The large garden and the tall gates in front made the others seem miles away. Besides being his first permanent house and a place for his daughter to come to, the house could become a repository for all the memories he had kept so carefully for more than forty years. He wanted to construct a vault where the records of his life in Bristol, of his time in vaudeville, of his films and marriages, of his investments and of his successes would always be at hand, a place for the memorabilia of Archie Leach.

He told the columnist James Bacon, "I had lots of problems over the years, but mostly they were Archie Leach's problems, not Cary Grant's. You might say that Archie Leach sat in a movie one day and said, 'Why don't I relax like Cary Grant?'" That was precisely what he now intended to do.

He had also decided to help Dyan Cannon get work in Hollywood. He telephoned his old friend Mike Frankovich, Columbia's head of production, and said, "Mike, you know you promised me that you're going to give Dyan a crack at it. . . ."

A slightly bewildered Frankovich replied, "A crack at what?"

"You're making this picture *Bob and Carol and* . . . There must be a role in it for her."

Frankovich said he would think about it. But when he talked to Paul Mazursky, the film's writer and director, the young Englishman told him, "We've already interviewed her and turned her down." At Frankovich's suggestion Mazursky talked to Dyan Cannon again, and finally cast her.

The job kept Grant's daughter and her mother in Los Angeles for some months, but Grant could not stop Dyan Cannon from looking elsewhere for other roles. Nor could he prevent her from taking an interest in more and more experimental forms of psychiatry, including that propounded by the Esalen Institute, a group psychotherapy center in northern California that figured in her film *Bob and Carol and Ted and Alice*. She also tried Arthur Janov's primal scream therapy, which called for her to shut herself in a padded room and to scream whenever she felt tense. The thought that his daughter might be shuttled relentlessly around the country, dumped in hotel rooms or looked after in rented houses depressed Grant. He wanted Jennifer in Hollywood. The man who had fretted meticulously over his films for more than thirty years now had only one creation to fuss over, a small girl with clear eyes.

Harry Fain went to court to try to modify the custody agreement Judge Wenke had handed down at the time of Grant's divorce, and in October 1969 he was successful. He negotiated a new agreement with Frank Belcher, Cannon's lawyer, whereby Grant would be allowed to have Jennifer on alternate weekends from Friday evening until Sunday noon, as well as every Monday afternoon between three and six o'clock. She was also to be allowed to stay with him for half the Christmas holidays, for one month of each of her summer holidays and for all the Easter holidays on alternate years. It was more than Grant had dared hope for.

Even more significantly, the court accepted Grant's suggestion that neither he nor Cannon should be allowed to take Jennifer out of California without the specific permission of the other, and without providing precise details of where they were going. So from now on, if Dyan wished to spirit his daughter away to Europe, or even to New York, he would have to know about it. If he did not, his wife would be breaking the law.

After the judgment, Cary Grant told one inquisitive reporter in Boston, "I have no commitments for the future and anticipate none. It would have to be something very special to get me out of my 'retirement.' "

Gradually, Hollywood realized that Cary Grant would never again walk onto a sound stage to make a film.

As if to mark their acceptance of the fact, his friends in the movie industry recommended he be given a special honorary Oscar at the forty-third Academy Awards ceremony which was due to be held in the Dorothy Chandler Pavilion on April 7, 1970. Gregory Peck, as president of the Academy, was organizing the awards, and he had asked Grace Kelly if she would make the presentation. The gold statuette would bear the special inscription, CARY GRANT—FOR HIS UNIQUE MASTERY OF THE ART OF SCREEN ACTING WITH THE RESPECT OF HIS COLLEAGUES.

It was a distinction the Academy had bestowed on few in the past. Greta Garbo had been given a special Oscar "for her unforgettable screen performances" in 1954, and in 1969 producer Arthur Freed had been honored. It was, perhaps, not quite as good as winning in competition, but still it was recompense for the Oscars this star's performances had helped to win for Leo McCarey, James Stewart, Ethel Barrymore, Joan Fontaine, Sidney Sheldon and Peter Stone, who as he collected his own Oscar in 1965 for the script of *Father Goose,* had said, "Thank you to Cary Grant who keeps winning these things for other people."

When he heard of the proposed tribute, Cary Grant was delighted. The old ghost of the neglected outsider had almost been put to rest.

As had happened so often before, however, when everything seemed settled and going nicely, something unpleasant occurred. In the first weeks of 1970, Grant heard that Cynthia Bouron, a former actress who had worked for a time as a producer at Universal, was claiming that he was the father of the child to which she was about to give birth. Bouron, thirty-five years old with two children from previous marriages, announced that if her baby was a boy she was going to name him Cary Grant. She had already named her English collie dog after him.

As the Academy Awards drew nearer, rumors about the story filled Hollywood. Grant, however, was in New York at the Fabergé offices, or visiting his mother in England, or staying in Jamaica with Noel Coward, anywhere but home. All Hollywood held its breath. The Los Angeles newspapers kept silent for six weeks, but on March 20, fewer than three weeks before the Oscar ceremony, the *Los Angeles Times* reported Cynthia Bouron's claim and disclosed that she had given birth to a baby girl, whom she had christened Stephanie Andrea Grant. On the birth certificate Bouron had put the name of the father as Cary Grant, age sixty-six, occupation, actor.

Still Grant said nothing. His lawyer, Stanley Fox, announced on his behalf, "As far as I'm concerned, there is no validity to the charge." Gradually, the details of Cynthia Bouron's life emerged. First married in Paris to a dentist, she had taken as her second husband the actor Milos Milocevic, once a stunt man working for the French star Alain Delon. In January 1966, Milocevic had murdered Mickey Rooney's wife Barbara when she had threatened to leave him and had then killed himself. Not long afterward, Bouron had been arrested for burglary but was found not guilty. One former friend called her a "con woman," while others said that she merely was one of those women whose life was spent following movie stars around. As these facts became public, most people in Hollywood believed Cary Grant should ignore the scandal.

Nevertheless, barely a week before the ceremony, he asked the organizers of the Academy Awards to withdraw his name as the recipient of a special Oscar, and said that in any case he would not attend the ceremonies. Sheilah Graham reported that he had given "personal reasons" for his decision and that there were those in the Academy who thought the award should not be made. But Gregory Peck stood firm. "We don't take back the award if the recipient isn't going to be present," he said, and set about doing all he could to persuade Cary to change his mind.

The Hollywood press was in no doubt. "He should not distinguish the muckraking by not making an appearance," the *Citizen News* said angrily. "The real tragedy is that Cary Grant, because of these scandalous stories, not even worthy of a weekly tabloid, has been deprived of accepting an Oscar he so richly deserves."

In the end it was Howard Hughes, the one man whose advice Cary Grant had always sought and whose attitudes toward privacy and secrecy he had long shared, who persuaded him to accept the Oscar. The billionaire, now growing increasingly reclusive himself, living on the top floor of the Desert Inn Hotel in Las Vegas protected by Mormon guards and communicating only on the telephone, told his friend that there was every reason for not turning down the award. He deserved it. He should have had it before. Hang the publicity.

Nervously, Cary Grant returned to Los Angeles. Other Hol-

lywood stars had lived through paternity su
claims, and he accepted that he now migh
same. He would say later, "I'm lucky, I guess,
badly as some, Frank Sinatra for example, or E
Errol." He spent the night before the cerem
Cannon, rehearsing his speech.

For the ceremony the next night Peck had p
Sinatra to stand in for Grace Kelly, who was unable to attend—although she had come to Los Angeles especially for the
occasion. As Grant stepped forward, the singer told him, "It
was awarded for sheer brilliance of acting." The tears mounted
in Grant's eyes as his friend went on, "Cary has so much skill
that he makes it all look easy."

Grant looked down at the polished wood dais in front of him,
away from the television cameras, and paused. The vast television audience, as well as the crowd of actors in the arena in
front of him, did not know what to expect. Few of them had
ever heard him say anything that was not in a script.

Slowly he started to speak. "You know I may never look at
this without remembering the quiet patience of the directors
who were so kind to me, who were kind enough to put up with
me more than once, some of them even three or four times.
There were Howard Hawks, Hitchcock, the late Leo McCarey,
George Stevens, George Cukor and Stanley Donen. And the
writers. There was Philip Barry, Dore Schary, Bob Sherwood,
Ben Hecht, dear Clifford Odets, Sidney Sheldon and more recently Stanley Shapiro and Peter Stone. Well, I trust they and
all the other directors, writers and producers, and leading
women, have all forgiven me what I didn't know."

As the audience got to its feet to give him a standing ovation,
he concluded, "You know I've never been a joiner or a member
of any, of a particular, social set, but I've been privileged to be
a part of Hollywood's most glorious era."

As he received his special Oscar, that glorious era came to an
end. The days of light comedy, elegance and style, of beautiful
costumes and dazzling women, of heroes and villains, belonged
to a past age, to a part of the movie industry that had imper-
ceptibly died. Motion pictures were never again to offer their
audiences such gentle and delicate pleasures.

After Grant had walked off the stage, John Schlesinger's *Midnight Cowboy* was awarded the Oscar as best picture of the year. Dyan Cannon had lost by only a narrow margin as best supporting actress for *Bob and Carol and Ted and Alice.*

Cary Grant knew that he had given his last professional performance. In the back of his limousine on the way home to Beverly Hills, he slipped on his black-rimmed glasses and thought of Jennifer.

Even while he traveled for Fabergé, shaking hands effortlessly with department store perfume buyers and turning on his accustomed charm, she was never out of his mind. When Dyan Cannon moved into the exclusive Malibu Colony, he walked the beach there, gazing up at her small wooden house with vast glass windows. Some mornings he would wave at no one in particular, hoping Jennifer would see him.

He had rented a house nearby just to be near his daughter, but on weekends when she stayed with him he would take her back to Beverly Hills and the nursery he had built for her. During the afternoons she stayed with him, he would curl up with her on the bed to encourage her to take a nap. This tall man of sixty-six, the star of more than seventy films, would lie with the tiny child in his arms for hours. If anyone asked him why he did it, he would say simply, "If it helps her to sleep, it's worth it."

He had become more cautious and more discreet as he had grown older, less prepared to be seen with beautiful young women who might be attracted to him. He did not want any more Cynthia Bourons.

Grant had denied Bouron's claim that he was the father of her daughter and refused to pay her "a reasonable sum" in child support. When she would not take a blood test after being asked to do so by the Los Angeles court, her paternity suit was dismissed. But this woman was to remain one of the most mysterious people in his life. Three years later, on October 30, 1973, her dead body was found in the trunk of a car in a supermarket parking lot. She had been beaten to death with a claw hammer. The North Hollywood detectives assigned to the case never interviewed Cary Grant, but they did note in their official report that her daughter Stephanie "appears to be of strong Negro blood" and that "friends of the victim state she would often pick up men at bars or restaurants." But the murder of Cynthia was one of only two of the twenty-two homicides in the North Hollywood police division in 1973 that were never solved.

Grant did form one or two new attachments. In 1971 he met Maureen Donaldson, a young English gossip writer and former nanny whose father was a London fireman, and they started to live together in Malibu and Beverly Hills. His friends thought he might want to marry again simply to show that he could provide a stable home for his daughter, but the romance with Donaldson fluctuated too much for that. Meanwhile, Dyan had hired a van with padding inside so that she would have somewhere to scream when she was away from her home in Malibu.

His daughter preoccupied Grant. He was still fighting to keep her as near to him as he could. At the end of his month with her in the summer of 1971, he filed a custody suit, alleging that her mother had been living in Europe and New York and had ignored his requests that she should come back to California. But nothing happened until the following March when he heard that Dyan Cannon had agreed to star in the new Columbia film *Shamus*, opposite Burt Reynolds, to be made in New York. Once again, four years after their divorce, Cary Grant and Dyan Cannon found themselves arguing in court.

This time, however, the hearings were held in private. Judge Jack T. Ryburn ordered that the small windows in the court's doors be sealed up so that no photographers could take pictures; and he allowed Grant and Cannon to remain in court during lunch to avoid being photographed, although they were not to eat together. Grant lunched in the court itself while Cannon sat in the jury room.

Cary Grant claimed that he should be allowed joint custody of their daughter so that if his former wife went away, Jennifer could stay with him. He also asked that if Jennifer did stay with him, he should not be forced to pay his former wife $500 a month for a nanny and that his maintenance payments to her of $1,500 a month should be halved to $750. Throughout the hearings, Harry Fain repeated the claim that he had first made in court four years earlier, that his client "loves his daughter and is keenly concerned for her welfare." He also said that Grant was prepared to devote all his time to her. It was absolutely true.

Dyan Cannon feared that her former husband's meanness and his obsession with their daughter might well ruin her own life. That was why she had decided to petition the court to let her take Jennifer with her to New York, but Judge Ryburn did not agree. He ruled that Jennifer should remain in California, with her father taking her to New York for at least two visits. He also said that neither Cannon nor Grant should be allowed to use the private back doors of the court to escape the press and the public. He saw no reason why these two bickering parents, famous though they were, should be treated differently from the rest.

Grant was jubilant. It looked as though he would finally be given joint custody of Jennifer, and he could plan to spend every evening waiting for her to come back from school, every weekend showing her how to ride. Within eight weeks he had sold the rights to his last films with Universal for more than $2 million. *Operation Petticoat, That Touch of Mink, Charade* and *The Grass Is Greener* were all included, as was *Penny Serenade,* the only one of his earlier films to which he still retained the rights. He had no more connection to the movie business. He even was willing to disappoint George Barrie, who had found a script that would have suited the actor perfectly and which Barrie wanted his new Brut Productions to make. It was called *A Touch of Class.* But Grant simply told him, "If the script had been given to me ten years ago, I'd have made it in a second. I thought about it, but I realized I was too old for it."

He continued, however, to protect his business interests. In April 1972 he issued a suit for a million dollars against Twentieth Century-Fox for including a scene from *Monkey Business* in their film *Marilyn* without his permission, claiming it lessened his "professional status and earning power as a motion picture star." He invested in a property development in Malaga in southern Spain, and another one near Shannon in Ireland. He thought Jennifer might like to stay in one or another of these places when she grew older. He also joined the board of MGM but concentrated on the company's hotels, not its films. Principally, though, he devoted himself to Jennifer.

Now she was really the only woman in his life, for on January 22, 1973, Elsie Maria Leach died quietly in her sleep in a Bristol nursing home, fewer than two weeks before her ninety-sixth birthday. Cary Grant went back to Bristol to bury her next to the other man she had never made happy, her husband.

"She never smoked, she never drank and she ate very lightly," Grant said later. "But even in her later years she refused to acknowledge that I was supporting her. One time I took her some fur coats. I remember she said, 'What do you want from me now?' I said, 'It's because I love you.' And she said something like, 'Oh you . . .' She wouldn't accept it."

When he got back to Los Angeles after the quiet funeral, he declared, "With the past gone now, I have the future ahead with my daughter." More than six months would pass before he could bring himself to go back to Bristol and begin the painful process of sorting through his mother's things and selling her house. "To do it sooner would have seemed like hurrying her away."

Eventually, he took most of the smaller mementos back to Beverly Hills and added them to the thousands of others he had accumulated over the years. He would frequently retire to the fireproof vault, shut the door and look back over the past. There were photographs of his parents, his wives and Jennifer, old marriage certificates and divorce papers, passports and press clippings, presents from Noel Coward and Cole Porter, his father's watch and his mother's rings, all neatly labeled and meticulously kept, the mementos of the life of Archie Leach stored in a house belonging to Cary Grant.

In general, he divided his time between Malibu and Beverly Hills. Maureen Donaldson was still the most frequent of his companions; there were servants to look after him; he traveled a little for Fabergé; he supervised his investments; he went to baseball games on Monday evenings. He thought about getting married again, but in the end he could not forget that every one of his wives had left him.

As he was to tell *The New York Times*, "I don't know why, they got bored with me, I guess, tired of me. I don't know. Maybe I was making the mistake of thinking that each of my wives was my mother, that there would never be a replacement once she left. . . . I'm not at all proud of my marriage record, but I have wanted a family for years. I finally have this one child, and I will do whatever I can for her. I want Jennifer to give one man love and confidence and help. It has taken me many years to learn that I was playing a different game entirely. My wives and I were never one, we were competing."

As his seventieth birthday arrived, Cary Grant resolved to survive, come what might, to see his daughter become a woman. He had always looked after himself, eating carefully, resting regularly, having messages whenever he could and going to bed before ten on most evenings, but now he stuck to that routine even more unremittingly.

Offers to return to the movies kept on coming in. MGM wanted him to do a remake of *Grand Hotel;* any number of books and scripts arrived for him to look at; Warren Beatty tried for weeks to get him to appear in his film *Heaven Can Wait* for any fee he cared to ask (he had already cast Dyan Cannon in a role that was to get her an Oscar nomination), but Grant refused, just as he refused Joe Mankiewicz's suggestion that he appear in his film version of Anthony Shaffer's thriller *Sleuth*.

All around him the Hollywood he had known was dying. Cole Porter, Leo McCarey and Noel Coward were already gone and, in April 1976, Howard Hughes died on his way back to his home in Texas. Other stars of his generation were retiring. Fred Astaire preferred to go to the races, James Stewart was working less and less, and so was David Niven. Irene Dunne was not working at all, and neither was Loretta Young. Howard Hawks was not making movies. George Cukor was not working regularly, and neither was Hitchcock. Only Katharine Hepburn seemed indefatigable.

Cary Grant was afraid of death. He had resisted a hernia operation for some time in case he might not survive the surgery.

In June 1977, when he could not put it off any longer, he insisted on having a local anesthetic so that he would know what was happening. He also insisted that no women should be allowed into his room. He shaved himself in preparation for the operation and would let only men look after him. He was still, after all, one of Hollywood's greatest romantic stars, and he saw no reason to have his image tarnished in any way.

On one of his trips to London for the annual Fabergé sales conferences, he met a young public relations officer, Barbara Harris, at the Royal Lancaster Hotel overlooking Hyde Park, where the company usually held its meetings. His affair with Maureen Donaldson was drawing to an end, and he still enjoyed the company of beautiful young women. He was attracted to the brown-haired, sensible woman with her calm expression and open face. She had been born in Tanganyika, where her father had been a member of the British colonial service, but the family had returned to England from Africa in 1963 and Barbara had lived there with them since.

When he returned to Beverly Hills, Grant telephoned her every week, trying to persuade her to come to California. For the next two years he telephoned and flew over on visits, always charming, always courteous, as perfect a suitor as he had been in his films. They went to small English pubs together, had quiet dinners, and she introduced him to her mother. Finally, in the summer of 1978, she agreed to go back to California to live with him.

"I was absolutely terrified of the age difference. Before I went, I thought, at great length, about the possibility of being without him. But I decided to go through with it because, otherwise you don't enjoy the time you do have, which is precious." Grant was fifteen years older than her own father had been when he died in 1979, but she felt that she understood him. Unlike Dyan Cannon, Barbara Harris did not feel overwhelmed.

For his seventy-fifth birthday, she baked a cake for the quiet celebration that they were to have together. No one had done that for him in a very long time. She seemed happy not only to bake for him but happy to answer the telephone for him, to arrange his trips, to drive his car, to answer his letters and to organize the renovation of the house in Beverly Hills. She was not afraid of his moods or of the memories he kept in the fireproof vault hidden behind the secret panels. "I think of us as being the same age."

In May 1979, however, Cary Grant had cause to remember that he and Barbara Harris were not the same age. His former wife Barbara Hutton was taken to the Cedars-Sinai Medical Center in Beverly Hills with pneumonia, and he was worried. Even though she had married four times after their divorce, Grant was the only one of her seven husbands she kept in touch with regularly. She had spent the past six years living barely a mile away from him in a magnificent permanent suite at the Beverly Wilshire Hotel. They talked on the telephone constantly, he had helped her whenever she needed it and he had comforted her when her only son, Lance, had been killed in a plane crash in 1972. She always said, "I loved Cary the most. He was so sweet, so gentle. It didn't work out but I loved him."

On Friday, May 12, only a week after she was released from Cedars-Sinai, Barbara Hutton died of a heart attack at the age of sixty-six. The slight, blond woman whom he had first met on the *Normandie,* who was surrounded by enormous wealth but very little happiness, had died alone. Grant didn't want a similar fate, nor did he wish to die in a strange city surrounded by servants as his old friend Howard Hughes had done. He could hardly bring himself to acknowledge his second wife's death. He preferred to remember her as she had been, frail, sloe-eyed and constantly fascinated by the world.

Despite the memorabilia he kept, Cary Grant disliked being publicly reminded of the past. He went to the American Film Institute's dinner to honor Alfred Hitchcock only with reluctance. That part of his life was behind him. He had not set foot on a sound stage or in front of a camera for more than a dozen years, and he told one reporter, "I not only will not view any of my own pictures but I rarely go to any other movie unless it is a Disney film that my daughter wants to see. I don't read most novels either. I enjoy reality too much. I can use the time learning more French, being with Jennifer, doing a lot of riding, a little swimming and tending to business."

Yet he had fought long and hard to become a star, and he still liked to play that role in public, to look ageless, to be accorded the deference due to one of Hollywood's aristocrats. He would appear briefly from time to time at private parties for the elite of the movie business and then retreat again, leaving them waiting for more. For him a star should always remain aloof, above all attempts to persuade him to give television interviews, for example. "I'm not selling anything," he explained, "not running for office, I don't really care to be in the limelight." He made a brief appearance in MGM's compilation film *That's Entertainment, Part Two,* but mainly as a favor to MGM's president, Kirk Kerkorian. He did not relish the occasion any more than he liked going to the Cannes Film Festival. "I don't look at my old movies," he explained a little stiffly. "If I did, I'd be rather disappointed."

Meanwhile he decided to get married for the fifth time. He discovered that, in California, if a couple had lived together for three years they did not need a marriage license and could be married privately by a judge, which appealed to his sense of secrecy. Early in 1981, he asked his daughter, Jennifer, "Look, how would you feel if I asked Barbara to marry me? I'm getting on. I need her."

His fifteen-year-old daughter's eyes clouded with tears, and for a moment he wondered if she thought he was doing the wrong thing. But the tears came only because she was happy.

"For goodness sake," he told her, "don't say anything to Barbara. I might not have the courage to ask her."

Frank Sinatra and Fred Astaire had both married their young partners, and he and Barbara saw them regularly, just as they saw Ronald Reagan and his wife Nancy, Grace Kelly and Prince Rainier. "We were mixing with a lot of married people," he said later. "I felt we enjoyed each other's company. It was I who approached her, not the other way around. It took me a long time to decide I wanted to get married again."

He was also sick of the rumors that still pursued him. In September 1980 TV and film comedian Chevy Chase, whom Grant had never met, had accused him on the television show *Tomorrow* of being homosexual, saying "What a gal" on the air. Although such a smear was not new, it still upset him enough

301

to make him file a suit for slander and claim $10 million in damages. As he said some eighteen months later, "I guess anyone that's publicized is not allowed to be a fairly decent individual. Whether it's for envy or whatever, it perpetuates itself. At my age, though, it doesn't matter. Every dinner table is filled with gossip. True or untrue, I'm old enough not to care."

On April 15, 1981, Cary Grant married again. Barbara Harris, happy and composed, stood beside him in front of a judge on the terrace of their house looking out across Beverly Hills. She had no bridesmaids and wore a simple cream silk dress. The only witnesses were her new stepdaughter, Jennifer Grant, Stanley Fox and his wife, and Grant's butler and his wife. As soon as the brief ceremony was over, the newly married couple led the small group inside for a wedding lunch which Harris herself had prepared that morning because she did not want to "let our secret out." That afternoon the new Mr. and Mrs. Grant left for a short honeymoon with Frank and Barbara Sinatra at their estate in Palm Springs. However ageless he may have appeared, Cary Grant was now seventy-seven years old, and he did not want to be alone.

EPILOGUE

Is it possible to succeed without
any act of betrayal?
                    Jean Renoir

So many are gone. Gable, Cooper, Bogart and Flynn have followed Valentino, Chaplin and Keaton into the myths of Hollywood's past alongside Harlow, Garland and Monroe. Only a
handful of greats remain. Garbo is still alone and in New York.
Dietrich is in Paris, Colbert in Barbados. Only Astaire and
Rogers, Davis, Stewart and Hepburn seem to shine as brightly
in the memories of moviegoers as Cary Grant. In the aristocracy of the movies they have a stature all their own.

Yet few people pause to wonder what is the price these leg-
ends have been called upon to pay for their eminence and
fame. The tragic deaths are plain enough, the suicides and
overdoses; but for those who survive, the pressures of stardom
never disappear. To become and remain a star is a unique and
painful process. Millions desire it, few understand the reality,
the silent hour before the dawn when anguish and doubt in-
vade.

Cary Grant once remarked, "Everyone tells me I've had such
an interesting life, but sometimes I think it's been nothing but
stomach disturbances and self-concern." It is a description that
Bud Schulberg recognized in *What Makes Sammy Run*, one of the
best novels ever written about Hollywood, when he said,
"Sometimes I think the three chief products this town turns out
are moving pictures, ambition and fear."

Archie wanted to become a star. He wanted to forget the
past, to win the affection his mother had seldom given him and
to gain the sense of identity that applause alone could bring. It
meant that he existed, that he deserved to be loved. But the
price stardom exacted was a subtle and prolonged torture. Be-

303

cause Archie Leach realized that he was loved only as Cary Grant, he found it all the more difficult to retain a hold on his own personality. To reveal who he really was might threaten his reputation, weaken his grasp on fame.

In Michael Balcon's unforgettable British film *Dead of Night,* Michael Redgrave plays a ventriloquist with a strange, haunted dummy. The dummy is Redgrave's own creation, brutal, terrifying, yet fascinating and hypnotic. Gradually, as the story unfolds, the dummy assumes a life of its own, more grotesque and terrifying than anything its creator could have imagined. There is a parallel here with the way in which Archie Leach slipped into the costume and style of Cary Grant. Archie Leach became more and more convinced that he was not real. The invented Cary Grant came to dominate the real person who had started life as a vulnerable boy in Bristol.

But the desire to remain a star, to sustain the illusion so carefully created on the screen, was stronger than the fears. If the price was depression and insecurity, then so be it. In private, at least, Cary Grant could be Archie Leach, could respect the separation between the two parts of his character. He could try to put the dummy into a case and forget it.

Being a star, however, guaranteed the one thing that being Archie Leach could not, immortality. The tall, dark and handsome figure on the screen became the reality. One screenwriter who worked with Grant at the end of his career described him as "like a house on the back lot of a Hollywood studio, enormously impressive from the front, but when you open the door you realize that there is nothing behind it. But I don't know if he knows that himself." The same view is echoed by some of the actors who worked with him.

His meticulous creation of a screen personality and his determination to remain a star have demanded intense concentration. As one woman friend described it, "He agonizes constantly about his interior. Sometimes he hurts people unwittingly because he is so self-absorbed."

Certainly his determined retreat into himself wrecked his marriage to Betsy Drake. "The marriage was lived on Cary's terms," she said after their separation. "It was terribly frustrating to be married to him because he's a very self-sufficient man." David Niven once recalled that, when he and his wife used to visit Grant in Palm Springs on the weekend, "he'd vanish, and we'd find him hanging from parallel bars, or doing push-ups, or in a trance on the floor mesmerizing his big toe. . . . He keeps great chunks of himself in reserve."

The self-discipline and constant worry that he brought to his screen career led him to remain aloof and remote, to protect the separation between Cary Grant and Archie Leach by a reticence that fueled incessant rumors. And in Hollywood rumors are the blood that sustains the beast. It loves myths, but also likes to be able to say it knows the truth behind the myths. In these circumstances, inevitably, rumor invaded Grant's life, and he came to abhor it.

Of course, much that was said about him was at least partly true. Cary Grant, no doubt about it, is extremely cautious with money. He dislikes buying meals for other people and prefers to "go dutch." He habitually examines restaurant bills to see that he has not been cheated, and he keeps his own hospitality very noticeably within bounds. Director Billy Wilder once remarked, "I don't know anyone who's been inside his house in the last ten years."

Grant dislikes owning houses except as investments. Yet his shrewdness and bargaining ability have made him one of Hollywood's richest actors, probably worth more than $40 million if he were to realize all his assets. He was earning $300,000 a picture in 1946, and at the end of his career his income was estimated to exceed $800,000 a year in royalty payments alone. "I like money," he once wrote. "Anybody know anyone who doesn't? You do? He's a liar."

Grant also likes the sense of what money can buy. He greatly admired Howard Hughes, copying his style of life with its preference for the telephone, intense privacy and dislike of needless spending. He enjoyed the company of Aristotle Onassis and is still friendly with Prince Rainier of Monaco. He likes to prove to those less fortunate than himself that he is a success. He once paid for an old co-worker from vaudeville to come to Hollywood and took him around in his chauffeur-driven car "to show him how well I was doing." It was the action of a man who needs constant reassurance.

Cary Grant has never found relationships with others easy. He has a self-conscious depersonalized view of himself and assumes that other people regard themselves in the same way. He has usually tried to manipulate the women he has known. Many of them speak of his habit of dictating to them, choosing their clothes, telling them not to wear makeup, to act demurely and never to talk about him to others. Dyan Cannon used to call him The Master, so determined was he that she should obey his commands. Yet he is also frightened of women.

The Hollywood columnist Sheilah Graham, who confessed to being attracted to him herself, remarked, "He is always embarrassed when I tell him every woman I know swoons for him. In spite of his friendliness he remains aloof. He may confide in you one day, but the next day, when you expect more of the same, he will be cool and on the friendly adviser plateau again, and you'd better not bring up the confidences of yesterday. And you know he is still an unsure man, even when he is advising you so sincerely how to live your life."

Coexisting with Archie Leach's pathological fear of poverty was his fear of any woman who might replace his mother, his horror of the thought of marrying his mother. For almost thirty years he deliberately chose women who were blond and blue eyed, the very opposite of his mother in looks. This contradiction may lie at the heart of his extraordinary appeal on the screen, where he seems both frightened of, and fascinated by, women.

Because women have certainly terrified him, he has sought out the company of men on many occasions. He preferred to live with Randolph Scott at the start of his career when other eligible young bachelors were living alone, and that too has fueled the rumors about him. Hollywood has reported for years that Grant has had bisexual leanings, and on occasions he has answered back. Once he told *The New York Times,* "When I was young and a popular star, I'd meet a girl with a man and maybe she'd say something nice about me and then the guy would say, 'Yeah, but I hear he's a fag.' It's ridiculous, but they say it about all of us."

The implication of bisexuality in a leading man in Hollywood today carries nothing like the stigma, or the danger of ruin, that it did in the days of Adolph Zukor or Louis B. Mayer, when the faintest hint of any such scandal could ruin an actor's career. Yet even today the movie industry prefers its stars to hide their vices from the public gaze, and they have no option but to protect themselves as best they can. Grant's pending $10 million slander suit against Chevy Chase for accusing him of homosexuality has still not come to court, even though the proceedings were announced in October 1980.

One of Grant's defenses has been to take great care that he avoids the suggestion that he is in any way feminine. He has usually refrained from wearing any makeup on the set, preferring to rely on his perpetual suntan; and he has always seemed less than happy in films like *Bringing Up Baby* or *I Was A Male War Bride,* which called for him to perform in women's clothes. Pauline Kael has commented, "He is never so butch, so beefy and clumsy a he-man, as in his female impersonations."

His experiments with LSD also harmed his reputation. Some maintained that they harmed him physically too, affecting his mind, impairing his memory and making his retirement inevitable. Certainly his experiments with the drug puzzled some of his friends. David Niven maintained that they were half-horrified and half-made-envious by what Grant had willingly subjected himself to, and went on to say, "It seemed to the rest of us a most hazardous trip for Cary to have taken." But he remained unrepentant about it.

"My intention," he said recently, "was to help make me happy. I suppose everything we do in life, or should do in life, is a consequence of happiness. A man would be a fool if he looked for anything else. LSD's not a drug for addicts. No self-respecting addict would take LSD. The nightmares come out of you." His experiments with the drug and his enthusiasm for it clearly represent part of the battle between the character he created on the screen and Archie Leach. Indeed, it was during his experiments with LSD that he tried to reconcile the two halves of his personality. He himself said in 1963, "I have spent the greater part of my life fluctuating between Archie Leach and Cary Grant, unsure of either, suspecting each."

307

Through the drug, he said, "I discovered that I had created my own pattern and I had to be responsible for it. I had to forgive my parents for what they didn't know and love them for what they did pass down. It was absolute release." It also encouraged Archie Leach to think he could coexist with Cary Grant, but the contradiction and the separation between the characters never disappeared.

Cary Grant has always dressed elegantly in public. He keeps his wardrobe in precise order; every suit and jacket is fastidiously stored, and his clothes are carefully protected. He has usually worn his own clothes in his films. On the set of *Indiscreet* in 1958 he wore a coat he had bought in 1935, and he has always taken pride in buying the best quality clothes to insure that they last for years. He is often uncomfortable in such formal clothes at home, however. There he habitually prefers jeans and open-necked shirts. In recent years he has taken to wearing caftan tops that his fifth wife, Barbara Harris, has made for him, with white jeans and black velvet slippers.

The director Richard Brooks has said that "Cary finds it difficult to accept anything from anyone, gifts, compliments or even love, because he feels the moment you accept anything you are obligated." It is a sentiment that he shared with his mother. Barbara Harris has put it, "There is a dominance in Cary, of course. You can't expect someone who has been at the top of his career for so long not to have it . . . but Cary's basic personality is one of extreme understanding. He is a complex man, extremely kind and intelligent. He has wonderful humor in him. But I think sometimes when people are dominant, it is out of shyness or not feeling at ease in a situation."

He can also be extremely generous, buying his friends sudden and unexpected gifts. He bought Dyan Cannon a sable coat after their acrimonious divorce, and there are other instances of this trait. He maintains that his reputation for meanness is undeserved. "I'm sure that I have that reputation because I don't gamble or go to nightclubs or give huge parties," he once explained, "and because I don't believe in giving gifts at Christmas. I give presents when I feel like it." He refused to tell his daughter, Jennifer, about Santa Claus, saying, "I don't see any reason to perpetuate unrealities."

He hates being taken for a ride. His friend Robert Arthur, who worked with him in his last years at Universal, said, "Cary's anger becomes almost a phobia when he thinks he is being taken advantage of because he is Cary Grant."

A curious and comic instance of this occurred when he was staying at the Plaza Hotel in New York. He had ordered coffee and English muffins to be sent up to his room for breakfast. When they arrived, there were only three half slices and not four.

"I asked the waiter why, and he didn't know. So I called the head of room service, who also didn't know. I went up the line, assistant manager to manager. No one could explain." So he telephoned the hotel's owner, Conrad Hilton, in Beverly Hills, "but his office told me he was in Istanbul."

Undeterred, he then telephoned Hilton in Istanbul to ask why he had been brought only three half slices of muffin at the Plaza in New York when the menu clearly stated "muffins."

"Conrad knew the answer," he recalled later. "It seems a hotel efficiency expert had decreed that all guests left the fourth slice of muffin on their plate. As a plate cleaner upper I was appalled." And he proceeded to tell Hilton that he should immediately alter his menu to read "muffin and a half."

"It cost me several hundred dollars in phone calls," he added, "but ever since I have always gotten four slices of muffin at the Plaza."

The same obsessive strain led him to take swimming lessons late in life because he wanted to swim "perfectly," to take riding lessons to insure that once he started to ride he would do so "perfectly," to try and dress "perfectly" and to look for perfection in his wives. As David Niven put it, "Cary's enthusiasm has made him search for perfection in all things, particularly in the three that meant most to him, filmmaking, physical fitness and women."

His dislike of cadgers and of those who want something for nothing lies behind his lifelong battle with autograph hunters. He claims that he is "only rude to rude autograph seekers," but he does not deny that he does everything he can to avoid giving autographs. On one occasion a fan whom he refused asked, "Who the hell do you think you are?" and was told coolly, "I know who I am. I haven't the vaguest idea who you are, and furthermore I don't care to know." While on the set of *Operation Petticoat,* he even charged for the autographs he gave and donated the money to motion picture charities with the comment, "Paying makes people aware of the value of what they're getting."

His privacy is paramount to him. When he was honored by Ronald Reagan in December 1981 for his contributions to the performing arts, he told the *Washington Post,* "I'm very self-conscious about being on display. Now, on a movie set, that's different. That's all right. That's your office really, and there was no intrusion there by outsiders."

Almost the only story about himself that he has not minded being perpetuated is his reported reply to a magazine editor's telegram in the early 1960's. When asked, "How old Cary Grant?" he is supposed to have replied, "Old Cary Grant fine, how you?" A few years back he told his friend Roderick Mann, "That story has been attributed to various people over the years. I wish I could say it was true, but it's not." Instead, he comments, "I'm actually rather dull, for all I do is relax. I was an idiot until I was forty, an actor, a bore, wrapped up in himself."

Whatever Archie Leach's private fears, Cary Grant's reputation as one of the screen's most brilliant and seductive comedians is undimmed. The director Frank Capra called him Hollywood's greatest farceur. Mae West could say to him in 1933, "Why don't you come up sometime, see me?" and thirty years later Audrey Hepburn could say, "Won't you come in for a minute? I don't bite, you know, unless it's called for." The critic Pauline Kael wrote, "Everyone likes the idea of Cary Grant. Everyone thinks of him affectionately, because he embodies what seems a happier time, a time when we had a simpler relationship to a performer. We could admire him for his timing and his nonchalance, we didn't expect emotional revelations from Cary Grant, we were used to his keeping his distance, which, if we cared to, we could close in idle fantasy. He appeared before us in radiantly shallow perfection, and that was all we wanted from him. . . . We didn't want depth from him, we asked only that he be handsome and silky and make us laugh."

This judgment has been echoed by almost every performer who ever worked with him. James Stewart described him as "a great comedian, a nice man and a loyal one," and went on, "I didn't know him awfully well, but I liked him." Katharine Hepburn once described him as "a delicious personality who has learned to do certain things marvelously well." More recently she said, "He was great fun to act with and laughter reigned around him, a wonderful comedian and always a lively approach to the material. I did not really know him socially," she added, "as neither of us was much on going out. I think he liked working with me. He could catch the ball and run with it. Too bad he quit. A lovely talent. I learned a lot from him."

Doris Day explained, "He looks into your eyes, not into your forehead or your hair as some people do. He can make love to me on the screen when he's ninety." Laraine Day described him as "a marvelous man to appear with," though "in the evenings it was like you were with a different person." And Samantha Eggar said, "He taught me a lot about comedy, he was marvelously professional." Yet she too found him "an elusive pimpernel."

David Niven called him "the most truly mysterious friend I have. A spooky Celt really, not an Englishman at all. Must be some fey Welsh blood in there someplace. Gets great crushes on people like the late Countess di Frasso, or ideas like hypnotism. Has great depressions and great heights when he seems about to take off for outer space." Deborah Kerr regards him as "one of the outstanding personalities in the history of cinema."

Before he died, the director George Cukor paid tribute to Grant's talent by saying, "He really is the great exponent of a very subtle kind of human comedy, having learned the most difficult thing in the world, light comedy. For it to work it must have human appeal." And speaking for a younger generation of directors, Peter Bogdanovich said, "What made him so desirable as a player and so inimitable was the striking mixture of a comedian's talents with the looks of a matinee idol."

Bogdanovich continued, "When all the elements are right,

his presence becomes an indispensable part of a masterpiece; Cukor's *The Philadelphia Story*, Hawks's *His Girl Friday*, Hitchcock's *North by Northwest* and *Notorious*. The ideal leading man, the perfect zany, the admirable dandy and the most charming rogue; except in his earliest years at Paramount, he was never allowed to die at the end of a film, and with good reason, who would believe it? Cary was indestructible."

Stanley Kramer said, "Cary Grant has no peer in comedy or suspense. His reputation is the highest in the history of Hollywood, one of the *legitimate* Hollywood greats!"

Producer Robert Arthur explained, "Cary always represented quality, and because he made everything look so easy we've tended to underestimate him." Like many of his oldest friends, Arthur is protective of Grant, conscious of the impact that invasions of privacy have had on him over the years. "He's always been a very private person and wanted to remain one." It is a view shared by another of his old friends, Lord Bernstein, chairman of the British Granada Television Corporation, who calls him "a very private man."

Robert Arthur explained his friend's retirement by saying, "Cary had always almost preferred the business of making films to the acting, and the old Hollywood that he had been brought up in was slowly dying around him. He was fastidious about everything, and he did not want to make what he thought might be 'tasteless films.'" None of his close friends sees any contradiction between his directorships of Fabergé, of which he is a large shareholder, or MGM, and his career in films. The writer Sol Saks said, "He always knew the grosses of his films, and he was proud that he had made very few flops."

Grant is also proud of the fact that twenty-eight films of his opened at Radio City Music Hall, where they grossed more than $12 million, making him the most popular performer in that theater's fifty-year history, his nearest rivals being Katharine Hepburn and Fred Astaire.

Unlike some other Hollywood stars of his generation, Grant has never been tempted to return to Broadway and the stage. He has persistently turned down offers and maintains that he hardly goes to the theater, just as he seldom reads novels or sees movies. What he values above all else, he tells people, is his time. He told Roderick Mann in 1978, "I doubt if I have more than seventy thousand hours left and I'm not about to waste any of them."

José Ferrer is convinced "that behind that joking elegant exterior there lurked tortured emotional depths that would have led to fine serious acting," and adds, "Obviously, fear of failure or some insecurity about his ability, or just plain indifference to such a career prevented him from extending his range." Grant once told him, "They won't accept me in serious roles, Joe; they want me to make them laugh."

It was to prove a tragic waste for the film industry. Only Alfred Hitchcock, in his two films *Suspicion* and *Notorious,* ever came near to capturing part of what might have been possible. Archie Leach's fears and insecurities had to be hidden if the world was to admire Cary Grant. His wives would be the only people ever to see the contradiction at close quarters.

The actor who told Ingrid Bergman in *Notorious,* "I've always been scared of women, I'll get over it," put his trust in his wives. It was not misplaced. Barbara Hutton remained devoted to him until the end of her life. As he was to say, "We always stayed in touch; I was the only husband who never took a dime from her," and she maintained that he was the one of her seven husbands whom she loved the most. Virginia Cherrill, who now lives in Santa Barbara, California, with her fourth husband, offered to appear as a character witness for him during his divorce from Dyan Cannon. Betsy Drake, who has moved to Europe, has never said anything critical about him since their separation. Even Dyan Cannon, who stated after her divorce, "I was looking for a Daddy. I married Daddy. He even looks like my father," has reestablished a reasonably cordial relationship with her former husband. He called her after his fifth marriage in 1981 to suggest it was time she got married again, and has never spoken negatively of her. In this, he has shown himself more forbearing than some of his friends, many of whom blame her for the fracture of his public image and feel that, whatever his private feelings, she caused him unnecessary unhappiness.

Both Grant and Cannon are proud of their dauthter, Jennifer, now nearly eighteen. "Jennifer is very well adjusted when you consider what she has had to put up with," one of Grant's friends observed. "She has enormous common sense and hasn't been overwhelmed by the war that seemed to be constantly going on between her parents over her custody. She is more secure than either her mother or her father." In spite of Hollywood's appetite for younger leading ladies, Jennifer Grant has shown no signs of wanting to become an actress.

Grant's determination to provide a secure home for his daughter transformed Cary Grant's life by making him settle down. Now he takes her to the Magic Castle, a Hollywood club given over to magic and magicians and one of the few public places where he feels at ease, and he sometimes takes her with him to baseball games on Monday evenings with his wife, Barbara. And his business trips were always carefully planned in order not to curtail the time he could spend with her.

The actor who told Ginger Rogers in *Monkey Business*, "You're only old when you forget you're young," has seldom had a day's illness. He swims a little, rides a little and rests regularly. He and his wife live happily and calmly in their white painted house looking down over Beverly Hills, which still has the perimeter wall that Howard Hughes built for it. They play a card game together called Spite and Malice. Grant maintains it is "a great way for getting rid of your hostilities," and they watch television. He avoids meeting strangers. "I prefer to stay at home with my wife."

When *Soupy Sales*, a children's program in which celebrities often appear for the sole purpose of having a custard pie thrown at them, heard he was one of its fans, the producers called to ask him if he would appear. Grant, now nearly eighty, told them, "Gee, I'd love to, fellas, I watch the show all the time, but you know I never do television, so . . ." The separation between the public man and the private world is still studiously maintained.

In the years since the public experiments with LSD brought the voice of Archie Leach to the surface, it has been quietly but relentlessly suppressed. Yet some of Archie's characteristics remain: fear of disorder, determination to remain in control, a tendency to wash constantly. But the young man from Bristol is a quieter fellow now. The decades of fretting over scripts, arguing over contracts and billing, worrying about performances are long gone. As the actor himself puts it, "Archie Leach the dropout/runaway from Bristol studied men like Noel Coward and became Cary Grant."

Archie Leach no longer need be allowed to survive. He may whisper occasionally in the silence of the night, but Cary Grant no longer needs to pay attention. Archie Leach could be allowed to wither and die, but whether he has or not, only he and Cary Grant know.

FILMOGRAPHY

Cary Grant appeared in the following feature films:

1. *This Is the Night*. Paramount Publix, 1932. Directed by Frank Tuttle; screenplay by George Marion, Jr., based on the play *Naughty Cinderella* by Avery Hopwood; starring Lily Damita, Charlie Ruggles, Roland Young, Thelma Todd. Running time 75 minutes.
2. *Sinners in the Sun*. Paramount Publix, 1932. Directed by Alexander Hall; screenplay by Vincent Lawrence, Waldemar Young, and Samuel Hoffenstein, based on a story by Mildred Crane; starring Carole Lombard, Chester Morris, Adrienne Ames, Alison Skipworth. Running time 70 minutes.
3. *Merrily We Go to Hell*. Paramount Publix, 1932. Directed by Dorothy Arzner; screenplay by Edwin Justin Mayer; starring Sylvia Sidney, Fredric March, Adrienne Allen, George Irving. Running time 83 minutes.
4. *Devil and the Deep*. Paramount Publix, 1932. Directed by Marion Gering; screenplay by Benn Levy, based on a story by Harry Hervey; starring Tallulah Bankhead, Gary Cooper, Charles Laughton, Paul Porcasi. Running time 73 minutes.
5. *Blonde Venus*. Paramount Publix, 1932. Directed by Josef von Sternberg; screenplay by Jules Furthman and S. K. Lauren, based on a story by Josef von Sternberg; starring Marlene Dietrich, Herbert Marshall, Dickie Moore, Gene Morgan. Running time 85 minutes.
6. *Hot Saturday*. Paramount Publix, 1932. Directed by William Seiter; screenplay by Seton I. Miller; starring Nancy Carroll, Randolph Scott, Edward Woods, Lillian Bond. Running time 73 minutes.

7. *Madame Butterfly*. Paramount Publix, 1932. Directed by Marion Gering; screenplay by Josephine Lovett and Joseph Moncure March; starring Sylvia Sidney, Charles Ruggles, Sandor Kallay, Irving Pichel. Running time 86 minutes.
8. *She Done Him Wrong*. Paramount Publix, 1933. Produced by William Le Baron; directed by Lowell Sherman; screenplay by Harvey Thew, John Bright, adapted from Mae West's play, *Diamond Lil;* starring Mae West, Gilbert Roland, Noah Beery, Owen Moore. Running time 68 minutes.
9. *Woman Accused*. Paramount Publix, 1933. Directed by Paul Sloane; screenplay by Bayard Veiller, based on a *Liberty* magazine article; starring Nancy Carroll, John Halliday, Irving Pichel, Louis Calhern. Running time 72 minutes.
10. *The Eagle and the Hawk*. Paramount Publix, 1933. Directed by Stuart Walker; screenplay by Bogart Rogers and Seton I. Miller, based on a story by John Monk Saunders; starring Fredric March, Jack Oakie, Carole Lombard, Sir Guy Standing. Running time 74 minutes.
11. *Gambling Ship*. Paramount Publix, 1933. Directed by Louis Gasnier and Max Marcin; screenplay by Max Marcin and Seton I. Miller; starring Benita Hume, Roscoe Karns, Glenda Farrell, Jack La Rue. Running time 72 minutes.
12. *I'm No Angel*. Paramount Publix, 1933. Produced by William Le Baron; directed by Wesley Ruggles; screenplay and original story by Mae West; starring Mae West, Edward Arnold, Ralf Harolde, Gertrude Michael. Running time 87 minutes.
13. *Alice in Wonderland*. Paramount Publix, 1933. Directed by Norman Z. McLeod; screenplay by Joseph L. Mankiewicz and William Cameron Menzies, based on a novel by Lewis Carroll; starring Charlotte Henry, Richard Arlen, Gary Cooper, W. C. Fields. Running time 90 minutes.
14. *Thirty Day Princess*. Paramount Publix, 1934. A B. P. Schulberg Production; directed by Marion Gering; screenplay by Preston Sturges and Frank Partos; starring Sylvia Sidney, Edward Arnold, Vince Barnett, Henry Stephenson. Running time 74 minutes.
15. *Born to Be Bad*. United Artists, 1934. A Twentieth Century

Production (William Goetz and Raymond Griffith); directed by Lowell Sherman; screenplay by Ralph Graves; starring Loretta Young, Jackie Kelk, Henry Travers, Russell Hopton. Running time 61 minutes.

16. *Kiss and Make Up*. Paramount Publix, 1934. A B. P. Schulberg Production; directed by Harlan Thompson; screenplay by Harlan Thompson and George Marion, Jr.; starring Helen Mack, Genevieve Tobin, Edward Everett Horton, Lucien Littlefield. Running time 80 minutes.

17. *Ladies Should Listen*. Paramount Publix, 1934. Produced by Douglas MacLean; directed by Frank Tuttle; screenplay by Claude Binyon, Frank Butler and Guy Bolton; starring Frances Drake, Edward Everett Horton, Rosita Morena, Nydia Westman. Running time 62 minutes.

18. *Enter Madame*. Paramount Publix, 1935. Produced by A. Benjamin Glaser; directed by Elliott Nugent; screenplay by Charles Brackett and Gladys Lehman; starring Elissa Landi, Lynne Overman, Sharon Lynn, Frank Albertson. Running time 81 minutes.

19. *Wings in the Dark*. Paramount, 1935. Produced by Arthur Hornblow, Jr.; directed by James Flood; screenplay by Jack Kirkland and Frank Partos; starring Myrna Loy, Roscoe Karns, Hobart Cavanaugh, Dean Jagger. Running time 75 minutes.

20. *The Last Outpost*. Paramount, 1935. Produced by E. Lloyd Sheldon; directed by Charles Barton and Louis Gasnier; screenplay by Philip MacDonald, based on a story by F. Britten Austin; starring Claude Rains, Gertrude Michael, Kathleen Burke, Akim Tamiroff. Running time 75 minutes.

21. *Sylvia Scarlett*. RKO Radio, 1936. Produced by Pandro S. Berman; directed by George Cukor; screenplay by Gladys Unger, John Collier and Mortimer Offner; starring Katharine Hepburn, Brian Aherne, Edmund Gwenn, Natalie Paley. Running time 95 minutes.

22. *Big Brown Eyes*. Paramount, 1936. Produced by Walter Wanger; directed by Raoul Walsh; screenplay by Raoul Walsh and Bert Hanlon; starring Joan Bennett, Walter Pidgeon, Isabel Jewell, Lloyd Nolan. Running time 76 minutes.

23. *Suzy.* MGM, 1936. Produced by Maurice Revnes; directed by George Fitzmaurice; screenplay by Dorothy Parker, Alan Campbell, Horace Jackson and Lenore Coffee; starring Jean Harlow, Franchot Tone, Lewis Stone, Benita Hume. Running time 95 minutes.

24. *Wedding Present.* Paramount, 1936. Produced by B. P. Schulberg; directed by Richard Wallace; screenplay by Joseph Anthony, based on a story by Paul Gallico; starring Joan Bennett, George Bancroft, Conrad Nagel, William Demarest. Running time 81 minutes.

25. *The Amazing Quest of Ernest Bliss* (US title, *Romance and Riches*). Garrett-Klement Pictures, 1936. Produced and directed by Alfred Zeisler; screenplay by John L. Balderston; starring Mary Brian, Peter Gawthorne, Iris Ashley. Running time 70 minutes.

26. *When You're in Love* (GB title, *For You Alone*). Columbia, 1937. Produced by Everett Riskin; directed by Robert Riskin; screenplay by Robert Riskin, based on an original idea by Ethel Hill and Cedric Worth; starring Grace Moore, Aline MacMahon, Henry Stephenson, Thomas Mitchell. Running time 110 minutes.

27. *The Toast of New York.* RKO Radio, 1937. An Edward Small Production; directed by Rowland V. Lee; screenplay by Dudley Nichols, John Twist and Joel Sayre; starring Edward Arnold, Frances Farmer, Jack Oakie, Donald Meek. Running time 109 minutes.

28. *Topper.* MGM, 1937. A Hal Roach Production; directed by Norman Z. McLeod; screenplay by Jack Jevne, Eric Hatch and Eddie Moran, based on a novel by Thorne Smith; starring Constance Bennett, Roland Young, Billie Burke, Alan Mowbray, Hedda Hopper. Running time 98 minutes.

29. *The Awful Truth.* Columbia, 1937. Produced and directed by Leo McCarey; screenplay by Viña Delmar and Leo McCarey, based on a play by Arthur Richman; starring Irene Dunne, Ralph Bellamy, Alexander D'Arcy, Cecil Cunningham. Running time 89 minutes.

30. *Bringing Up Baby.* RKO Radio, 1938. Produced and directed by Howard Hawks; screenplay by Dudley Nichols and

Hagar Wilde, based on a story by Hagar Wilde; starring Katharine Hepburn, Charlie Ruggles, Barry Fitzgerald, May Robson, Walter Catlett. Running time 102 minutes.

31. *Holiday* (GB titles, *Free to Live; Unconventional Linda*). Columbia, 1938. Produced by Everett Riskin; directed by George Cukor; screenplay by Donald Ogden Stewart and Sidney Buchman, based on a play by Philip Barry; starring Katharine Hepburn, Doris Nolan, Lew Ayres, Edward Everett Horton. Running time 93 minutes.

32. *Gunga Din.* RKO Radio, 1939. Produced by Pandro S. Berman; directed by George Stevens; screenplay by Joel Sayre and Fred Guiol, based on a story by Ben Hecht and Charles MacArthur and adapted from the poem by Rudyard Kipling; starring Victor McLaglen, Sam Jaffee, Joan Fontaine, Douglas Fairbanks, Jr. Running time 115 minutes.

33. *Only Angels Have Wings.* Columbia, 1939. A Howard Hawks Production; directed by Howard Hawks; screenplay by Jules Furthman and Howard Hawks; starring Jean Arthur, Richard Barthelmess, Rita Hayworth, Thomas Mitchell. Running time 121 minutes.

34. *In Name Only.* RKO Radio, 1939. Executive producer Pandro S. Berman; directed by John Cromwell; screenplay by Richard Sherman; starring Carole Lombard, Kay Francis, Charles Coburn, Helen Vinson. Running time 94 minutes.

35. *His Girl Friday.* Columbia, 1940. Produced and directed by Howard Hawks; screenplay by Charles Lederer, based on the play *The Front Page* by Ben Hecht and Charles MacArthur; starring Rosalind Russell, Ralph Bellamy, Gene Lockhart, Helen Mack. Running time 92 minutes.

36. *My Favorite Wife.* RKO Radio, 1940. Produced by Leo McCarey; directed by Garson Kanin; screenplay by Bella and Samuel Spewack; starring Irene Dunne, Randolph Scott, Gail Patrick, Ann Shoemaker. Running time 88 minutes.

37. *The Howards of Virginia* (GB title, *The Tree of Liberty*). Columbia, 1940. Produced and directed by Frank Lloyd; screenplay by Sidney Buchman, based on the novel *The Tree of Liberty* by Elizabeth Page; starring Martha Scott, Sir Cedric Hardwicke, Alan Marshal, Irving Bacon. Running time 115 minutes.

38. *The Philadelphia Story.* MGM, 1940. Produced by Joseph L. Mankiewicz; directed by George Cukor; screenplay by Donald Ogden Stewart, based on the play by Philip Barry; starring Katharine Hepburn, James Stewart, Ruth Hussey, John Howard, Roland Young. Running time 112 minutes.

39. *Penny Serenade.* Columbia, 1941. Produced by Fred Guiol; directed by George Stevens; screenplay by Morrie Ryskind, based on a story by Martha Cheavens; starring Irene Dunne, Beulah Bondi, Edgar Buchanan, Ann Doran. Running time 120 minutes.

40. *Suspicion.* RKO Radio, 1941. Directed by Alfred Hitchcock; screenplay by Samson Raphaelson, Joan Harrison and Alma Reville, based on the novel *Before the Fact* by Francis Iles; starring Joan Fontaine, Sir Cedric Hardwicke, Nigel Bruce, Dame May Whitty. Running time 99 minutes.

41. *The Talk of the Town.* Columbia, 1942. Produced by George Stevens and Fred Guiol; directed by George Stevens; screenplay by Irwin Shaw and Sidney Buchman, based on a story by Sidney Harmon; starring Jean Arthur, Ronald Colman, Edgar Buchanan, Glenda Farrell. Running time 118 minutes.

42. *Once Upon a Honeymoon.* RKO Radio, 1942. Produced and directed by Leo McCarey; screenplay by Sheridan Gibney, based on a story by Leo McCarey; starring Ginger Rogers, Walter Slezak, Albert Dekker, Albert Bassermann. Running time 116 minutes.

43. *Mr. Lucky.* RKO Radio, 1943. Produced by David Hempstead; directed by H. C. Potter; screenplay by Milton Holmes and Adrian Scott, based on a story by Milton Holmes; starring Laraine Day, Charles Bickford, Gladys Cooper, Alan Carney. Running time 100 minutes.

44. *Destination Tokyo.* Warner Brothers, 1943. Produced by Jerry Wald; directed by Delmer Daves; screenplay by Delmer Daves and Albert Maltz, based on a story by Steve Fisher; starring John Garfield, Alan Hale, John Ridgely, Dane Clark. Running time 135 minutes.

45. *Once Upon a Time.* Columbia, 1944. Produced by Louis F. Edelman; directed by Alexander Hall; screenplay by Lewis Meltzer and Oscar Saul; starring Janet Blair, James Gleason,

Ted Donaldson, William Demarest. Running time 89 minutes.
46. *None but the Lonely Heart.* RKO Radio, 1944. Produced by David Hempstead; directed by Clifford Odets; screenplay by Clifford Odets, based on a novel by Richard Llewellyn; starring Ethel Barrymore, Jane Wyatt, June Duprez, Barry Fitzgerald. Running time 113 minutes.
47. *Arsenic and Old Lace.* Warner Brothers, 1944. Produced and directed by Frank Capra; screenplay by Julius J. Epstein and Philip G. Epstein, with help from Howard Lindsay and Russell Crouse, based on the play by Joseph Kesselring; starring Josephine Hull, Jean Adair, Raymond Massey, Priscilla Lane, Jack Carson, Peter Lorre, Edward Everett Horton. Running time 118 minutes.
48. *Night and Day.* Warner Brothers, 1946. Produced by Arthur Schwarz; directed by Michael Curtiz; screenplay by Charles Hoffman, Leo Townsend and William Bowers; starring Alexis Smith, Monty Woolley, Ginny Sims, Jane Wyman, Mary Martin. Running time 130 minutes.
49. *Notorious.* RKO Radio, 1946. Produced and directed by Alfred Hitchcock; screenplay by Ben Hecht; starring Ingrid Bergman, Claude Rains, Louis Calhern, Madame Leopoldine Konstantin. Running time 103 minutes.
50. *The Bachelor and the Bobby-Soxer* (GB title, *Bachelor Knight*). RKO Radio, 1947. A Dore Schary Production; directed by Irving Reis; screenplay and original story by Sidney Sheldon; starring Myrna Loy, Shirley Temple, Rudy Vallee, Ray Collins. Running time 94 minutes.
51. *The Bishop's Wife.* RKO Radio, 1947. A Samuel Goldwyn Production; directed by Henry Koster; screenplay by Robert E. Sherwood and Leonardo Bercovici, based on a novel by Robert Nathan; starring Loretta Young, David Niven, Monty Woolley, James Gleason. Running time 105 minutes.
52. *Mr. Blandings Builds His Dream House.* RKO Radio, 1948. Produced by Dore Schary; directed by H. C. Potter; screenplay by Norman Panama and Melvin Frank, based on a novel by Eric Hodgkin; starring Myrna Loy, Melvyn Douglas, Reginald Denny, Connie Marshall. Running time 94 minutes.
53. *Every Girl Should Be Married.* RKO Radio, 1948. Produced by

Don Hartman and Dore Schary; directed by Don Hartman; screenplay by Stephen Morehouse Avery and Don Hartman, based on a short story by Eleanor Harris; starring Betsy Drake, Franchot Tone, Diana Lynn, Eddie Albert. Running time 84 minutes.

54. *I Was a Male War Bride* (GB title, *You Can't Sleep Here*). Twentieth Century-Fox, 1949. Produced by Sol C. Siegel; directed by Howard Hawks; screenplay by Charles Lederer, Leonard Spiegelgass and Hagar Wilde, based on a story by Henri Rochard; starring Ann Sheridan, Marion Marshall, Randy Stuart, William Neff. Running time 105 minutes.

55. *Crisis*. MGM, 1950. Produced by Arthur Freed; directed by Richard Brooks; screenplay by Richard Brooks, based on a story by George Tabori; starring José Ferrer, Paula Raymond, Ramon Novarro, Gilbert Roland. Running time 95 minutes.

56. *People Will Talk*. Twentieth Century-Fox, 1951. Produced by Darryl F. Zanuck; directed by Joseph L. Mankiewicz; screenplay by Joseph L. Mankiewicz, based on the play *Dr. Praetorius* by Curt Goetz; starring Jeanne Crain, Finlay Currie, Walter Slezak, Hume Cronyn. Running time 109 minutes.

57. *Room for One More*. Warner Brothers, 1952. Produced by Henry Blanke; directed by Norman Taurog; screenplay by Jack Rose and Mel Shavelson, based on a book by Anna Perrott Rose; starring Betsy Drake, Iris Mann, George Winslow, Lurene Tuttle. Running time 97 minutes.

58. *Monkey Business*. Twentieth Century-Fox, 1952. Produced by Sol C. Siegel; directed by Howard Hawks; screenplay by Ben Hecht, I.A.L. Diamond and Charles Lederer; starring Ginger Rogers, Charles Coburn, Marilyn Monroe, Hugh Marlowe. Running time 97 minutes.

59. *Dream Wife*. MGM, 1953. Produced by Dore Schary; directed by Sidney Sheldon; screenplay by Sidney Sheldon, Herbert Baker and Alfred L. Levitt; starring Deborah Kerr, Walter Pidgeon, Betta St. John, Buddy Baer. Running time 98 minutes.

60. *To Catch a Thief*. Paramount/Alfred Hitchcock, 1955. Produced and directed by Alfred Hitchcock; screenplay by John Michael Hayes, based on a novel by David Dodge; starring

Grace Kelly, Jessie Royce Landis, John Williams, Brigitte Auber. Running time 103 minutes.

61. *The Pride and the Passion.* United Artists/Stanley Kramer, 1957. Produced and directed by Stanley Kramer; screenplay by Edward and Edna Anhalt, based on the novel *The Gun* by C. S. Forester; starring Frank Sinatra, Sophia Loren, Theodore Bikel, John Wengraf. Running time 130 minutes.

62. *An Affair to Remember.* Twentieth Century-Fox, 1957. Produced by Jerry Wald; directed by Leo McCarey; screenplay by Delmer Daves and Leo McCarey; starring Deborah Kerr, Richard Denning, Cathleen Nesbitt, Neva Patterson. Running time 114 minutes.

63. *Kiss Them for Me.* Twentieth Century-Fox, 1957. Produced by Jerry Wald; directed by Stanley Donen; screenplay by Julius Epstein, based on the novel *Shore Leave* by Frederick Wakeman and the play by Luther Davis; starring Jayne Mansfield, Suzy Parker, Leif Erickson, Ray Walston. Running time 103 minutes.

64. *Indiscreet.* Warner Brothers, 1958. A Grandon Production; produced and directed by Stanley Donen; screenplay by Norman Krasna, based on his play *Kind Sir;* starring Ingrid Bergman, Cecil Parker, Phyllis Calvert, Megs Jenkins. Running time 100 minutes.

65. *Houseboat.* Paramount/Scribe, 1958. Produced by Jack Rose; directed by Mel Shavelson; screenplay by Jack Rose and Mel Shavelson; starring Sophia Loren, Martha Hyer, Harry Guardino, Paul Petersen. Running time 112 minutes.

66. *North by Northwest.* MGM, 1959. Produced and directed by Alfred Hitchcock; screenplay by Ernest Lehman; starring Eva Marie Saint, James Mason, Jessie Royce Landis, Leo G. Carroll. Running time 136 minutes.

67. *Operation Petticoat.* Universal, 1959. A Granart Company Production; produced by Robert Arthur; directed by Blake Edwards; screenplay by Stanley Shapiro and Maurice Richlin; starring Tony Curtis, Joan O'Brien, Dina Merrill, Gene Evans. Running time 124 minutes.

68. *The Grass Is Greener.* Universal, 1960. A Grandon Production; produced and directed by Stanley Donen; screenplay by

Hugh and Margaret Williams, based on their play; starring Deborah Kerr, Robert Mitchum, Jean Simmons, Moray Watson. Running time 104 minutes.

69. *That Touch of Mink.* Universal/Granlex/Arwin/Nob Hill, 1962. Produced by Stanley Shapiro and Martin Melcher; executive producer Robert Arthur; directed by Delbert Mann; screenplay by Stanley Shapiro and Nate Monaster; starring Doris Day, Gig Young, Audrey Meadows, Dick Sargent, John Astin, Alan Hewitt. Running time 99 minutes.

70. *Charade.* Universal/Stanley Donen, 1964. Produced and directed by Stanley Donen; screenplay by Peter Stone, based on a story by Peter Stone and Marc Behan; starring Audrey Hepburn, Walter Matthau, James Coburn, George Kennedy. Running time 113 minutes.

71. *Father Goose.* Universal, 1964. A Granox Company Production; produced by Robert Arthur; directed by Ralph Nelson; screenplay by Peter Stone and Frank Tarloff; starring Leslie Caron, Trevor Howard, Jack Good, Verina Greenlaw. Running time 116 minutes.

72. *Walk, Don't Run.* Columbia, 1966. A Granlex Production; produced by Sol C. Siegel; directed by Charles Walters; screenplay by Sol Saks, based on a story by Robert Russell and Frank Ross: starring Samantha Eggar, Jim Hutton, John Standing, Miiko Taka. Running time 114 minutes.

INDEX